For Reference

Not to be taken from this room

African American Almanac

African American Almanac

**Volume 2
Society**

Jay P. Pederson and Kenneth Estell, Editors

U·X·L

An Imprint of Gale Research Inc.

African American Almanac

Jay P. Pederson and Kenneth Estell, *Editors*

Staff

Carol DeKane Nagel, *U·X·L Developmental Editor*
Thomas L. Romig, *U·X·L Publisher*

Amy Marcaccio, *Acquisitions Editor*

Barbara A. Wallace, *Permissions Associate (Pictures)*
Margaret A. Chamberlain, *Permissions Supervisor (Pictures)*

Mary Kelley, *Production Associate*
Evi Seoud, *Assistant Production Manager*
Mary Beth Trimper, *Production Director*

Mary Krzewinski, *Cover Designer*
Cynthia Baldwin, *Art Director*

The Graphix Group, *Typesetter*

This publication is a creative work fully protected by all applicable copyright laws, as well as by misappropriation, trade secret, unfair competition, and other applicable laws. The editors of this work have added value to the underlying factual material herein through one or more of the following: unique and original selection, coordination, expression, arrangement, and classification of the information. All rights to this publication will be vigorously defended.

Copyright © 1994
U·X·L
An Imprint of Gale Research Inc.

All rights reserved, including the right of reproduction in whole or in part in any form.

™ This book is printed on acid-free paper that meets the minimum requirements of American National Standard for Information Sciences—Permanence Paper for Printed Library Materials, ANSI Z39.48-1984.

ISBN 0-8103-9239-9 (Set)
ISBN 0-8103-9240-2 (Volume 1)
ISBN 0-8103-9241-0 (Volume 2)
ISBN 0-8103-9242-9 (Volume 3)

Printed in the United States of America

Published simultaneously in the United Kingdom
by Gale Research International Limited
(An affiliated company of Gale Research Inc.)

I(T)P™
The trademark **ITP** is used under license.

ADVISORY BOARD

Alton Hornsby, Jr.
Professor of History
Morehouse College

Jean Blackwell Hutson
Former Curator and Director
Schomburg Center for Research in Black Culture

William C. Matney, Jr.
Public Affairs Coordinator
U.S. Bureau of the Census

Carole McCullough
Professor of Library Science
Wayne State University

Brenda Mitchell-Powell
Editor
Multicultural Review

Jessie Carney Smith
University Librarian
Fisk University

READER'S GUIDE

African American Almanac features a comprehensive range of historical and current information on African American life and culture. Organized into 26 subject chapters, including Civil Rights, The Family and Health, and Science, Medicine, and Invention, the volumes contain more than three hundred black-and-white photographs and maps, a glossary of terms used in the text, a selected bibliography, and a cumulative subject index.

Other titles of interest:

African American Biography profiles three hundred African Americans, both living and deceased, prominent in fields ranging from civil rights to athletics, politics to literature, entertainment to science, religion to the military. A black-and-white portrait accompanies each entry, and a cumulative subject index lists all individuals by field of endeavor.

African American Breakthroughs: Five Hundred Years of Black Firsts provides fascinating details on hundreds of "firsts" involving African Americans. The volume is arranged in subject categories, and entries summarize events and include brief biographies of the people involved. *African American Breakthroughs* features illustrations, a timeline of firsts, and a thorough index.

African American Chronology explores significant social, political, economic, cultural, and educational milestones in black history. Arranged by year and then by month and day, the chronology spans from 1492 to modern times and contains more than one hundred illustrations, extensive cross references, and a cumulative subject index.

Comments and Suggestions

We welcome your comments on *African American Almanac* as well as your suggestions for topics to be featured in future editions. Please write: Editors, *African American Almanac*, U·X·L, 835 Penobscot Building, Detroit, Michigan 48226-4094; call toll-free: 1-800-877-4253; or fax: 313-961-6348.

CONTENTS

Advisory Board v
Reader's Guide vi
Picture Credits xv
Words to Know xvii

Volume 1: History

1 **Flashbacks: The Birth and Rise of the African American, 1492-1993** 1
   Columbus's Great Discovery to the Beginnings of Colonial America 1
   The Pilgrim Landing to the American Revolution 2
   The Independence of a Nation to the Emancipation of a Race 4
   The Death of Lincoln to the Birth of King 4
   The Depths of the Depression to the Dawn of the Civil Rights Movement 8
   The Montgomery Boycott to the Death of King 11
   The Newton Trial to the Miami Riots 15
   The Rise of the Black Middle Class to Jackson's Second Running 16
   New Heights, New Lows 19

2 **Motherland: A Survey of African South of the Sahara** 21
   A Brief History 21
   Africa Today 23
   Country Profiles
      West Africa 24
      West Central Africa 35
      Northeast Africa 40

CONTENTS

    East Africa 43
    Southeast Central Africa 46
    Southern Africa 49
    East African Island Nations 52

3 Neighbors: Blacks in the Western Hemisphere 55
  A Brief History 55
  The Caribbean Today 55
  Country Profiles
    The Caribbean 56
    Central America 68
    South America 70
    North America 73

**4 Words: Letters, Laws, Speeches, Songs, and Other Chronicles of
African American History, 1661-1993** 75

5 Places: African American Landmarks around the United States 124
  The Midwest 125
  The Northeast 135
  South Central States 152
  The Southeast 159
  The West 170

Further Reading 183
Index 185

Volume 2: Society

6 Slavery: From the Beginnings of America to the End of the 19th Century 213
  African Roots of Slavery 213
  The Growth of Slavery in Colonial America 217
  Slavery in the New Nation 218
  Expansion of Slavery 220
  Antislavery Movements 222
  The Abolition Movement 222
  The Underground Railroad 224
  Civil War 224
  Civil Rights at the End of the Civil War 225

CONTENTS

7 Civil Rights: The Struggle That Shaped the Hearts and Minds of African Americans 227
    Reconstruction and Civil Rights 227
    Civil Rights in the Twentieth Century 229
    Boycotts, Marches, Sit-ins, and Demonstrations: Civil Rights in the 1960s 232
    "Letter from Birmingham Jail" 232
    Urban Tension and Civil Disorder 235
    The Fading of Militancy and a New Civil Rights Era 241
    Racism in the 1980s 242
    1993 and Beyond 243

8 Black Nationalism: Nation Building 245
    Early Black Nationalism in the United States 246
    The Flowering of the Movement 249
    Black Nationalism in the Twentieth Century 250
    Black Nationalism Today 253

9 Law: The Legal Status of African Americans 255
    Thurgood Marshall: A Beacon of Black Hope 255
    The Rights of African Americans: The First Hundred Years 256
    Civil Rights Following the Civil War 258
    The Twentieth Century and Full Legal Status for African Americans 262
    Twentieth-Century Supreme Court Decisions 262
    Justice Wins Out: The Medgar Evers Murder Case 266

10 Politics: The Voter and Elected Officeholder 267
    Black Politics during the Years of Slavery 268
    The Convention Movement 269
    Reconstruction and Backlash 271
    The Twentieth Century and Jim Crow 273
    World War II and the Election of Adam Clayton Powell, Jr. 275
    The Civil Rights Movement Leads to Breakthrough Gains for African Americans 277
    Politics in the 1990s 280
    Blacks and the Clinton Administration 280

11 National Organizations: In Unity There Is Strength 282
    Early Black Organizations 283
    Twentieth-Century Organizations 284

CONTENTS

12 Population: The Growth and Settlement of a Race 295
    A New Land, a New People 295
    Emancipation and Migration 297
    The Great Migration 298
    Population Growth Since 1980 300
    The Present and Future 300
    Current Demographics 301
    The Future of the Black Population 304

13 Jobs and Money: The African American Labor Force and Economic Outlook 305
    Middle Class and Underclass 305
    Family Structure and Family Income 307
    Poverty 309
    The Role of the Government 312
    Current Trends 314

14 Entrepreneurship: Risk-taking and the Creation of Wealth 315
    Entrepreneurship before the Civil War 316
    Entrepreneurship after the Civil War 318
    Black Agriculture: A Story of Decline 319
    Black Entrepreneurs in the Post-Civil Rights Era 324
    Growth Industries 324
    Recent Trends 326
    Modern-Day Milestones: A Look Back and a Look Forward 327

15 The Family and Health: The Backbone of the Community 329
The Family
        Hopeful Appraisals 329
        Different Shapes, Different Sizes 333
        Families and Money 334
        Family Structure and Stability 336
        Violence and Other Problems of the Inner-City Family 336
        The Great Society: A Failure? 338
        Number and Size of Families 339
        Families in Poverty 341
        The Elderly 341

    Marriage and the Shortage of Black Men 341
    Fertility and Births 342

Health
    Birth 344
    Child Health 344
    Sickle Cell Anemia 345
    AIDS 345
    Cigarette, Alcohol, and Drug Use 346
    Life Expectancy 346
    Homicide and Death by Accident 347
    Suicide 347
    Health Care 348
    Solutions 348

16 Education: The Force That Liberates 349
    Education through the Church 349
    African Free Schools in New York and Philadelphia 350
    Freedmen's Organizations and Agencies 351
    Independent Schools in the Late Nineteenth Century 353
    Early Black Institutions of Higher Education 354
    Early Promoters of African American Studies 356
    The End of Segregation in Public Education 356
    Black Colleges in the Twentieth Century 360
    Independent Schools in the Late Twentieth Century 360
    Current Problems, Needs, and Trends 361

17 Religion: The Tie That Binds 365
    The Old and the New 365
    Christian Missionary Efforts 366
    Early Black Congregations 367
    Black Female Religious Leadership 371
    Black Churches during Reconstruction 372
    Black Churches in the Twentieth Century 374
    Current Trends 375
    Black Denominations 379

Further Reading 387
Index 389

CONTENTS

Volume 3: Culture

18 Literature: African American Writers, Scholars, and Poets 417
    The Oral Tradition 419
    Early African American Writers 419
    The Harlem Renaissance 423
    African American Writers after the Harlem Renaissance 425
    The Black Arts Movement 425
    Post-1960s Literature and the Rise of Black Women Writers 427

19 Performing Arts: The African American in the Performing Arts 429
    African Americans and the Performing Arts 429
    The Earliest Plays with African American Actors 430
    Minstrel Shows 431
    Reclaiming the Black Image: 1890 to 1920 432
    The Development of Black Performers from the Harlem Renaissance
        through the 1950s 434
    Dramatic Theater in the 1950s 436
    Black Dance 437
    The Black Comedian 438
    The Civil Rights Movement and Its Affect on Black Performers 438
    Modern Black Musicals 440
    Modern Black Dance 441
    Modern Black Comedy 444

20 Film and Television 446
    Film
        The Silent Era 448
        Oscar Micheaux and Early Independent Filmmaking 449
        The 1930s and the Dawn of Musicals 450
        World War II and the 1940s 452
        Dorothy Dandridge and the 1950s 453
        The Reign of Sidney Poitier 453
        Black Power, Black Direction, and Blaxploitation 455
        Comedy: The Hottest Trend of the 1980s 456
        Spike Lee and a New Era of Filmmaking 459

Television
- *I Spy* 464
- The 1970s and the Rise of Programs for Blacks 466
- The 1980s 470
- Current Programming 472

21 Media: The African American Press and Broadcast Media 473
Newspaper and Magazine Publishers 473
Broadcasting
- Radio 478
- Television 481
- Public Television 484
- Public Radio 485
- Cable Television 485

Book Publishers
- Religious Publishers 485
- Institutional Publishers 487
- Commercial Publishers 489

22 Music: Popular, Jazz, and Classical 490
Popular Music
- Gospel: The Root of Popular Music 490
- The Rise of Rhythm and Blues 493
- Rock and Roll 496
- Blacks and Country Music 497
- Soul: The Mirror of a Decade 498
- Motown: The Capital of Northern Soul 499
- Funk 501
- Rap: A Voice from the Streets 502

Blues and Jazz
- Ragtime and Blues 504
- New Orleans Jazz 504
- Early Recordings and Improvisation 505
- The Jazz Tradition 507

Classical
- Slave Music 511
- Art Music in the Nineteenth Century 511
- Classical Music in the Twentieth Century 512

xiii

CONTENTS

23 Fine and Applied Arts: The African American Artist **518**
    Black Artists in Early America 519
    African American Artists in the Harlem Renaissance 521
    African American Artists since the Depression 522
    The Search for an African American Identity 524
    Architecture and the Applied Arts 524
    Museums and Galleries since the 1960s 526
    Black Milestones and Major Black Exhibits 529

24 Science, Medicine, and Invention: African American Contributions to Science .. **533**
    Early Scientists and Inventors 534
    Scientists and Inventors in the 20th Century 535
    Highlights in Medicine 539

25 Sports: The African American Amateur and Professional Athlete **542**
    Baseball 543
    Basketball 546
    Football 547
    Boxing 549
    Women in Sports 551
    Current Issues in Sports for African Americans 552

26 Military: African American Servicemen and the Military Establishment **556**
    The American Revolution and the Revolutionary War (1775-83) 556
    The War of 1812 557
    The Civil War (1861-65) 557
    United States Colored Troops (USCT) 558
    The Indian Campaigns (1866-90) 560
    The Spanish-American War (1898) 561
    World War I 564
    The Interwar Years (1919-40) 565
    World War II 565
    The Move toward Equality in the Ranks 572
    The Korean War 573
    Vietnam 574
    The 1970s and 1980s 576
    The Persian Gulf War 577

Further Reading 581
Index 583

PICTURE CREDITS

The photographs and illustrations appearing in *African American Almanac* were received from the following sources:

Courtesy of the Library of Congress: pp. 3 (upper left), 4, 7, 91, 97, 107, 181, 214, 215, 219, 220, 221, 224, 226, 233, 246, 258, 259, 270 (lower right), 273 (lower right), 283, 317, 319, 351, 353, 431, 534, 558; **AP/Wide World Photos:** pp. 10, 12, 14, 18, 19, 20, 51, 86, 94, 108, 113, 122, 140 (lower right), 144, 146, 153, 155, 157, 161, 171, 231, 235, 244, 254 (upper right), 260, 262 (upper left), 262 (upper right), 265, 269 (upper left), 270 (upper left), 275, 281, 286, 291 (lower right), 292, 293 (lower right), 312, 318, 324 (lower right), 326 (lower right), 328, 356, 359, 374, 377, 378, 382, 418, 419, 427, 428 (upper left), 434 (lower right), 437, 440 (upper left), 440 (lower right), 443, 444, 447, 450, 451, 457, 458, 460, 462, 463, 467, 470, 471, 482, 483, 484, 492, 495 (lower right), 497, 498, 499, 502, 503, 505, 508, 514, 516, 527, 538, 543 (upper right), 546 (upper left), 547, 548, 550 (lower right), 551 (upper left), 552, 553, 554, 555, 560, 576, 577, 578, 579; **UPI/Bettmann:** pp. 13, 28, 105, 112, 120, 230, 238, 254 (upper left), 256, 280, 288, 291 (upper left), 293 (upper left), 307, 428 (upper right), 452, 468, 469, 478, 506, 513, 525, 541, 544, 549, 551 (lower right); *Harper's Magazine:* pp. 22, 147; **United Nations:** pp. 27, 33, 36, 42, 44, 48, 59, 61, 63 (upper left), 63 (lower right), 65, 67, 71, 385; **National Museum of African Art:** pp. 31, 35, 39; **Courtesy of Fisk University:** pp. 77, 95, 247, 272, 354 (lower right), 371, 422 (lower right), 430; **Bettmann Archive:** pp. 89, 172, 229 (lower right), 357, 453, 504, 535 (lower right), 559; **Courtesy of the Consulate General of Jamaica:** p. 102; **NBC:** 110, 466, 500; **The Granger Collection, New York:** p. 138; **The Schomburg Center for Research in Black Culture, the New York Public Library:** pp. 158, 512, 545; **Courtesy of the National Park Service:** p. 166, 168; **U.S. Navy:** 174, 572; **Denver Public Library, Western Collection:** pp. 176, 180; **Archive Photos/Lass:** p. 223; **Archive Photos:** pp. 252, 271, 384, 454, 455, 456, 459, 465, 515, 543 (upper left); **Courtesy of the NAACP:** pp. 264, 285, 290, 311, 320 (lower right), 331; **Courtesy of the New York Public Library:** pp. 269 (lower right), 434 (upper left), 495 (upper left); **Surlock Photographers:** p. 274; **Courtesy the National Archives:** pp. 284, 303, 521; **Reproduced by

PICTURE CREDITS

permission of The Stanley B. Burns, M.D. Collection: pp. 299, 379; **NASA:** p. 306; **Photograph by Sue Stetler:** p. 309; **Photograph by Kenneth Estell:** pp. 310, 334, 336; **Photograph by Andy Roy:** pp. 314, 324 (upper left), 326 (upper left); **Courtesy of the Walker Collection of A'Lelia Bundles:** p. 320 (upper left); **Photograph by Brian V. Jones:** 330, 333, 341; **Courtesy of the Bethune Museum and Archive:** p. 354 (upper left); **Photograph by Bruce Giffin:** p. 362; **Photograph by Beverly Hardy:** p. 364; **The National Portrait Gallery, The Smithsonian Institution:** p. 370; **Archive Photos/American Stock Photos:** p. 373; **John Duprey/*NY Daily News:*** p. 381; **Springer/Bettmann Film Archive:** pp. 423, 493; **Courtesy of the Arthur B. Spingarn Collection, Moorland-Spingarn Research Center, Howard University:** p. 424 (upper left); **Courtesy WABC-TV, New York:** p. 442; **Courtesy of The Associated Publishers:** p. 475; **Archive Photos/Frank Driggs Collection:** p. 494; **Courtesy of Columbia Records:** p. 496; **Courtesy of the William Morris Agency:** p. 509; **Courtesy of *Downbeat:*** p. 510; **National Museum of American Art, Washington D.C./Art Resource, N.Y.:** pp. 520 (upper left), 523, 531; **General Motors, Public Relations Department:** p. 526; **Reuters/Bettmann:** p. 546 (lower right); **Photograph by Carl Nesfield:** p. 550 (upper left); **U.S. War Department/National Archives:** p. 563, 564; **U.S. Army:** p. 567, 569, 573.

WORDS TO KNOW

A

abolition: the destruction or ending of slavery; an *abolitionist* is a person or a group in favor of putting an end to slavery, or the principles behind such a person or group

abstain: to refrain from doing; *abstinence* is the act of voluntary avoiding a certain behavior

acquittal: a court decision freeing one of charges; to be *acquitted* is to be cleared of all charges, to be declared not guilty

aesthetics: the study or theory of beauty as it relates to art

affiliates: those businesses or persons associated or connected with an organization

affirmative action: a policy designed to correct the effects of racial and sexual discrimination through hiring quotas and other measures; sometimes negatively referred to as "reverse discrimination"

agrarian: relating to farming, agriculture, or agribusiness

alliance: a close partnership or association

alma mater: (Latin for *fostering mother*) the particular school or college a person attended

alumni: persons who have attended or graduated from a particular school or college

American Dream: the concept that all Americans, given equal opportunities, may strive for personal and financial success

anchor: in broadcasting, to serve as chief reporter of a newscast

annex: to add or attach

anthropology: the study of humans, including their characteristics, culture, and customs

anti-Semitism: discrimination or prejudice against Jews

apartheid: a policy of racial separation

applied arts: fields in which art serves a dual function, such as graphic or fashion design

apprehension: an understanding of an issue; fear that something bad will occur; capture or arrest

appropriations: funds set aside for a specific purpose

arbiter: one who judges or decides

archaeologists: scientists who study past civilizations, especially by a process of careful digging called excavation

WORDS TO KNOW

archipelago: a group of islands

archives: a place where important papers, documents, and other memorabilia are kept; the papers, documents, and memorabilia that are kept in such a place

arias: melodies in an opera, oratorio, or cantata created especially for a solo voice

Armageddon: the place referred to in the Biblical Book of Revelation where the last battle is to be fought between the forces of good and evil; the time of the last battle; also referred to as the *apocalypse*

aspirations: ambitions

assimilate: to become like or similar to, to join

attaché: a person with special duties, particularly in connection with international relations

autonomous: independent or self-governing

avant-garde: new and nontraditional

B

bequest: money or other personal property that is awarded by means of a will; the act of giving money or personal property

Black Muslim movement: also called the Nation of Islam; a religious movement, begun by W. D. Fard and furthered by Elijah Muhammad, that preached black self-sufficiency and worship of Allah. Among the most famous converts to the Black Muslims were Malcolm X and Muhammad Ali

Black codes: unfair rules and laws directed at African Americans following emancipation

Bohemianism: living outside the conventions of society

bourgeoisie: a social class between the wealthy and the working class; the middle class

boycott: a refusal by an individual or group to buy, sell, or use products or services

C

capital: money, property, and other valuable assets that are used to start and sustain a business

cardiovascular: the system that links the heart and blood vessels

catafalque: a wooden framework used to hold a coffin during elaborate funerals

catalysts: persons or objects that bring about events or results

caucus: a group of politicians or a meeting of political party leaders

ceded: formally transferred or surrendered

census: an official count of the population that also includes information about age, sex, race, economic status, etc.

CEO: *C*hief *E*xecutive *O*fficer; the highest executive of a company or organization

charter: a document that outlines the goals of a group

chattel: persons regarded as fixed items of personal property

choreography: the arrangement or step-by-step planning of a dance

civil disobedience: nonviolent resistance to a policy or law; first popularized by Indian leader Mohandas (Mahatma) Gandhi

clichés: unoriginal statements or ideas

coalition: a group united in purpose

collateral: a form of security that is offered to a lender until a loan is repaid

commercialism: business focused purely on profit

compromise: something blending qualities of two different things

compulsory: necessary or required

confrontations: bold face-to-face meetings

conglomerate: a large corporation that owns several smaller businesses in a number of different industries

WORDS TO KNOW

connoisseurs: those who take keen enjoyment in their field of expertise

conscientious: ruled by what one thinks to be right

consecrated: made or *ordained* a bishop through a religious ceremony; made or declared sacred

consensus: general agreement

conservatism: a political movement or philosophy that stresses less government and more private enterprise

conspiracy: a plot to work together in secret, especially for harmful or unlawful purposes

constituency: the group of voters an elected official serves

constitutionality: legality in relationship to the laws and principles set forth in the Constitution

controversial: subject to argument or debate

conversion: the change from lack of faith to religious faith; the change from one religion to another

corporations: businesses, formed with permission of the state or federal government, that have the power to own property and make contracts

coup: (short for the French *coup d'état*) a quick seizure of power, often by military force

crossover: the ability to please or appeal to more than one group

curators: heads of museums or special collections

curriculum: the standard information, teaching plan, and testing for a course or major field of study; the entire teaching program of a given school or college

D

defected: left because of disagreement

demographics: the census characteristics of a population, broken down by geographic regions

denigrated: belittled

denomination: a specific religious body or organization (for example, Baptist, Methodist, or Catholic); *denominational* means having to do with a specific religious group, the opposite of *nondenominational*

deportation: the sending away, by official order, of an undesirable alien

deposed: removed from office

derive: come from

dialect: a spoken language specific to a region or group

diaspora: a scattering or dispersion of people who share a common background

dictatorships: governments ruled by absolute power; the opposite of democracies

dilemma: a serious problem, usually one for which there are two equally difficult choices

dioceses: a religious district presided over by a bishop; large or prominent religious districts are called *archdioceses*

disenfranchised: the poor or disadvantaged

dissenting: in legal matters, a *dissenting* opinion is one that differs from the majority, or ruling, opinion; dissenting opinions are offered by justices who think their fellow members on the bench have made an error in their ruling

documentary: a nonfiction (true-to-life) film

dominion: the power to rule; a territory that is ruled

downsizing: trimming, through plant closings, layoffs, etc., to make a business healthier and more profitable

E

ecumenical: anything promoting the unity of Christian churches

WORDS TO KNOW

effigy (to burn in): to publicly burn an image of a person in protest

emancipation: to be freed from the control of another

enact: to pass into law

enclave: a territory or group that is surrounded by a larger territory or group

endowment: a gift, generally money, to an institution or person; a natural talent or ability

entrepreneurship: the business quality of undertaking risk for the sake of earning a profit

equatorial: near or of the equator, the imaginary line equidistant from the North and South Poles

equity: value or worth, as in money, property, stocks, etc.

eulogized: praised after death

Eurocentric: concerned primarily with European or Western culture

evangelists: literally, bringers of good news; those fervently devoted to spreading the gospel

execution: the act of legally putting to death; carrying out of a task

exile: a person who by force or choice lives outside his country; the condition of living outside a country

exodus: literally, a going out; a massive migration or departure of a people

exonerated: declared not guilty

exploitation: unfair use of an individual or group

F

fascism: government by a one-party dictatorship

fertility: the state of being able to produce children, determined by age and other factors

feudal: a system popular in Europe during the Middle Ages in which serfs were bound for life to work the land and were, in turn, protected by overlords

fine arts: fields in which art stands alone, such as painting or sculpture

flamboyant: flashy and exciting

franchise: in sports, a team that is granted membership in a league

fugitive: a person who flees from danger or from the law

G

generative: capable of continuing, through reproduction, etc.

genocide: the destruction or killing of an entire race

genre: a type of literary form, such as a poem, story, novel, essay, or autobiography

glaucoma: an eye-related disorder that can, if untreated, cause a total loss of vision

Gothic: a style of architecture that stresses pointed arches and steep roofs; a style of fiction that suggests horror, mystery, and gloom; anything ornate

H

Harlem Renaissance: a flowering of black literature and performing arts during the 1920s in which Harlem served as the artistic capital

heptathlon: a track and field contest consisting of seven separate events

I

illiterate: a person who cannot read or write; the phrase *functional illiterate* refers to those whose reading and writing abilities are less than adequate

impeached: brought before a hearing on charges of wrongdoing

importation: to bring into a new region goods that are then usually sold

WORDS TO KNOW

inauguration: the formal ceremony by which a person is placed in office; to be *inaugurated* is to be formally sworn into office

incumbent: the current office-holder

indemnity: protection

indentured servant: a person bound by contract to work for another for a certain length of time; during the early period of American history, both black and white indentured servants were commonly used and were usually forced to work for seven years before they gained their freedom

indigo: a plant of the pea family; the blue dye obtained from such a plant

inducted: enrolled or entered into

inevitably: predictably

infringement: the act of overstepping boundaries and intruding on another's

injunction: an order from the court either prohibiting or demanding a certain action

innovators: in the performing arts, those who introduce new methods and styles and thereby change the direction of the field

inoculation: an injection, aimed at disease prevention, that causes a mild form of the disease; the injection forces the body to build up an immunity to a later attack of the actual disease

institution: a person, thing, idea, or practice that has taken root or settled into habit

insurmountable: not able to be overcome

integration: the bringing together of races, classes, or ethnic groups that were previously separated; bringing a group into equal membership in society

interpretive: bringing out the meaning or importance of

intimidation: to scare or make timid by means of threats or violence

intravenous: directly into a vein

involuntary servitude: the institution of forcing people to work for their freedom; also called indentured servitude

ironically: in a manner opposite of what is expected

J

Jim Crow: a reference (taken from a minstrel song) to laws and practices supporting the segregation of blacks and whites

jurisdiction: legal territory

L

laypersons: nonordained church members; also referred to as the *laity*

leveraged buyout: the purchase of a company in which most of the sale price is financed using borrowed money

liable: responsible by law

liberal arts: a course of study that provides a broad background in literature, philosophy, languages, history, and abstract sciences; the opposite of a vocational or technical course of study

literacy: the ability to read and write

litigation: the process of filing and pursuing a lawsuit

liturgical: having to do with the order and nature of public worship, including the songs, rituals, readings, prayers, and sermon that form a religious service

lynching: murder without trial, frequently by hanging

M

maligned: spoken ill of

manumission: liberation from slavery; to be *manumitted* is to be freed from slavery

WORDS TO KNOW

Maroons: black slaves who escaped and formed communities in the mountains, swamps, and forests of the southern colonies

Mason-Dixon line: generally thought of as the line that divides the North and the South; named after surveyors Charles Mason and Jeremiah Dixon, who in 1767 settled a dispute over the east-west boundary between Pennsylvania and Maryland and the north-south boundary between Maryland and Delaware

Masonic: having to do with Masons or Freemasons, an international organization dedicated to universal brotherhood, charity, and mutual aid

media: a plural noun signifying all types of communication (radio, television, newspapers, etc.)

median: the midway point in a series of numbers (half of the numbers being above and half below); not to be confused with average

metaphor: a figure of speech in which one thing is identified with another

Middle Passage: the trade route from West Africa across the Atlantic Ocean to the West Indies and the East Coast of America

militant: aggressive; prepared to fight

minstrel: an entertainer typically associated with a traveling comic variety show, such as the Christy Minstrels (from which the word comes)

misogyny: hatred of women

monarchy: a government ruled by a king or queen or other person of royal birthright. Constitutional monarchies are limited in power, but absolute monarchies are essentially dictatorships

monographs: scholarly books or articles on a single subject

Monroe Doctrine: the policy established by President James Monroe that said the United States would not allow European interference in the affairs of America or her neighbors

mosaics: pictures composed of small bits of stone, glass, tile, etc.

mulatto: a person who has one black and one white parent; any person of black-white ancestry

multicultural: concerned with minority as well as majority cultures

N

nationalism: a movement to achieve independence; patriotism; a *nationalist,* in black studies, is one who believes in the creation of black power through a politically and economically strong black nation

negritude: the awareness among blacks of their cultural heritage

neoclassical: art or literature dating from the mid-seventeenth to mid-eighteenth century that revived the classic forms and styles of ancient Greece and Rome

niche: a desirable place; in business terms, typically a safe market not threatened by competitors

O

odyssey: epic journey

ordained: established or invested with the title of minister, priest, rabbi, and so forth

orthodox: traditional; conforming to established doctrine

ostracized: banished

P

pacify: to satisfy or calm

Pan-Africanism: a theory or movement embracing cooperation and unity among African nations and among all African peoples

WORDS TO KNOW

parodied: poked fun at through imitation

patents: legal and exclusive rights to produce, use, and sell what one has invented

pathology: the condition and results of a disease

patois: a differing form of a standard language

patron: a person, usually wealthy, who finances and supports another person, cause, or institution; *patronage* is that support given

pending: not yet decided or determined

per capita: per person

petition: a formal, signed request

philanthropists: those who share their wealth with various humanitarian, or charitable, causes

plaintiffs: those filing a lawsuit (*defendants* are those being accused or sued by the plaintiffs)

plasma: the fluid part of blood

plebiscite: an expression of the people's will, by ballot, on a political issue

posthumous: after death

poverty: the condition of being poor; the government determines poverty according to a poverty index based on monetary income alone; in 1990 a family of four was considered to be in poverty if the household income was less than $13,359

predecessors: those who have gone before, usually said of influential persons

prenatal: taking place before birth

proclamation: an official announcement

prohibit: to forbid or make illegal; something *prohibited* is not allowed by law

prolific: highly energetic and productive

propaganda: ideas and information used to further or to hinder a movement or cause

propagation: expansion from person to person, place to place; reproduction or multiplication

prosperity: wealth

protectorate: a weaker state that is governed by a stronger state

proteges: persons guided, taught, or shaped by generally older and more influential persons

provision: something set aside for the future; a section in a legal document that outlines a special condition or requirement

psychedelic: causing intense stimulation of the mind

pueblo: a close-knit village of sun-dried bricks and stone built by Native Americans in the southwestern United States; Pueblo Indian cultures include the Hopi and Zuni

pundits: experts or authorities on given topics

R

ratify: to approve or pass

ratio: the relationship of one quantity to another, expressed in a fraction or percentage

recession: a general decline in business activity that translates into more layoffs, fewer new jobs, and decreases in household spending power

referendum: a direct vote by the people

repatriationist: one who believes in returning to the country of origin

repeal: to cancel

repertoire: songs or pieces within a musician's or group of musicians' typical performance program

repertory: a group that alternates the works (from their *repertoire*) that they perform

repression: the act of keeping back, putting down, or holding down

resolutions: statements of intent

retaliation: to respond in kind, as in "an eye for an eye"

retrospective: an exhibit that looks back at an artist's development

rhetoric: especially effective speaking or writing; alternately, language that is flashy but insincere

WORDS TO KNOW

rigorous: very strict or challenging

S

savanna: a grassland

schism: a split or break within an organization, usually as a result of serious disagreement

secession: withdrawal from an organization

secular: relating to worldly things, as opposed to religious or spiritual things

segregation: the separation or isolation of a race, class, or ethnic group into a restricted area

seminary: a school where one is trained to become a minister, priest, or rabbi

separatism: a policy of keeping the races apart in all matters

seriocomic: mixing serious and comic elements

servitude: slavery

sociologist: one who studies human society

sole proprietorships: businesses in which the owner is also the chief operator

sovereignty: having dominion status or control over a nation

speaking in tongues: a gift of the Holy Spirit described in the New Testament (see Acts 2:4 and 1 Corinthians 12-14)

stereotypes: simple and inaccurate images of a person, group, etc.

stigmatizes: marks or brands unfavorably

subservient: inferior or subject to rule by another

suppression: keeping from happening or being known

supremacy: the state of having the most power or authority; a *supremacist* is one who believes in the superiority of a certain group

surveillance: continual observation

syncopated: shifted in beat from what is regularly accented to what is regularly unaccented

syndicated: sold and presented through many *media* outlets

syphilis: a venereal, or sexually transmitted, disease that can lead to a weakening of the bones, nerve tissue, and heart

T

temperance: in general, the quality of self-restraint; historically, movements promoting moderation, total avoidance, or prohibition of alcoholic liquor

tenure: a permanent right to a position, as in teaching

thesis: in education, a long, formal research paper

timpanist: a player of kettledrums (timpani)

tumultuous: troubled or characterized by upheaval

U

ultimatum: a final offer that, if rejected, will leads to a specific consequence

unalienable: secure from being transferred or taken away

unanimously: in total agreement

uncompromising: unwilling to change one's principles or alter one's behavior

unconstitutional: not permitted or spelled out in the United States Constitution; one of the primary duties of the Supreme Court is to determine whether laws or customs are constitutional or unconstitutional

Underground Railroad: a secret network of safe places, such as houses or barns, where runaway slaves could hide on their way north; these safe places were called "stations," and the people who operated them were called "conductors"

V

v.: an abbreviation for versus, a term used to separate opposing forces, such as the plaintiff and the defendant in a lawsuit

valets: personal servants who take care of clothes, help one dress, etc.

vaudeville: a form of entertainment consisting of skits, dances, songs, and other performances

versatile: multitalented

viability: ability to grow and prosper

Victorian: a nineteenth-century style of architecture characterized by largeness and ornamentation; anything dating from the reign of Queen Victoria (1837-1901)

virtuoso: someone with extraordinary skill in a given field

vulnerable: open to attack or injury

W

West Indies: a large group of islands, including the Bahamas, Puerto Rico, Jamaica, Cuba, Haiti, and the Virgin Islands, that lies between North and South America and to the east of Central America

Western Hemisphere: that half of the world containing the continents of North and South America; also called the New World

women's suffrage: a movement for the right of women to vote

African American Almanac

6
Slavery

From the Beginnings of America to the End of the Nineteenth Century

> **FACT FOCUS**
>
> - Between ten and twenty million Africans arrived in the New World as slaves.
> - One of every six or seven slaves died during the dreadful **Middle Passage**.
> - Another one of every three or four slaves died during a harsh period of training in the West Indies.
> - By 1790, African Americans represented nearly 20 percent of the U.S. population.
> - Although the overseas slave trade ended in 1808, slavery continued within the United States until the end of the Civil War.

"I was conductor of the Underground Railroad for eight years and I can say what most conductors can't say—I never ran my train off the track or lost a passenger."—Harriet Tubman, inscription on the Harriet Tubman Memorial, Auburn, New York

African Roots of Slavery

West Africa was the birthplace of three powerful tribal empires, the Ghana, Mali, and Songhai. Although all were highly developed civilizations, these empires upheld the custom of slavery.

As early as the ninth century, the Ghanaian king was trading slaves to Arab merchants for goods from the Mediterranean and the East. As the centuries passed, the mud-walled city of Timbuktu (now part of modern-day Mali) became both a university and the famous southern hub of trade across the Sahara Desert. Horses, steel, and woven goods came south and were purchased with gold, ivory, cotton, and slaves.

When fifteenth-century Portuguese explorers became the first modern Europeans to reach West Africa by sea, they found that slave trading was well established, as it was back in Portugal. The opening of a direct sea

SLAVERY

The first Africans arrived in Jamestown, Virginia, as indentured servants in 1619, a year before the pilgrims landed at Plymouth Rock

WORDS TO KNOW

assimilate: to become like or similar to, to join

ceded: formally transferred or surrendered

chattel: persons regarded as fixed items of personal property

controversial: subject to argument or debate

dilemma: a serious problem, usually one for which there are two equally difficult choices

indigo: a plant of the pea family; the blue dye obtained from such a plant

manumission: liberation from slavery

Middle Passage: the trade route from West Africa across the Atlantic Ocean to the West Indies and the East Coast of America

ratify: to approve or pass

repeal: to cancel

surveillance: continual observation

unalienable: secure from being transferred or taken away

valets: personal servants who take care of clothes, help one dress, etc.

route immediately changed things for the worse, however. Once the Portuguese began trading guns for captives, the slave trade became a vicious trap. If an African king refused to raid for slaves, the traders would cut off his gun supply, making his own people defenseless against the raids of others.

African slaves were, in fact, much more highly regarded by their fellow Africans than by the Europeans. Many such slaves were well educated and multitalented. African slavery was not based on race. The kings of Dahomey (modern-day Benin) were known to choose the sons of slaves to succeed to the throne. Only in the Western Hemisphere did race become the badge of slavery: the slave's heaviest chain was the color of his skin.

Servants, Free Persons, and Slaves

In 1619, 20 Africans accompanied the Europeans who landed at Jamestown, Virginia. These people were not slaves but

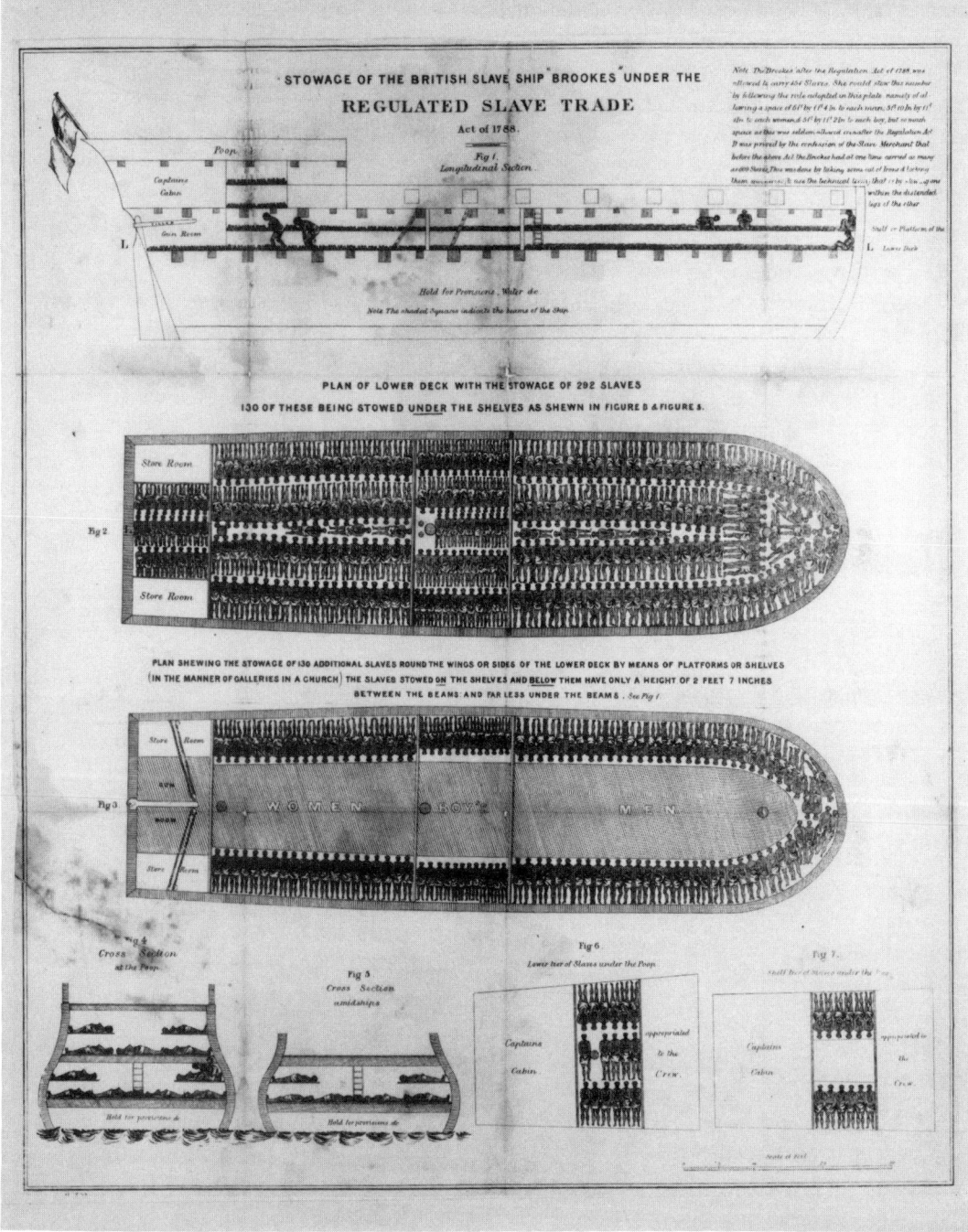

The layout of a slave ship

215

SLAVERY

indentured servants. Upon completing their contracts they were free to enjoy the liberties and privileges of the other colonists.

The first black American born in the colonies, William Tucker, shared with the other settlers the common birthright of freedom. The slave Anthony Johnson apparently became free about 1622. He later imported five servants of his own, for which he obtained 250 acres from the colonial government. Another black American, a carpenter named Richard Johnson, imported two white servants and received 100 acres.

By 1650 there were about 300 Africans, most of them indentured servants, in the American colonies. It is unclear when the first actual African slaves arrived on American shores. But from the 1640s Africans were increasingly regarded as **chattel**. In 1641 Massachusetts became the first state to make slavery legal, and the institution gradually spread among the original 13 colonies.

Rhode Island had an antislavery ordinance, but the colonists openly disobeyed it. Only Pennsylvania maintained a strong opposition to slavery. By the 1650s Africans

---

1492 Pedro Alonzo Niño, whom some historians think was black, sails with Christopher Columbus to the New World.

1502 Portugal sends black slaves to the New World.

1526 The first group of Africans sets foot on what is now the United States. Led by a Spanish explorer, they arrive in South Carolina.

1619 A Dutch ship carries twenty blacks to Jamestown, Virginia.

1620 The *Mayflower* arrives at Plymouth, Massachusetts.

1641 Massachusetts becomes the first colony to legalize slavery.

1700 There are approximately 28,000 slaves in the English colonies.

1750 Over 236,000 slaves now live in colonial America.

1775 The first **abolitionist** society is organized in Philadelphia, Pennsylvania.

1776 The Continental Congress approves the Declaration of Independence, minus a paragraph against slavery written by Thomas Jefferson.

1777 Vermont becomes the first state to abolish slavery altogether.

1790 The first census records that there are 757,000 blacks in the United States. This number represents close to one-fifth of the total population. Less than one-tenth of all blacks are free.

1793 Eli Whitney, a white inventor from Massachusetts, obtains a patent for his cotton gin. Whitney's machine makes cotton growing a very profitable business; as a result, the slave system expands, especially in the South.

1841 Frederick Douglass, a runaway slave, begins his career as a popular speaker and writer.

1863 President Abraham Lincoln signs the Emancipation Proclamation.

1865 The Civil War ends.

were commonly sold for life. As white indentured servitude began to end, the flow of African labor into the colonies accelerated. Southern planters began strictly enforcing the slave system.

One practical reason for this unfortunate system was that escaped slaves of African origin could be more easily detected than whites. Another less commonsense reason why the colonists began to base slavery on race was their unfounded belief that African cultures were primitive and pagan. Based on this belief, whites justified forcing imported blacks into labor in the name of civilized, Christian culture. Even after black Americans were Christianized, however, their slave status was not altered.

The Trans-Atlantic Slave Trade

The number of Africans who reached the Americas is estimated at between ten and twenty million. About 600,000 Africans were imported during the sixteenth century, two million in the seventeenth century, five million in the eighteenth century, and three million in the nineteenth century. In addition to those who reached the Americas must be added the enormous number who died in passage. It is estimated that 15 percent of those who were shipped to the Americas died of disease on the overcrowded boats of the "Middle Passage," and that another 30 percent died during the brutal training period faced in the West Indies before being shipped to the American mainland.

The Growth of Slavery in Colonial America

Although the northern colonies had little local need for slave labor, they played a prin-

> **SPECIAL FOCUS**
>
> The majority of African slaves came from the areas of these nations:
>
> Benin • Burkina Faso • Cameroon • Congo • Gabon • Gambia • Ghana • Guinea • Ivory Coast • Liberia • Nigeria • Senegal • Sierra Leone • Togo

cipal role in the slave trade. By 1700 black Americans in New Hampshire, Massachusetts, Rhode Island, and Connecticut numbered only 1,000 among a population of 90,000. In the middle colonies (New York, New Jersey, Pennsylvania, and Delaware), the population formed a larger percentage because there were a number of small slaveholders who employed slaves as farm laborers, domestics, and craftsmen. In New York, slaves comprised 12 percent of the population during the mid-eighteenth century. The Quakers of Pennsylvania protested that slavery violated the principles of Christianity and passed laws prohibiting the slave trade in 1688, 1693, and 1696, but the British parliament overruled these statutes in 1712.

Most slaves, of course, lived in the South. The southern colonies were divided between the tobacco-producing provinces of Maryland, Virginia, and North Carolina and the huge rice and **indigo** plantations of South Carolina and Georgia. (Georgia, founded in 1733, prohibited slavery until the British government took control of it in 1752.)

The growth of a plantation economy and the concentration of a large number of black Americans in the southern states led Virginia (1636) and then the other states to form all white militias. The terror of slave uprisings led the slaveholders to devise ever harsher slave codes. Ultimately, a slave could not own anything, carry a weapon, or leave his plantation without a written pass. Murder, rape, arson, and many other offenses were punishable by death. Small offenses were commonly punished by whipping, maiming, and branding. In the South a slave was not given the right to defend himself against a white, and as far north as Virginia it was not possible for a white to be convicted for the murder of a slave.

The American Revolution

During the course of the American Revolution, many colonies granted freedom to slaves in return for military service. Rhode Island passed the first slave enlistment act in February 1778, raising a regiment that served heroically in many important battles. In 1780 Maryland became the only southern state to enroll slave troops, while South Carolina and Georgia flatly refused even to arm their slaves. While slave conscripts were at first assigned to combat support, they were often armed in the heat of battle. Black Americans were often enlisted for longer terms than whites, and by the latter years of the war many of the most seasoned veterans were black soldiers. At the end of the war about 5,000 black Americans had been freed through military service.

The United States Constitution

The United States Constitution, which was passed in 1788, provided the nation with basic political principles. Most important were: 1) the belief that all people are created equal and possess certain **unalienable** rights and 2) that government receives its power from the people.

> **SPECIAL FOCUS**
>
> States that abolished slavery following the Revolutionary War:
>
> Vermont, 1777
> Massachusetts, 1783
> Connecticut and Rhode Island, 1784
> New York, 1785
> New Jersey, 1786
> Pennsylvania, 1789

Unfortunately, black Americans were not afforded the rights and privileges of the Constitution. At the time, many whites believed that people of African descent were racially inferior and unable to **assimilate** themselves into society. Article I, section 2 of the Constitution specified that all persons not free should be counted as three-fifths of a person for the sake of tax purposes, and article I, section 9 allowed the slave trade to continue until 1808.

Slavery in the New Nation

In 1793 Eli Whitney invented the cotton gin, a processing machine that led to a huge increase in cotton growing and cotton buying and also increased the demand for slaves in cotton-producing states. In 1800 there were nearly 900,000 African slaves in the United States. By 1810 there were 1.1 million. Although the slave trade technically stopped in 1808, it is estimated that from then until 1860 more than 250,000 more slaves were illegally imported. Furthermore, nothing prevented owners from selling or trading slaves *within* the country, and the breeding of slaves for sale became a specialized business.

SLAVERY

Slave auction notice

By the mid-eighteenth century, three-fourths of the cotton produced in the world came from the United States. Profits from cotton were so great that vast plantations were hacked from the wilderness, allowing large numbers of slaves to work the fields. With the outbreak of the Civil War there were nearly four million slaves in the United States. Nearly three-fourths of them worked on cotton plantations.

Slave Life

Slavery was by its very nature brutal. The more fortunate slaves tended to work on family-sized farms or had positions as house servants. Much depended on the kindness of the master. On the larger plantations slaves were divided between house and field hands. The former were responsible for groundskeeping, gardening, house cleaning, general maintenance, and caring for the slave owner's children. House servants were frequently allowed to practice such trades as metalworking, masonry, and tailoring. Some became skilled musicians. Some even became doctors.

Body slaves (specialized house servants) served their masters as **valets** and personal messengers, and from this closeness friendships sometimes developed. But the daily lives of house servants had little in common with those of the field-workers.

On larger plantations with 25 or more slaves, the only contact between field hands and whites occurred through the overseer, who often adopted cruel measures to maintain control. Many planters believed the largest profits were to be made by working a slave to death in eight or ten years and then buying a new one. Even tenderhearted masters often had little contact with their field-workers. So long as the overseer returned a profit no questions were asked.

Most slaves could only expect to live with the bare necessities of food, clothing, and shelter. Food was often limited to a bucket of rice or corn per week with no meat. Clothing was basic in design and made of coarse materials. Often, large families were expected to live in a cramped, windowless, mud-floored shack.

Only holidays broke the routine, although in some cases slaves were able to hunt, fish, or garden in the hours after work.

The Denmark Vesey Conspiracy

The mistreatment of slaves in the years after the Revolutionary War led to an atmosphere of suspicion and terror. Masters lived in constant fear of uprisings, and devoted much time to surveillance. Slave codes, too, became increasingly strict.

219

SLAVERY

Slaves outside their quarters

In 1800 a black American named Denmark Vesey purchased his freedom and from about 1817 planned a slave revolt in Charleston, South Carolina. The revolt was scheduled to begin on July 14, 1822. With the help of five other black Americans, Vesey was able to recruit as many as 5,000 slaves before word of the revolt leaked out. Vesey then moved the date forward to June 16, but again word was leaked. The state militia gathered and began an intense search. In the end, 4 whites and 131 blacks were arrested. Vesey and 36 others were hanged. As news of the conspiracy spread, southern states continued to toughen their slave laws.

Expansion of Slavery

Slavery in the Northwest Territory

In the early seventeenth century, the

SLAVERY

> **CAUTION!!**
>
> **COLORED PEOPLE**
> **OF BOSTON,** ONE & ALL,
> You are hereby respectfully CAUTIONED and advised, to avoid conversing with the
>
> **Watchmen and Police Officers of Boston,**
>
> For since the recent ORDER OF THE MAYOR & ALDERMEN, they are empowered to act as
>
> **KIDNAPPERS**
> **AND**
> **Slave Catchers,**
>
> And they have already been actually employed in KIDNAPPING, CATCHING, AND KEEPING SLAVES. Therefore, if you value your LIBERTY, and the *Welfare of the Fugitives* among you, *Shun* them in every possible manner, as so many *HOUNDS* on the track of the most unfortunate of your race.
>
> **Keep a Sharp Look Out for KIDNAPPERS, and have TOP EYE open.**
>
> APRIL 24, 1851.

Poster warning blacks of the ever-present danger of slave catchers

French began to settle in the area that is now Illinois, Indiana, Michigan, Ohio, Wisconsin, and part of Minnesota. Beginning in the mid-eighteenth century, the British also began settling in the area. In July 1787, to protect American interests, Congress passed the Northwest Ordinance, which established a government for the Northwest Territory and provided terms under which states could be formed for entrance into the Union. The ordinance also contained **controversial** provisions. One outlawed slavery and servitude in the territory, and the other provided for the return of fugitive slaves to the states from which they had escaped.

The farmers who had brought slaves into the territory were angered by the clause prohibiting slavery and petitioned Congress for its **repeal.** The prohibition against slavery was practically ignored when the Illinois and Indiana territories established a system under which any person owning slaves could bring them into the region and place them under lifetime service. Among the restrictions placed on these servants were laws forbidding independent travel without a pass as well as independent public gatherings.

The Missouri Compromise

In April 1803 the United States paid $15 million for the Louisiana Territory, an area that had been settled by the French in the late seventeenth century. Many southerners hoped to extend slavery into the vast new territory and it was widely expected that Missouri would be admitted to the Union as a slave state.

A series of heated debates erupted over the extension of slavery in the region. But in 1821 the Missouri Compromise was reached. This agreement allowed Missouri to enter the Union as a slave state and Maine to enter as a free state.

Texas and the Mexican American War

The territory of Texas was part of the Louisiana Purchase, but by 1819 it had become part of Mexico. Mexico provided land grants to American settlers (many of whom brought their slaves with them), and soon Americans outnumbered the Mexicans of the region. In 1836 Texas declared its independence from Mexico and requested to join the United States. The possibility of another slave state entering the Union stirred fresh debate. On March 1, 1845, President John Tyler signed a joint resolution of Congress to admit Texas as a slave state. In 1846 Mexican and American troops clashed in Texas, and the United States declared war on the Republic of Mexico. The war ended in 1848, with Mexico surrendering its claims to Texas, and with the United States having acquired all of the region extending to the Pacific Ocean.

Antislavery Movements

Quakers and Mennonites

Early opposition to slavery was generally based on religious beliefs. The Quakers (or the Society of Friends) and Mennonites were two of the first groups to oppose the practice in the United States. Primarily settled in Pennsylvania, both groups were also to be found in the South. They practiced simple living, modest dress, and nonviolence. In 1652 the Quakers passed a resolution against lifetime servitude, and in 1688 the Mennonites did the same. With the continued rise of slavery in the South, many Quakers protested and moved north into Indiana and Ohio.

The Free African Society

In 1787 the Free African Society was organized in Philadelphia by two black Americans, Richard Allen and Absalom Jones. Allen later founded the Bethel African Methodist Episcopal Church, and Jones became the rector of an African Protestant Episcopal Church. The society provided economic and medical aid, supported abolition, and communicated with African Americans in the South. Like the many other African American organizations that followed, the society was rooted in religious principles. Throughout the nineteenth century, a number of mutual aid societies—that provided loans, insurance, and various other services—also sprang up in black communities.

The American Colonization Society

In 1816 the American Colonization Society was organized in Washington, D.C., with the goal of encouraging the resettlement of black Americans in Africa. Although much support for the society was well meant, some of it came from those who feared a large free black population in the United States.

Congress provided funds for the transportation of freed slaves to the west coast of Africa and assisted in negotiations with African chiefs who **ceded** the land that became Liberia. While Northerners contributed support and donations to the society, southern patrols threatened freedmen into emigrating. In 1822 the first settlers landed at a site on the western coast of Africa, which was later named Monrovia after President James Monroe. In 1838 the Commonwealth of Liberia was formed and placed under the administration of a governor appointed by the society.

The Abolition Movement

The earliest abolition societies were the Pennsylvania Society for Promoting the Abolition of Slavery, formed in Philadelphia in 1775, and the New York **Manumission** Society, formed in that city in 1785. Before the 1830s a number of antislavery societies arose in both the North and the South. After that time, other such societies arose alongside the women's rights organizations as part of a general social reform movement.

SLAVERY

Cotton, picked by African Americans, is weighed

The American Anti-Slavery Society was formed in Philadelphia in 1833. After attending one of the society's meetings, Quaker abolitionist Lucretia Coffin Mott formed the Philadelphia Female Anti-Slavery Society with the assistance of Elizabeth Cady Stanton. Mott and her husband, James, were active in the Underground Railroad and various other antislavery activities, and James served as a delegate to the World Anti-Slavery Convention.

The press was the primary weapon of the antislavery movement. In 1827 the journalists Samuel Cornish and John Russwurm launched *Freedom's Journal*, the first African American newspaper. In 1831 editor and lecturer William Lloyd Garrison published the first issue of the *Liberator*. Other antislavery papers followed, including *Anti-Slavery Record*, the *Emancipator, Human Rights,* and the *Northern Star*, launched by black abolitionist leader Frederick Douglass.

While many of the antislavery organizations were dominated by whites, African Americans such as Douglass played an important role in the abolition movement. Other notable black leaders were Alexander Crummell, Sarah Mapp Douglass, Charlotte Forten, Henry Highland Garnet, Sojourner Truth, and David Walker. Most of these

SLAVERY

Slaves believed to have used the Underground Railroad to escape the South

leaders were committed to cooperative relations with whites and opposed separatist doctrines. However, some of the more militant abolitionists, including Garnet and Walker, stressed the possibility of violence in the struggle against slavery.

The Underground Railroad

A vast network of individuals and groups developed throughout the country to help black Americans escape from slavery. Abolitionists provided "stations" (food, shelter, and financial assistance), while experienced "conductors" (often themselves runaway slaves) led thousands of "passengers" to freedom in the Northern United States, Canada, and the Caribbean. Most of the movement occurred at night, with passengers hiding in the barns and homes of sympathetic whites and black Americans during the day. Two of the most famous conductors were Josiah Henson and Harriet Tubman.

Civil War

In 1860 Abraham Lincoln, a northern Republican, was elected president. At that time the country was still bitterly divided over the issue of slavery. Because Lincoln had voiced opposition to the expansion of slavery prior to his election, Southerners became even more fearful that their legal right to own slaves would be taken away. In 1860 South Carolina severed its ties with the Union. Georgia, Florida, Alabama, Mississippi, Louisiana, and Texas soon followed. In February 1861 the seven states drew up a constitution and elected Jefferson Davis as president of the Confederate States of America.

As northern leaders sought a means of preserving the nation, southern troops seized federal installations, post offices, and customs houses. In April 1861 Confederate forces took one of the last Union holds in the south, Fort Sumter in Charleston Harbor, South Carolina. Lincoln was forced to respond and for the next four years the Civil War raged.

Black American Soldiers in the Civil War

From the beginning of the war, black Americans engaged in the fighting, although Lincoln at first refused officially to employ them in the Union army. Lincoln faced a **dilemma:** if he freed all slaves, as the abolitionists encouraged him to do, he risked offending the border slave states that remained supportive of the Union. These were Delaware, Maryland, Kentucky, and Missouri. In a letter to journalist and political leader Horace Greeley, Lincoln stated:

> If I could save the Union without freeing any slave, I would do it; if I could save it by freeing all the slaves, I would do it; and if I could save it by freeing some and leaving others alone, I would also do that. What I do about slavery and the colored race, I do because I believe it helps save the Union.

During the summer of 1862, Lincoln began to feel that freeing the slaves would be necessary to realizing victory over the South, and on January 1, 1863, he issued the Emancipation Proclamation, which freed all slaves living in Confederate states.

The rebel Confederate states, however, felt no need to honor Lincoln's proclamation, and conditions changed little for southern slaves during the war. And, because the proclamation did not apply to Union states or the areas under occupation by Union forces, 800,000 northern blacks remained slaves as well.

The Civil War lasted until April 1865. By the end of the war, more than 360,000 Union soldiers and 258,000 Confederate solders were dead. Twenty-one black Americans received the Medal of Honor and untold numbers of others had made sacrifices for the cause.

Civil Rights at the End of the Civil War

Following the war Republicans, who controlled the Congress, took up the cause of the newly freed black Americans. Between 1865 and 1875 they led a movement to pass three amendments to the Constitution and a string of civil rights and Reconstruction laws. The Thirteenth Amendment, **ratified** December 18, 1865, abolished slavery and involuntary servitude. The Fourteenth Amendment, ratified July 28, 1868, guaranteed citizenship and provided equal protection under the laws. The Fifteenth Amendment, ratified March 30, 1870, was designed to protect the right of all citizens to vote.

The Fifteenth Amendment, however, was unsuccessful. Many state and local govern-

Freed blacks leaving the South following the Civil War

ments created voting regulations that ensured that black Americans would not be allowed to vote: these included grandfather clauses, which allowed an individual to vote only if his grandfather had voted; literacy tests; poll taxes; and "white primaries," which were held prior to general elections and in which only whites were permitted to vote.

The last of the early civil rights acts, passed by Congress in 1875, prohibited discrimination in public places. However, an 1883 Supreme Court ruling concluded that this act was unconstitutional on the grounds that the Fourteenth Amendment did not authorize Congress to pass laws against discrimination by private individuals, including owners of hotels, theaters, and restaurants. The Court's ruling brought an end to federal efforts to protect the civil rights of black Americans until the mid-twentieth century.

7

Civil Rights

The Struggle That Shaped the Hearts and Minds of African Americans

"Injustice anywhere is a threat to justice everywhere."—Martin Luther King, Jr.

Throughout American history, blacks have struggled to obtain basic civil rights. The mutinies by Africans during the Middle Passage, the numerous slave uprisings in the New World, the founding of the Free African Society, abolitionism, the Civil War, and emancipation, the civil rights marches and black power rallies of the twentieth century—the struggle has tried and shaped the hearts, minds, and souls of African Americans.

Reconstruction and Civil Rights

The first civil rights laws were passed following the Civil War. They went hand in hand with the Thirteenth (1865), Fourteenth (1868), and Fifteenth Amendments (1870). The last of these laws to be passed was the Civil Rights Act of 1875, which outlawed discrimination in public places and on forms of public transportation. On paper, at least, African Americans during this Reconstruction era could no longer be deprived of their freedom or their basic rights as citizens.

However, by 1877 it was clear that Reconstruction had failed. In February of that year, the presidential election of 1876 was being contested in Washington, D.C. Representatives of Republican candidate Rutherford Hayes agreed to meet with Southern Democrats, who supported Samuel Tilden.

Tilden had actually won the most popular votes by a narrow margin (less than 170,000). But as a result of fraud and violence in Louisiana, South Carolina, and Florida, the Hayes-Tilden election results were in doubt.

After months of arguing, the two political parties reached a complicated agreement. The Democrats supported Hayes's election as president in exchange for several Republican promises. The most important one involved removing the last federal troops who were supporting the government's Reconstruction policies in the South. In effect, the trade-off signalled the rise of the solid South, where racist customs and laws reigned for the next 80 years.

Hence, it was no wonder that large numbers of Southern blacks chose to head West

CIVIL RIGHTS

(mostly to Kansas) in what came to be known as the "Exodus of 1879." Of course many blacks, due to poverty and other reasons, remained in the South. Their situation only worsened when, in 1883, the U.S. Supreme Court ruled that the Civil Rights Act of 1875 was unconstitutional.

Antilynching Efforts

One of the most savage practices of this era was **lynching,** which was not limited to the South or to blacks. However, by the late nineteenth and early twentieth century, lynching had become a weapon whites used primarily against blacks, for crimes both real and imagined.

Between 1882 and 1890 approximately 1,750 African Americans were lynched in the United States. Ida B. Wells-Barnett, a journalist and social activist, became one of the leading voices in the antilynching crusade by writing and lecturing throughout the United States against the practice of lynching. Despite her efforts, and those of numerous others who followed, lynching was not eliminated from the American landscape until the 1960s.

Legal Segregation

In 1896 the U.S. Supreme Court was faced with the issue of segregation on public transportation. A Louisiana state law, typical of others in the South, said that "equal but separate" accommodations for blacks and whites should be maintained in all public facilities. When Homer Adolph Plessy, a

---

1866 The Civil Rights Act of 1866 is passed in an attempt to protect African Americans from **Black Codes** and other unjust laws.

1868 The Fourteenth Amendment is passed, securing U.S. citizenship for African Americans.

1896 *Plessy* v. *Ferguson* upholds the doctrine of "separate but equal." **Jim Crow** segregation and white **supremacy** continue to thrive.

1909 The National Association for the Advancement of Colored People (NAACP) is founded in New York.

1948 President Harry S Truman integrates the armed forces.

1954 In the landmark case of *Brown* v. *Board of Education of Topeka, Kansas,* the U.S. Supreme Court rules **unanimously** that racial **segregation** is unconstitutional. The ruling overturned the "separate but equal" policies of the past.

1955 In Montgomery, Alabama, a black seamstress named Rosa Parks refuses to give up her seat to a white person. After she was arrested for violating Jim Crow segregation laws, a bus boycott, led by Martin Luther King, Jr., and others, launched the modern-day civil rights movement.

1963 More than 200,000 Americans of all races and colors gather at the Lincoln Memorial in the "March on Washington," the largest protest in the nation's history. King delivers his "I Have a Dream" speech.

CIVIL RIGHTS

Ida B. Wells-Barnett

Civil Rights in the Twentieth Century

Booker T. Washington and W. E. B. Du Bois

Around the turn of the century two men, Booker T. Washington and William Edward Burghardt Du Bois, emerged as leaders in the struggle for black political and civil rights.

Washington, an educator and founder of the Tuskegee Normal and Industrial Institute in Tuskegee, Alabama, strongly favored practical education and manual training as a means of developing the potential of African Americans. Tuskegee therefore provided vocational training and prepared its students to succeed financially in a segre-

Booker T. Washington

black man traveling by train from New Orleans to Covington, Louisiana, refused to ride in the "colored" railway coach, he was arrested.

In the *Plessy* v. *Ferguson* case, the Court declared that "separate but equal" accommodations were reasonable and that the Fourteenth Amendment of the Constitution could not be used to abolish social or racial distinctions or to force the two races to associate.

The Supreme Court had effectively trampled the Fourteenth Amendment, which was designed to give blacks specific rights and protections. The "separate but equal" doctrine paved the way for the segregation of African Americans in all walks of life.

CIVIL RIGHTS

W. E. B. Du Bois

WORDS TO KNOW

acquittal: a court decision freeing one of charges

Black Codes: unfair rules and laws directed at African Americans following emancipation

catalysts: persons or objects that bring about events or results

consensus: general agreement

injunction: an order from the court either prohibiting or demanding a certain action

integration: the bringing together of races, classes, or ethnic groups that were previously separated; bringing a group into equal membership in society

Jim Crow: a reference (taken from a minstrel song) to laws and practices supporting the segregation of blacks and whites

lynching: murder without trial, frequently by hanging

pending: not yet decided or determined

segregation: the separation or isolation of a race, class, or ethnic group into a restricted area

supremacy: the state of having the most power or authority

unanimously: in total agreement

gated society. In Washington's opinion, the goal of education was to provide African Americans with the means to become self-supporting.

Du Bois, a Harvard-educated historian, challenged what he thought were Washington's passive policies in a series of stinging essays and speeches. Du Bois promoted uplifting African Americans through educating a black elite, which he referred to as the "Talented Tenth," meaning the brightest tenth of the African American population. He believed that these African Americans should become especially learned so that eventually all of their brothers and sisters would benefit.

The Rise of Civil Rights Organizations

In 1905 Du Bois, along with a group of other black intellectuals, formed the Niagara Movement. The group's platform called for full citizenship rights for blacks and public recognition of their contributions to America's stability and progress. In 1909

CIVIL RIGHTS

Rosa Parks being fingerprinted after her arrest

the movement became known as the National Association for the Advancement of Colored People (NAACP).

The NAACP soon emerged as the first black organization with the expertise and finances to fight for justice in America's courts and legislatures. Another organization, the National Urban League, emerged from groups formed to aid blacks who had recently immigrated to Northern cities. The NAACP and the National Urban League were in many respects perfectly matched, for the former stressed civil rights, while the latter stressed jobs and job training. (See Vol. 2, Ch. 11: "National Organizations," for more information on this topic.)

A Slow Battle for Justice

The civil rights movement suffered many defeats in the first half of the twentieth century. Repeated efforts to obtain passage of federal antilynching bills failed. The all white primary system, which blocked Southern blacks from the political process, resisted numerous court challenges. And the Great Depression worsened conditions on farms and in ghettos. On the positive side, the growing political power of blacks in Northern cities and an increasing liberal trend in the Supreme Court foreshadowed the legal and legislative victories of the 1950s and 1960s.

Brown v. Board of Education of Topeka

The NAACP was responsible for much of the civil rights struggle throughout this period and had begun to chip away at the roots of legalized segregation in a series of successful lawsuits. A major victory for the NAACP came in 1954 when the U.S. Supreme Court ruled in *Brown* v. *Board of Education* that discrimination in education was unconstitutional. This decision overturned the Supreme Court's ruling in *Plessy* v. *Ferguson* (1896), which legalized the doctrine of "separate but equal" treatment for blacks.

Boycotts, Marches, Sit-ins, and Demonstrations: Civil Rights in the 1960s

Rosa Parks was one of the major **catalysts** of the 1960s civil rights movement. On December 1, 1955, Parks refused to give up her seat on a Montgomery bus to a white man, as the law then required. For this she was arrested and jailed. As a result of Parks's arrest, blacks throughout Montgomery refused to ride city buses. The Montgomery Bus Boycott, led by Martin Luther King, Jr., was highly successful and ultimately led to the **integration** of all Montgomery city buses.

Soon massive demonstrations swept across the South, supported by the King-led Southern Christian Leadership Conference (SCLC) and other nonviolent groups. In 1960 four North Carolina college students who had been denied service at a Greensboro lunch counter started the "sit in" movement. That same year, the Student Non-Violent Coordinating Committee (SNCC or "Snick") was created and would include among its members Julian Bond, H. Rap Brown, Stokely Carmichael, and John Lewis.

The civil rights movement of the 1960s mobilized blacks and sympathetic whites as nothing had ever done before, but it was not without cost. Thousands of people were jailed or lost their jobs because they defied Jim Crow laws. Homes and churches were regularly bombed. And riots, maimings, and murders occurred with alarming regularity.

On August 28, 1963, nearly 250,000 blacks and whites marched on Washington, D.C., to awaken the nation and to encourage the passage of **pending** civil rights legislation. The march was a cooperative effort of several civil rights organizations, including the SCLC, the Congress of Racial Equality (CORE), the NAACP, the Negro American Labor Council, and the National Urban League. It was during this demonstration in the shadow of the Lincoln Memorial, that King gave his "I Have a Dream" speech (see Vol. 1, Ch. 4: "Words," for an excerpt from this speech).

"Letter from Birmingham Jail"

On April 12, 1963 (Good Friday), Martin Luther King, Jr., was hauled off to jail by Birmingham Police Commissioner T. Eugene

CIVIL RIGHTS

Nearly 250,000 gather in Washington, D.C., August 1963

"Bull" Connor. At that time Birmingham was considered "the meanest city in the South" and Bull Connor, perhaps "the meanest police chief in the country."

King and the SCLC—after failing to gain national sympathy for their cause during an earlier nonviolent campaign in Albany, Georgia—had selected Birmingham as both the toughest and best place to begin dismantling the Jim Crow South. Their Birmingham campaign began on April 3 with a demand for desegregated public facilities and jobs for blacks. Daily meetings, sit-ins, and marches were the chosen tactics of the SCLC's "nonviolent army."

During the first week, some 300 blacks had been jailed. Surprisingly, Connor's police force displayed no signs of brutality. As the SCLC-led army dwindled, so too did the available bail money. Making matters even worse was the fact that many respected black citizens of Birmingham refused to join the protests.

Thus King was faced with a difficult decision. Should he lead another march—now forbidden by a state **injunction**—which would almost certainly place him in jail and would sentence the underfunded movement to dire straits? Or should he obey the injunction and thereby undermine the momentum of the movement?

King chose to march. Below is a portion of his famous letter written from jail, in which he responds to a published statement by eight white Alabama clergymen who urged patience, law and order, change in the courts, and, above all, no demonstrations:

> We have waited for more than 340 years for our constitutional and God-given rights. The nations of Asia and Africa are moving with jetlike speed toward gaining political independence, but we still creep at horse-and-buggy pace toward gaining a cup of coffee at a lunch counter. Perhaps it is easy for those who have never felt the stinging darts of segregation to say, "Wait." But when you have seen vicious mobs lynch your mothers and fathers at will and drown your sisters and brothers at whim; when you have seen hate-filled policemen curse, kick and even kill your black brothers and sisters; when you see the vast majority of your twenty million Negro brothers smothering in an airtight cage of poverty in the midst of an affluent society; when you suddenly find your tongue twisted and your speech stammering as you seek to explain to your six-year-old daughter why she can't go to the public amusement park that has just been advertised on television, and see tears welling up in her eyes when she is told that Funtown is closed to colored children, and see ominous clouds of inferiority beginning to form in her little mental sky, and see her beginning to distort her personality by developing an unconscious bitterness toward white people; when you have to concoct an answer for a five-year-old son who is asking: "Daddy, why do white people treat colored people so mean?"; when you take a cross-country drive and find it necessary to sleep night after night in the uncomfortable corners of your automobile because no motel will accept you; when you are humiliated day in and day out by nagging signs reading "white" and "colored"; when your first name becomes "nigger," your middle name becomes "boy" (however old you are) and your last name becomes "John," and your wife and mother are never given the respected title "Mrs."; when you are harried by day and haunted by night by the fact that you are a Negro, living constantly at tiptoe stance, never quite knowing what to expect next, and are plagued with inner fears and outer resentments; when you are forever fighting a degenerating sense of "nobodiness"—then you will understand why we find it difficult to wait....

Sources: Jakoubek, Robert, *Martin Luther King, Jr.* (1989) and Martin Luther King, Jr., *Why We Can't Wait* (1964).

At its height, the civil rights movement was the most important event taking place in America. Through demonstrations, sit-ins, marches, and speeches, the movement aroused widespread public indignation, thus creating an atmosphere in which it was possible to make positive changes in American society.

CIVIL RIGHTS

High pressure hoses are turned on demonstrators in Birmingham, Alabama, 1963

Urban Tension and Civil Disorder

Despite President Lyndon Johnson's "War on Poverty" and the passage of such important legislation as the Civil Rights Act of 1964 and the Voting Rights Act of 1965, civil rights laws and court decisions were slow to take effect. At the same time, the racial battleground was shifting dramatically.

Although the activities of the Southern-based Ku Klux Klan prompted swift and regular responses, more emphasis was now being placed on Northern and Western ghettos, where residents were concerned with the dire conditions of daily life.

For many, King's philosophy of **nonviolence** was losing its appeal, especially in light of the stirring, unapologetic militancy of Malcolm X. Malcolm's death at the hands of assassins in early 1965 only heightened the call of urban blacks for radical change and "black power" (a phrase popularized by SNCC leader Stokely Carmichael).

235

CIVIL RIGHTS

The Black Panther Party

Probably the most extreme—and certainly the most notorious—of the black power organizations was the Black Panther Party for Self-Defense, formed in Oakland, California, in 1966 by Huey Newton and Bobby Seale. Later members of the group included Carmichael, Eldridge Cleaver, Mark Clark, and Fred Hampton. As their name suggests, the Panthers supported the idea of black self-defense, especially against hostile police.

THE KU KLUX KLAN

Aside from fighting a general and longstanding tradition of legalized racism in America, one of the civil rights movement's greatest challenges has been to stem the power of the modern Ku Klux Klan. The Ku Klux Klan had been formed in Pulaski, Tennessee, following the Civil War, by whites in both the North and the South who wanted to withhold equal rights from blacks.

Three main Klan groups have flourished from the 1960s on. In *Klanwatch: Bringing the Ku Klux Klan to Justice* (1991), Bill Stanton records that the oldest and probably largest group (with an estimated 4,000 members) is the United Klans of America, established in 1961 near Tuscaloosa, Alabama. The other two groups, both founded in the 1970s in Louisiana, were the Knights of the KKK (estimated 2,000 members) and the Invisible Empire, Knights of the KKK (estimated 3,000 members). Together their reign of terror lasted well into the 1980s.

During the brief period from 1985 to 1987, the Klanswatch Project of the Southern Poverty Law Center reported 45 cases of arson and cross-burning as well as hundreds of acts of vandalism. (By 1990 Klan incidents had dropped markedly and overall membership stood at just 1,500.)

In one of the most extreme acts of modern Klan violence, 19-year-old Michael Donald of Mobile, Alabama, was randomly grabbed, beaten to death, and then hanged by local Klan members in 1981. In 1987 Donald's mother, Beulah Mae Donald, won a $7-million judgment against the Klan. The story of her successful struggle for justice won her the title "The Woman Who Beat the Klan."

Yet sympathy for Klan beliefs still persists among poor, angry whites. And the rise of the Neo-Nazi and skinhead movements would seem to indicate that racial hatred is still alive and well among various groups and in certain pockets of the country.

NONVIOLENCE

Nonviolence is a theory or movement based on the civil disobedience of American writer Henry David Thoreau (1817-1862) and the passive resistance of Hindu leader Mohandas K. Gandhi (1869-1948). It was championed by Martin Luther King, Jr., as an alternative to violence, which had as its goal the overthrow of unjust laws.

In his essay "Nonviolence and Racial Justice," which first appeared in 1957, King listed five points regarding nonviolence that could together bring about a better racial climate. In King's words nonviolence:

1) "is not a method for cowards; it *does* resist";
2) "does not seek to defeat or humiliate the opponent, but to win his friendship and understanding";
3) "is directed against forces of evil rather than against persons who are caught in those forces";
4) "avoids not only external physical violence but also internal violence of spirit. At the center of nonviolence stands the principle of love";
5) "is based on the conviction that the universe is on the side of justice."

They also provided food and instructional programs to inner-city children and demanded that the government make sweeping improvements in the areas of housing, employment, and education. Theirs was a largely unhappy history, however, for by 1970 most of the leading Panthers were either dead, serving time, or living in exile.

Urban Violence

There were signs within many cities across the nation that the peacefulness of the civil rights movement would not last. Urban riots and violent protest seemed inevitable. The relationship between protest, justifiable violence, and lawless riot is both complex and debatable. However, virtually everyone agrees on the circumstances that can lead to urban riots: unemployment, poverty, high levels of crime, and a general feeling of hopelessness among the people.

In May 1992 Congresswoman Maxine Waters addressed the Senate Banking Committee on the subject of the recent riots in south central Los Angeles, California. Perhaps she was right when she said:

> The verdict in the Rodney King case did not cause what happened in Los Angeles. It was only the most recent injustice—piled upon many other injustices—suffered by the poor, minorities, and the hopeless people living in this nation's cities. For years, they have been crying out for help. For years, their cries have not been heard.

The Harlem Riot (1964)

The first violent eruption to receive national attention during the 1960s occurred

CIVIL RIGHTS

Large sections of the black Watts community were burned during the 1965 riot

in Harlem in the summer of 1964. The Harlem riot exploded two days after a 15-year-old black youth was shot by an off-duty patrolman in the Yorkville section of New York City. Crowds of blacks roamed through the streets, breaking windows, looting stores, menacing police, and threatening the few white people they found in the area.

These crowds faced helmeted police patrols who fired volley after volley into the night air in a futile attempt to disperse the crowds. Compared to what was to come, the

Harlem casualty figures were small. One man died and 144 were injured.

The Watts Riot (1965)

The Watts section of southwest Los Angeles, a 20-square-mile black ghetto with an estimated population of 90,000, was the scene of one of the worst riots in the history of the United States. Thirty-four people were killed (including 28 African Americans) and nearly 900 were injured. Property damage due to looting and arson approached the staggering total of $225 million.

The incident that sparked the outburst occurred on August 11 when state highway patrolmen chased an automobile around a six-block area before arresting the motorist on a drunken driving charge. A crowd gathered as word of the arrest and rumors of brutality by the police spread. Rocks were thrown and more police were summoned to disperse the rioters. A semblance of order was restored early the next morning, but rioting again broke out on the evening of August 12. For the next four days, thousands of police and guardsmen served on riot duty.

The Long Hot Summer of 1967

From May 1 to October 1, the United States experienced the worst summer of racial disturbances in the country's history. More than 40 riots broke out and at least 100 other related incidents occurred.

The most serious eruptions were in Newark, New Jersey (July 12-17), where 26 people died, and in Detroit, Michigan (July 23-30), where 40 people died. Major trouble also surfaced in New York City; Cleveland, Ohio; Washington, D.C.; Chicago, Illinois; Atlanta, Georgia; and other cities.

On July 28 President Johnson assembled a National Advisory Commission on Civil Disorders. Commonly known as the Kerner Commission, the panel held hearings and investigations on the disturbances and, in a report released in 1968, made recommendations to stem future violence.

The Kerner Commission Report

When the President established his commission, he wanted three basic questions answered: 1) What happened? 2) Why did it happen? and 3) What can be done to prevent it from happening again?

The Kerner Commission Report begins with a basic conclusion that addresses the first two questions: "Our nation is moving toward two societies, one black, one white—separate and unequal." Later, in more detail, the report lists the many causes of civil disorder and pays special attention to police conduct and patrol practices. "Police misconduct," the report states, "cannot be tolerated even if it is infrequent. It contributes directly to the risk of civil disorder."

The report called for an end to the violence and "a national resolution" with "common opportunities for all within a single society." But it failed to concretely answer the president's third question: "We have learned much. But we have uncovered no startling truths, no unique insights, no simple solutions."

The Assassination Riots

Another wave of violence broke out in April 1968, just one month following the release of the Kerner Commission Report.

CIVIL RIGHTS

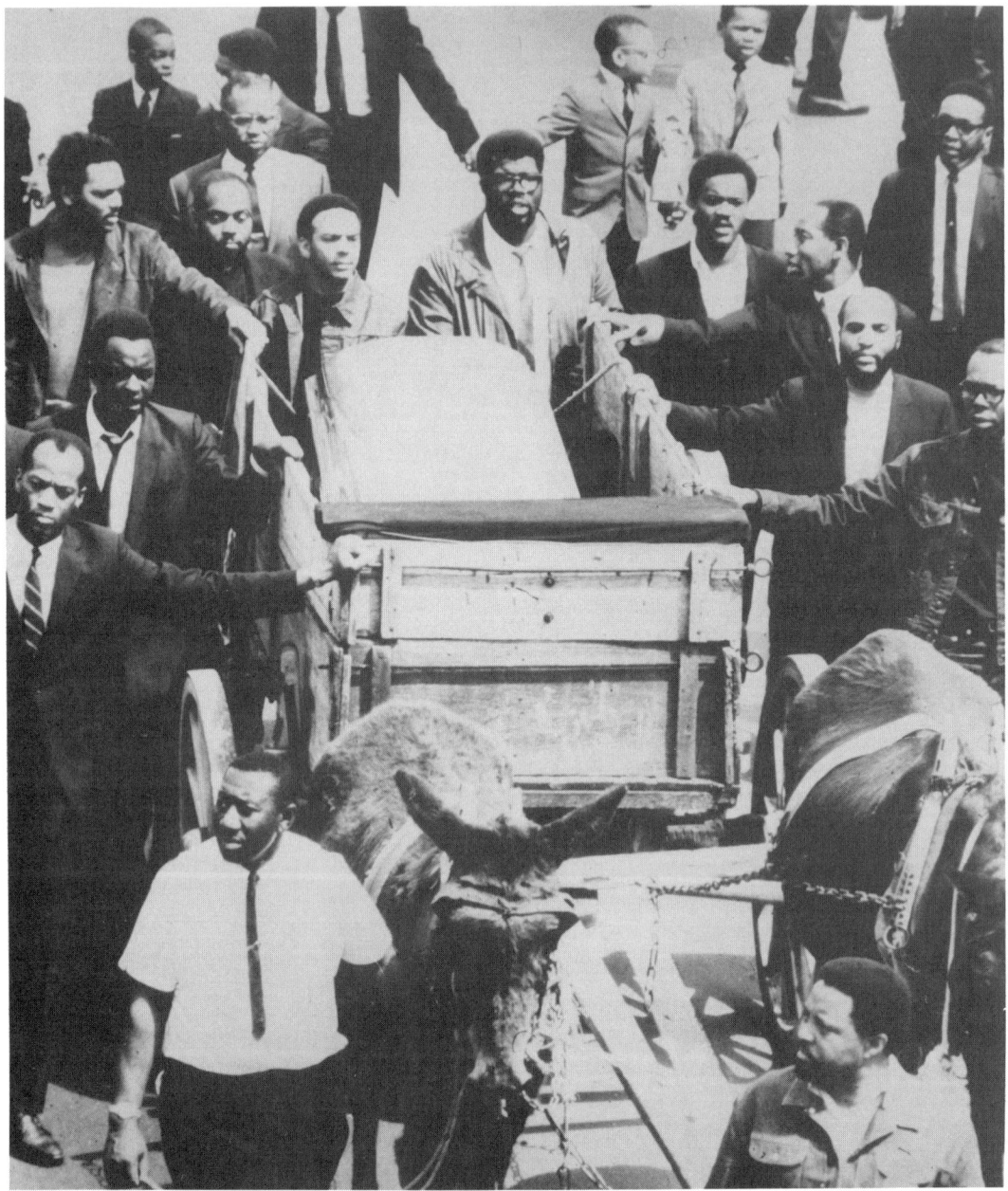

The funeral procession of Martin Luther King, Jr.

Sparked by the assassination of Martin Luther King, Jr., rioting occurred in at least 125 towns and cities across the country.

The government's prompt, stern reaction to these riots marked a turning point in black history and American politics. Unlike the response to earlier riots in Watts, Newark, and Detroit, troops were summoned immediately. Their numbers reached 70,000 and, for more than a decade, the frequency and intensity of outbreaks of urban violence decreased.

The Fading of Militancy and a New Civil Rights Era

Following the riots of 1968, militant black leaders, too, seemed to decline in influence. The summer of 1969, and those that followed, were "cool." Outbreaks became increasingly limited in duration and scope. However, many of the urban problems at the heart of the violence did not fade away.

By the mid-1970s it was evident that the civil rights movement had entered a new era. During the 1950s and 1960s the movement had achieved a number of long-awaited victories. More progress had been made in less time than in all the years since blacks first arrived in America. The legal structure that kept blacks in the back of the bus in the South and out of hotels, restaurants, and other public accommodations was outlawed. The segregation of public schools was effectively ended. The Voting Rights Act empowered millions of black voters and helped elect hundreds of Southern blacks to public office. Finally, the movement brought a fresh sense of pride to countless blacks, many of whom were beginning to shine as part of a new generation of black leaders.

> **SPECIAL FOCUS**
>
> Recipients of the Martin Luther King, Jr. Nonviolent Peace Prize, awarded by the Martin Luther King, Jr. Center for Nonviolent Social Change, Inc.
>
> 1973 Andrew Young
> 1974 César Chávez
> 1975 John Lewis
> 1976 Randolph Blackwell
> 1977 Benjamin E. Mays
> 1978 Kenneth D. Kaunda; Stanley Levison
> 1979 Jimmy Carter
> 1980 Rosa Parks
> 1981 The Honorable Ivan Allen, Jr.
> 1982 Harry Belafonte
> 1983 Sir Richard Attenborough; Martin Luther King, Sr.
> 1984 No award
> 1985 No award
> 1986 Bishop Desmond Tutu
> 1987 Corazon Aquino
> 1988 No award
> 1989 No award
> 1990 Mikhail Gorbachev
> 1991 No award
> 1992 No award
> 1993 Jesse Jackson

Progress through Politics

Unfortunately, the same national **consensus** that helped bring about the earlier legal civil rights victories could not be developed to deal quickly with the widespread social and economic problems of the black community. The glamour had gone out of the movement, which now lacked a strong, charismatic leader.

Power and progress through the rise of civil rights-minded black politicians—who championed desegregation, affirmative action, and inner-city investment policies—became the newest sign of hope for African Americans. In March 1972 Mayor Richard Hatcher welcomed 8,000 blacks to the city of Gary, Indiana. They had come to attend the first National Black Political Convention. The Congressional Black Caucus, formed in 1971, was further molded at the convention. Its influence became evident the following year when blacks won the mayorships of several large cities around the country, including Los Angeles, Detroit, and Atlanta. Although inner-city problems would continue, blacks now had a far greater voice in how these problems would be solved.

The Miami Riots of 1980

Just as the era of modern racial violence seemed to be over, another major series of riots shook the nation. This time Miami, Florida, was the scene of unrest. The spark that touched off the rioting was the **acquittal** of white Dade County police officers in the death of a black insurance man, Arthur McDuffie.

There was convincing evidence that the officers had inflicted a brutal beating on McDuffie after he was in their custody on a traffic violation. But an all-white jury freed the policemen and black anger spilled over into the worst riots in the nation since 1967. Five days later, ten blacks and seven whites were dead.

During the violence several national civil rights leaders, including Benjamin Hooks of the NAACP and Jesse Jackson of Operation PUSH (People United to Save Humanity), went to Miami in an effort to establish calm. However, as in the past, the peacemaking attempts of "establishment" black leaders were not effective and rioting continued until it had run its course.

The failure of black leaders to exert any influence over the rioters was indicative of the sheer intensity of the problems that still plagued the black community. Writer Francis Ward summed up this state of affairs several months later in *First World*:

> Miami was a dramatic but timely demonstration that [younger low-income blacks] have little if any confidence in black leadership, local or national. Black leadership has no message for the black dispossessed, no offer of jobs, education or new opportunities it can offer to lure the new generation of surly, angry blacks away from potential violence.

Racism in the 1980s

In the 1980s civil rights organizations found themselves faced with renewed racism, which exploded in well-publicized places such as Howard Beach and Forsyth County, and spread like an uncontrollable stain to many areas of the country.

Of particular concern was the marked increase of racially motivated incidents on college campuses throughout the nation.

The National Institute Against Prejudice and Violence listed 163 incidents over the school years 1986-87 and 1987-88. What lends special importance to these campus incidents is that they took place in a setting where diversity and tolerance have traditionally been welcomed.

Civil rights groups, most notably the NAACP and the National Urban League, continued to warn that racism drives a wedge between black and white America. But by the end of the 1980s the chasm seemed wider than it had at the beginning of the decade.

The Reagan Years

During President Ronald Reagan's eight years in office (1981-88), civil rights leaders grew increasingly fearful that the political climate was also changing for the worse. The Reagan Administration's promotion of self-help projects and increased black college graduation rang hollow with black leaders who wanted the government to turn its attention to the interests of the majority of blacks, such as employment, housing, and other fundamental needs. In addition, Reagan's three appointees to the U.S. Supreme Court created a clear conservative majority, with both immediate and long-reaching implications for overturning post-1960s civil rights decisions and laws.

However, a major symbolic victory was gained on January 20, 1986, when Martin Luther King, Jr.'s birthday was observed as a national holiday for the first time. Reagan had signed the controversial bill into law in 1983, though he himself initially opposed it.

1993 and Beyond

In August 1993 the thirtieth anniversary of the "March on Washington" was commemorated. African Americans had made enormous strides since the original march, and there were a number of still-lingering highlights from the past election years to build pride within the black community, including the back-to-back presidential campaigns of civil rights leader Jesse Jackson and a 14-seat gain in Congress in 1992. Barriers were still being shattered, as was evidenced by the election of the nation's first black female senator, Carol Moseley Braun.

Yet many problems remained, and America had still not rid itself of a tendency toward large-scale violence. On April 29, 1992, in Alameda County, California, a jury acquitted four Los Angeles police officers who had been captured on videotape beating black motorist Rodney King.

Within hours their acquittal sparked the most severe riot in U.S. history. It took place in predominantly black south central Los Angeles and lasted for three days. Blacks, whites, and Asians all believe that the police did not act quickly enough to restore order. In all, 53 people died in the rioting and billions of dollars in property and income were lost.

In November 1993 President Bill Clinton, when asked by Tom Brokaw on *Meet the Press* if the racial climate in urban America was better or worse than 10 years ago, responded:

I think for middle class people, it's much better. I think the level of comfort among people of different races is much higher. I think the appreciation

CIVIL RIGHTS

A woman prays for peace after three days of rioting in Los Angeles, May, 1 1992

for diversity is greater. I think for people who are outside the economic mainstream, it is much, much worse.

My God, we've got kids planning their funerals, 11-year-old kids. But the crying shame is that those people also want to be a part of mainstream America. I mean, look at these children. When they make these plans for their funerals, are they out there breaking the law?

And one thing I'd like to say to the rest of America is, you read those horrible stories about how many people get killed on the weekends. Most of the people who live in all those neighborhoods never break the law, work for a living, for modest wages, pay their taxes, trying to do right by their kids. I mean, this country is falling apart because we have allowed that—a whole group of us to drift away. It's not an underclass anymore, it's an outer class.

Clinton vowed as president to refocus attention on solving crime, drug addiction, and the breakdown of the family unit as a way to heal the nation.

8
Black Nationalism

Nation Building

"We are not engaged in domestic politics, in church building or in social uplift work, but we are engaged in nation building."—Marcus Garvey, in a 1922 speech delivered at Liberty Hall, New York City

"The goal has always been the same, with the approaches to it as different as mine and Dr. Martin Luther King's."—Malcolm X, in The Autobiography of Malcolm X *(1965)*

Civil rights and black nationalism have elements and goals in common, but they are not the same. The civil rights movement, as symbolized by Martin Luther King, Jr., consists of nonviolent protest and reform within the American social and political system. The black nationalist movement, as embodied by Black Muslim Malcolm X, consists of sharp criticism and the threat of violent retaliation. In contrast to the civil rights approach, the black nationalist approach emphasizes separation and self-help rather than integration and mutual help.

In the "Flashbacks" chapter, black nationalism is defined as "a movement to form a new black nation by transporting African Americans back to Africa." This was the black nationalism of Jamaican-born leader Marcus Garvey, who was supported by Malcolm X's father and thousands of others during the early decades of the twentieth century.

The founder of the Universal Negro Improvement Association (UNIA), Garvey is usually among the first African Americans who come to mind when discussing black nationalism. However, when Garvey arrived in Harlem in 1916 and began spreading his back-to-Africa gospel, he was not really championing something new. At least a century earlier, other disillusioned blacks were already attempting to provide a solution for an African American population that was powerless within a land and culture alien to its own. In the minds of its supporters, black nation-building was the only sensible reaction to the widespread domination of blacks by whites.

In its most modern sense, black nationalism (along with such related terms as **Pan-Africanism**) can be applied to any theory or movement that supports the advancement of African peoples everywhere. In this both King and Malcolm X, two of the greatest of all spokespersons for black rights and black pride, were united.

BLACK NATIONALISM

Paul Cuffe was an early black nationalist

Early Black Nationalism in the United States

Early black nationalism in the United States is associated with the activities of two successful businessmen: Paul Cuffe, a New Bedford, Massachusetts, sea captain; and James Forten, a Philadelphia sailmaker. These two figures hoped to foster Christianity, commerce, and civilization in Africa while providing a homeland for African Americans.

In 1811, aboard his ship *Traveller,* Cuffe sailed to Sierra Leone where he founded the Friendly Society. Through this organization, Cuffe hoped to help blacks return to the motherland. In 1815 he transported 38 colonists to Africa. Unfortunately, this was to be his last voyage.

> **WORDS TO KNOW**
>
> **abolition:** the destruction or ending of slavery
>
> **anti-Semitism:** discrimination or prejudice against Jews
>
> **deportation:** the sending away, by official order, of an undesirable alien
>
> **effigy** (to burn in): to publicly burn an image of a person in protest
>
> **eulogized:** praised after death
>
> **exodus:** literally, a going out; a massive migration or departure of a people
>
> **orthodox:** traditional; conforming to established doctrine
>
> **Pan-Africanism:** a theory or movement embracing cooperation and unity among African nations and among all African peoples
>
> **predecessors:** those who have come before
>
> **proteges:** persons guided, taught, or shaped by generally older and more influential persons
>
> **repatriationist:** one who believes in returning to the country of origin
>
> **separatism:** a policy of keeping the races apart in all matters

The American Colonization Society

Both Cuffe and Forten's **repatriationist** activities were brought to a halt in 1817, when Speaker of the House (and later Senator) Henry Clay, General (and later President) Andrew Jackson, and other white

Americans formed the American Society for Colonizing the Free People of Color in the United States, usually called the American Colonization Society.

The American Colonization Society had other prominent slaveholders among its leadership and boldly denied any sympathy for **abolition.** Consequently, large numbers of blacks loudly opposed the society, despite its creation of Liberia in West Africa in 1821 (Liberia won its independence in 1847). Cuffe died shortly after the society's founding, and Forten felt driven to silence, though he continued to believe that black Americans would "never become a people until they come out from amongst the white people." Those who continued to support repatriation, or who migrated under the sponsorship of the American Colonization Society, were sharply criticized.

The Free Black Response

Maria Stewart was among those free blacks who considered herself an African first but was nonetheless hostile to the colonization movement. She therefore insisted on her rights as an American. At the same time, she harshly denounced her racially divided adopted country.

In a similar vein, David Walker condemned colonization and emigration with the religious fervor of an Old Testament prophet. While upholding the separate destiny of blacks as colored citizens of the world, he also stressed that black and white Americans could be "a united and happy people."

Early Slave Revolts

In 1791 Toussaint L'Ouverture led a successful revolt against the French in the

Toussaint L'Ouverture, liberator of Haiti

Caribbean nation of Haiti, leaving the black population in control. In the United States, three major black revolutionaries attempted to do what Toussaint had done. The first was Gabriel Prosser.

In 1800 Prosser marshalled enormous support for a revolt to take place near Richmond, Virginia. The plan was discovered, however, and Prosser and several other slaves were executed.

Next came Denmark Vesey. A former slave, Vesey had bought his freedom, eventually becoming a Methodist minister. Through that office he recruited supporters for his plan to take over Charleston, South

BLACK NATIONALISM

Nat Turner's capture

Carolina. Vesey was prepared to put his plan into action in 1822. But like the Prosser scheme, Vesey's plan was betrayed by a slave who alerted white authorities. Vesey, too, died at the hands of executioners. Significantly, both Prosser and Vesey seemed to have had as their goals the creation of a black nation with ties to the Caribbean.

Finally, there was the singularly bloody but ultimately unsuccessful revolt of Nat Turner. A visionary and avid reader of the Bible, Turner believed that God wanted him to conquer Southampton County in Virginia. The Turner uprising took place in 1831 and resulted in the deaths of about 60 whites. Although Turner and 30 other blacks were executed, the aftermath left the South in constant fear, with authorities vigorously enforcing slave codes.

Northern Blacks and Free African Societies

For the most part, however, evidence of black nationalism in the United States was found among the free black population of the North. It was in the so-called Free African Societies, which sprang up in the black communities of New York, Boston, and Philadelphia, that the concepts of black identity and destiny were strongest.

During the 1830s and 1840s, black nationalist thinking was associated with religious leadership such as that provided by the bishop of the African Methodist Episcopal (AME)

Church, Richard Allen. Allen believed in a special God-given mission for black Americans as a people, but steadfastly opposed the American Colonization Society.

Peter Williams, leader of the Afro-American Group of the Episcopal Church in New York, took a more tolerant view of colonization. He **eulogized** Paul Cuffe and remained friendly with John Russwurm (an editor of the black newspaper *Freedom's Journal*), even after the latter emigrated to Liberia and was burned in **effigy** by anti-colonization protesters.

The Flowering of the Movement

During the 1850s and 1860s black nationalism began to flourish. To some degree the movement owed its rebirth to the Fugitive Slave Act (1850) and the *Dred Scott* v. *Sandford* court case (1858), two major legal defeats for antislavery crusaders. Support for emigration, which had been largely inactive since the death of Cuffe, began anew. A succession of colonization conventions were held.

The leaders of the movement were pastor and activist Henry Highland Garnet and physician and writer Martin R. Delany, who founded the African Civilization Society in 1858. Edward Wilmot Blyden, perhaps the chief nineteenth-century Pan-African theorist, migrated to Liberia in 1850. Alexander Crummell, another major Pan-African thinker, emigrated to Liberia through the sponsorship of the Domestic and Foreign Missionary Society of the Protestant Episcopal Church in 1853, but eventually became involved with the American Colonization Society. During the early years of

Martin R. Delany

the Civil War, *The Weekly Anglo-African* became the principal journal of the emigration movement.

Emigrationism died out during the peak years of Reconstruction following the Civil War. During this period, the black American population chose instead to take advantage of opportunities presented by emancipation.

However, from the mid-1870s to the World War I era the black condition steadily worsened in the South. The "Kansas **Exodus**" of the 1870s and the Oklahoma movement that established all-black towns during the 1890s were in some ways indicators of renewed black nationalism, for during this same period a number of back-to-Africa movements were organized.

Most prominent among these were the movements under Bishop Henry McNeal Turner and Ghanaian Alfred C. Sam. An outspoken critic of the U.S. Constitution, Turner firmly believed in a brighter future for blacks in Africa. In 1878 he was among the backers of a failed expedition involving about 200 blacks who went to Liberia in hopes of settling. Success did come in 1903, though, when he recruited African American stockbroker William Ellis to direct an expedition to Ethiopia.

By the time of Turner's death in 1915, Sam, supposedly an African chief, had already launched a colonization movement in Oklahoma. Forming emigration clubs and selling stock in his Akim Trading Company, the Ghanaian generated an enormous amount of excitement for his plans. In the summer of 1914, 60 blacks sailed for Ghana aboard Sam's ship, the S.S. *Liberia*. Shortly thereafter the movement failed due to British interference.

Black Nationalism in the Twentieth Century

Marcus Garvey and the UNIA

Marcus Garvey arrived in the United States from Jamaica in 1916. His timing could not have been better, for there was a large void to be filled following Turner's death and Sam's defeat. Garvey's Universal Negro Improvement Association was, according to some scholars, the largest organization-based movement ever to occur among black Americans.

Although Garvey was less successful as a repatriationist than some of his **predecessors,** he enjoyed tremendous success as a journalist, community organizer, and sponsor of economic development. His reputation became a source of great inspiration to many black leaders and spread among the masses of people in Africa and the Americas.

The Celebration of African Heritage

Cultural nationalism—the celebration of the "African personality" and the contributions of black people to world history—made its appearance in the mid-nineteenth century.

Abolitionist speaker Frederick Douglass shared with E. W. Blyden an admiration for the ancient Egyptians, who he believed to be of exactly the same racial type as African Americans. Toward the end of the century, such younger scholars as W. E. B. Du Bois were to make much of Egypt, Ethiopia, and Sudan as black regions that helped shape world civilization. Writers William H. Ferris and John E. Bruce, who like Du Bois were **proteges** of Alexander Crummell, sought to elevate the black race and to popularize the idea that black peoples of the upper Nile were, in fact, the first civilized peoples on earth. The writings of Joel Augustus Rogers, a sometime contributor to Marcus Garvey's newspaper *The Negro World,* represented the height of this school of thought.

During the 1930s new versions of cultural nationalism began to focus on the importance of West Africa, in addition to that of ancient Egypt. This development was partially due to the Negritude movement among French-speaking intellectuals, and also to the "Jazz Age" interest in Africa among white artists and social scientists.

MALCOLM ON BLACK NATIONALISM

Why Black Nationalism? Well, in the competitive American society, how can there ever be any white-black solidarity before there is first some black solidarity?... Even when I was a follower of Elijah Muhammad, I had been strongly aware of how the Black Nationalist political, economic and social philosophies had the ability to instill within black men the racial dignity, the incentive, and the confidence that the black race needs today to get up off its knees, and to get on its feet, and get rid of its scars, and to take a stand for itself.

One of the major troubles that I was having in building the organization that I wanted—an all-black organization whose ultimate objective was to help create a society in which there could exist honest white-black brotherhood—was that my earlier public image, my so-called "Black Muslim" image, kept blocking me. I was trying to gradually reshape that image. I was trying to turn a corner, into a new regard by the public, especially Negroes; I was no less angry than I had been, but at the same time the true brotherhood I had seen in the Holy World had influenced me to recognize that anger can blind human vision.

Every free moment I could find, I did a lot of talking to key people whom I knew around Harlem, and I made a lot of speeches, saying: "True Islam taught me that it takes *all* of the religious, political, economic, psychological, and racial ingredients, or characteristics, to make the Human Family and the Human Society complete.

"Since I learned the *truth* in Mecca, my dearest friends have come to include *all* kinds—some Christians, Jews, Buddhists, Hindus, agnostics, and even atheists! I have friends who are called capitalists, Socialists, and Communists! Some of my friends are moderates, conservatives, extremists—some are even Uncle Toms! My friends today are black, brown, red, yellow, and *white!*"

Source: Malcolm X with Alex Haley, *The Autobiography of Malcolm X* (1965).

The Nation of Islam, Malcolm X, and the 1960s

After the **deportation** of Marcus Garvey in 1925, black nationalism went into decline. The search for a black nationality was kept alive by such religious groups as the Black Jews of Harlem, the Moorish Science Temple, and the Nation of Islam, which was under the leadership of Elijah Muhammad.

BLACK NATIONALISM

Malcolm X addressing young civil rights workers in Selma, Alabama, February 1965

By far the most important of these groups was the Nation of Islam, or the Black Muslims. Founded in the 1920s by a mysterious black silk peddler named W. D. Fard or Wallace Fard Muhammad, the Nation preached black **separatism** and a black-centered gospel. Fard told blacks that they were members of a superior race that was descended from Muslims of Afro-Asia. Claiming to be a messenger from Allah, or God, he said he had been sent to reclaim his lost people and save them from the inferior race of "white devils" who had made their lives miserable. Christianity, he insisted, was a false religion used by white people to keep blacks enslaved.

During the Great Depression, an unemployed Detroit laborer named Elijah Poole became Fard's closest associate. When Fard suddenly disappeared in 1934, Poole (known by then as Elijah Muhammad) took control of the group. After serving time in federal prison for resisting the draft, Muhammad began rebuilding the Nation of Islam. During the 1950s and especially the 1960s, the Black Muslims saw their numbers increase dramatically.

The rise of Malcolm X, who became Elijah Muhammad's chief minister, did much to popularize black nationalism with young radical intellectuals during the early 1960s. After he split with Muhammad and made a pilgrimage to Mecca, Malcolm X abandoned black separatism but remained committed to black unity, power, and pride. Black nation-

MALCOLM X: "THE ANGRIEST BLACK MAN IN AMERICA"

Malcolm X (1925-1965) had a profound influence on both blacks and whites. Many blacks responded to a feeling that he was a man of the people, experienced in the ways of the street rather than the pulpit or the college campus. Many young whites responded to Malcolm's blunt, colorful language and unwillingness to retreat in the face of hostility.

Disillusioned with Elijah Muhammad's teachings and immorality, Malcolm formed his own groups, the Organization of Afro-American Unity and the Muslim Mosque Inc. In 1964 he made a pilgrimage to Islam's holy city, Mecca, and adopted the name El-Hajj Malik El-Shabazz. He also adopted views that were not popular with other black nationalists, including the idea that not all whites were evil and that blacks could make gains by working through established channels.

As a result of Malcolm's new views, he became the victim of death threats. On February 14, 1965, his home was firebombed; his wife and children escaped unharmed. A week later, Malcolm was shot and killed at the Audubon Ballroom in Harlem while preparing to speak. Three of the men arrested were later identified as members of the Nation of Islam.

Although Malcolm X is frequently identified with violence and always sensed that he would die violently, he never once resorted to violence as a Muslim leader. His *Autobiography* closes with these words:

If I can die having brought any light, having exposed any meaningful truth that will help to destroy the racist cancer that is malignant in the body of America—then, all of the credit is due to Allah. Only the mistakes have been mine.

---

alist attitudes persisted in some radical groups during the late 1960s but seldom showed any relationship to the black nationalist traditions of the nineteenth century.

Black Nationalism Today

In recent years, cultural black nationalists have shown a renewed interest in black nationalist history, especially as it relates to such figures as E. W. Blyden and Marcus Garvey. Both political nationalism in the tradition of Garvey and religious nationalism in the tradition of Muhammad, however, are less visible. Undoubtedly the most strident voice combining these two traditions is Louis Farrakhan.

BLACK NATIONALISM

Elijah Muhammad

Louis Farrakhan

A former calypso singer and accomplished violinist, Farrakhan joined the Nation of Islam at the urging of Malcolm X. Following Malcolm's break with Muhammad, Farrakhan soon became the Nation's leading minister. However, by the mid-1970s Muhammad's son had charted an **orthodox,** nonseparatist path for the Nation of Islam. Remaining true to the original doctrines of Elijah Muhammad, Farrakhan formed his own Nation, which by 1990 boasted some 10,000 members.

Although still plagued by charges of **anti-Semitism** (which surfaced due to remarks he made during his support of Jesse Jackson's 1984 presidential campaign) and warily viewed by mainstream whites and blacks, Farrakhan is both a powerful and resilient spokesperson for black nationalism.

9

Law

The Legal Status of African Americans

"Nothing will be settled with a gun. Nothing will be settled with a firebomb. And nothing will be settled with a rock, because the country cannot survive if it permits it to go unpunished. It's that simple. It takes no courage to throw a rock. Rather, it takes courage to stand up on your own two feet and look anyone straight in the eye and say, 'I will not be beaten.'"—Thurgood Marshall, in an address on May 4, 1969, to the students and faculty of Dillard University in New Orleans

Thurgood Marshall: A Beacon of Black Hope

Probably no other person symbolizes the legal advancement of African Americans as well as Thurgood Marshall (1908-1993). The son of a sleeping-car porter and the great-grandson of a slave, Marshall rose to the heights of the American justice system on the strength of his legal mind and his many successful battles for black rights.

While serving as chief counsel for the National Association for the Advancement of Colored People's (NAACP) Legal Defense and Education Fund, Marshall argued one of

> **WORDS TO KNOW**
>
> **black codes:** unfair rules and laws directed at African Americans following emancipation
>
> **constitutionality:** legality in relationship to the laws and principles set forth in the Constitution
>
> **dissented:** disagreed with the majority (in court cases, justices offer dissenting opinions when they think that their fellow members on the bench have made an error in their ruling)
>
> **inevitably:** predictably
>
> **involuntary servitude:** the institution of forcing people to work for their freedom; also called indentured servitude
>
> **ironically:** in a manner opposite of what is expected
>
> **supremacist:** one who believes in the superiority of a certain group
>
> **v.:** an abbreviation for versus, a term used to separate opposing forces, such as the plaintiff and the defendant in a lawsuit

255

Thurgood Marshall

the greatest cases in the history of the U.S. Supreme Court, *Brown* v. *Board of Education*. Thereafter, he seemed destined to become the nation's first black U.S. Supreme Court justice. (Of the 32 cases that he argued before the Supreme Court, Marshall won 29. Among his less well-known victories were *Sweatt* v. *Painter* [see below] and *Smith* v. *Allwright*.)

When President Lyndon B. Johnson announced his nomination of Marshall on June 13, 1967, he said: "I believe it is the right thing to do, the right time to do it, the right man and the right place. I believe he has already earned his place in history, but I think it will be greatly enhanced by his service on the court."

Throughout his career and his life, Marshall fulfilled Johnson's prediction. He was often identified as "Mr. Civil Rights," a nickname that paid tribute to his lasting devotion to the area of law most crucial to African American advancement. Although Marshall had his share of disappointments and setbacks prior to retiring in 1991, his career was nonetheless one hardly imaginable in the early years of American history.

The Rights of African Americans: The First Hundred Years

The United States of America was established with the declaration that "all men are created equal." But that vow ended at the color line: Freedom for all blacks would not come for another hundred years, and complete legal equality was still nearly two hundred years away.

The constitutional debates of the 1780s highlighted the nation's uncertainty about the race question. This was a nation founded on the principle of individual liberty, but that liberty did not extend to African slaves and their children.

In the 1790s the uncertainty continued. Should slaves be counted for purposes of representation? Should Congress have the power to outlaw slavery and the slave trade? Should an escaped slave be declared "free" in a free state? These were some of the questions that begged to be answered.

This country's inability to solve such matters openly and fairly was tied directly to the practice of African slavery. Although mired in a debate over the question of slavery, the drafters of the constitution avoided mentioning slavery in their final document. In effect, the founding fathers took the easy way out: They made no decisions regarding the race question.

Concerning the number of representatives to be assigned to each state, the Constitution originally counted the African slaves as "three-fifths of all other persons." The "three-fifths" clause foretold the history of the African American in the United States: Black Americans only partially shared in the promise of the new nation. The original Constitution also prevented the new federal government from ending the slave trade or from otherwise influencing matters of race before the year 1808.

Dred Scott v. Sandford (1856):
The Denial of African American Rights

It can be argued that no other case in American judicial history has achieved as much notoriety as the *Dred Scott* case. U.S. Army surgeon John Emerson lived in Missouri, a state that permitted slavery; Dred Scott was his slave. In 1834, as part of his duties, Emerson took Scott to Illinois, where

> **SPECIAL FOCUS**
>
> Clarence Thomas on Thurgood Marshall: "I am in awe of him because he played a major role in establishing that the Constitution applies to everyone. Without him, I wouldn't be here."
>
> *Source:* Todd Brewster, "One Man One Vote," *Life,* January 1992, p. 72.

1862 The Emancipation Act is passed.

1865 The Thirteenth Amendment, ending slavery and **involuntary servitude,** is passed.

1866 A Civil Rights Act providing all citizens (especially recently freed slaves) with basic liberties is passed.

1868 The Fourteenth Amendment, providing all citizens with the right to life, liberty, property, and equal protection under the law, is passed.

1870 The Fifteenth Amendment, designed to protect the right of all citizens to vote, is passed.

1875 A Civil Rights Act providing all citizens with equal access to public places is passed. The Act is declared unconstitutional by the United States Supreme Court in 1883.

1954 The ruling of the Supreme Court in *Brown* v. *Board of Education* overturns the "separate but equal" doctrine of *Plessy* v. *Ferguson.* Racial segregation in public schools is no longer constitutional.

1964 The Civil Rights Act of 1964 is passed, outlawing discrimination in public places.

1965 The Voting Rights Act of 1965 is passed, outlawing poll taxes and other schemes designed to prevent black citizens from voting.

Dred Scott

slavery was outlawed. The two later traveled to the Wisconsin Territory (specifically, to Fort Snelling in what is now Minnesota), where slavery was outlawed by the Missouri Compromise. In 1838 Scott returned to Missouri with Emerson. After Emerson's death in 1843, Scott, with the cooperation of Emerson's widow, sued for his freedom.

Scott's claim was based on the argument that his former residence in a free state and a free territory made him a free man. A Missouri state circuit court ruled in Scott's favor, but the Missouri Supreme Court later reversed that decision. The case eventually reached the U.S. Supreme Court, where five of the nine justices were Southerners.

By a vote of seven to two, the Supreme Court ruled that no African American, whether free or slave, could claim U.S. citizenship. It also held that Congress could not ban slavery in the U.S. territories. In addition, the decision contained what has become perhaps the most infamous line in American legal history. In his opinion, Chief Justice Roger Brook Taney wrote that blacks had "no rights which any white man was bound to respect."

This decision was a clear victory for those who supported slavery. Southerners had long argued that neither Congress nor the territorial legislature had the power to ban slavery from a territory; only states, they maintained, could exclude slavery.

Naturally, the *Dred Scott* ruling aroused resentment in the North and other parts of the country and moved the nation closer to civil war. It also influenced the introduction and adoption of the Fourteenth Amendment to the Constitution after the Civil War. The Amendment, which clearly overruled *Dred Scott,* not only offered citizenship to former slaves but also sought to give them full civil rights.

Civil Rights Following the Civil War

The years following the war produced the Civil War amendments (the Thirteenth, the Fourteenth, and the Fifteenth), each designed to empower former slaves. There now could be no dispute that citizenship in the United States was defined and protected by the national constitution and that state citizenship formed a part of that citizenship.

The passage of the Civil Rights Act of 1875 was a major contribution of this peri-

Engraving of blacks in Washington, D.C., celebrating the end of slavery

od. This act was intended "to protect all citizens in their civil and legal rights." Despite such general phrasing, the law was actually designed to protect newly freed slaves against unfriendly or possibly hostile whites (namely former slave owners and supporters of the Confederacy).

Civil Rights Withdrawn

In an effort to determine the **constitutionality** of the 1875 Civil Rights Act, the U.S. Supreme Court heard a series of civil rights cases. The Court then ruled that the 1875 Civil Rights Act was unconstitutional because it did not spring directly from the Thirteenth and Fourteenth Amendments to the Constitution.

In the view of the Court, the Thirteenth Amendment was concerned strictly with slavery and involuntary servitude. The Fourteenth Amendment, similarly, was limited in its power and did not give Congress the right to pass laws that overturned state laws or policies. In effect, this ruling denied blacks the very protections that were supposed to be contained in the postwar amendments.

A Jim Crow sign

Justice Harlan: A Lone Voice, Crying in the Wilderness

The vote in the *Civil Rights Cases* was eight to one. John Marshall Harlan was the single justice who **dissented.** At the time, Harlan was the court's only Southerner and a former slaveholder himself. **Ironically,** he had strongly opposed the Civil War amendments during the 1860s. But between that time and the time of the decision in the case, Harlan had undergone a profound change of heart.

In Justice Harlan's view, the purpose of the act "was to prevent *race* discrimination." The majority, according to Harlan, betrayed this purpose "by a subtle and ingenious verbal criticism." Justice Harlan was eloquent, but his was a lone voice, crying in the wilderness.

Neither the majority of the Supreme Court, nor the nation it represented, cared to do much else to promote the civil rights of its new black citizens. Harlan's stance in the *Civil Rights Cases* foreshadowed his more famous dissent in *Plessy v. Ferguson,* because the decision in the *Civil Rights Cases* led **inevitably** to the **black codes,** Jim Crow laws, and other examples of *de jure* (by law) segregation that came to define race relations in the United States.

Plessy v. Ferguson (1896) and the Growth of Segregation

The *Plessy* case tested the constitutionality of an 1890 Louisiana law providing for "separate but equal" railway carriages for whites and blacks. Homer Plessy was a black railroad passenger who refused to move out of a whites-only car; following his arrest, he challenged the state law.

In the majority opinion of the U.S. Supreme Court, "separate but equal" accommodations for blacks constituted a "reasonable" use of state power. Furthermore, it was said that the Fourteenth Amendment "could not have been intended to abolish distinctions based on color, or to enforce social equality, or a comingling of the two races upon terms unsatisfactory to either." This ruling greatly limited the influence of the national government in state affairs, especially with regard to race relations.

Again, with great eloquence, Justice Harlan dissented. He wrote:

> I am of the opinion that the statute of Louisiana is inconsistent with the per-

TWO AFRICAN AMERICAN JUSTICES, TWO DIFFERENT VISIONS OF JUSTICE

On July 1, 1991, President George Bush nominated Judge Clarence Thomas to fill the Supreme Court vacancy created by the retirement of Thurgood Marshall. Many African Americans opposed the choice of Thomas because he was viewed as a political conservative, one who had strongly opposed affirmative action programs while he headed the Equal Employment Opportunity Commission (EEOC) during the early 1980s. Then came the Anita Hill-Clarence Thomas hearings in October, in which University of Oklahoma law professor Hill accused Thomas of sexually harassing her while he was her supervisor at the EEOC. The hearings, which were televised nationally and sparked widespread debate about sexual harassment, left many in doubt about both Hill's and Thomas's credibility.

After the Senate confirmation votes were counted, Thomas was nominated by one of the narrowest margins in Supreme Court history. Like his fellow Supreme Court justices, Thomas was appointed for life and thus has considerable power in shaping the direction of American law. Many fear that past black victories may be undermined by his and other conservatives' presence on the Court. However, through 1993, Thomas largely maintained a low profile and avoided additional controversy; his opinions, though informed by his conservative views, are also guided by his great respect for the Constitution and the legal guarantees of the early civil rights movement.

sonal liberty of citizens, white and black, in that state, and hostile to both the spirit and letter of the Constitution of the United States. If laws of like character should be enacted in the several states of the Union, the effect would be in the highest degree mischievous. Slavery, as an institution tolerated by law, would, it is true, have disappeared from our country, but there would remain a power in the states, by sinister legislation, to interfere with the full enjoyment of the blessings of freedom; to regulate civil rights, common to all citizens, upon the basis of race, and to place in a condition of legal inferiority a large body of American citizens, now constituting a part of the political community called the People of the United States, for whom, and by whom through representatives, our government is administered. Such a

Clarence Thomas

Anita Hill

system is inconsistent with the guarantee given by the Constitution....

The Twentieth Century and Full Legal Status for African Americans

Although the legal picture for blacks remained clouded during the early part of the new century, a number of powerful black leaders had emerged to fight the ongoing battle for civil and economic rights. In their various ways, Booker T. Washington, W. E. B. Du Bois, A. Philip Randolph, and others helped fuel black aspirations and black unity while providing hope for a better future.

Nevertheless, it took numerous battles in the courts and Congress and years of civil rights protests before federal and state laws began to reflect the promise of equality contained in the original Constitution.

Twentieth-Century Supreme Court Decisions

Below is a sampling of U.S. Supreme Court cases, organized by topic, that represent legal victories for African Americans. For further case summaries that are of special importance to African Americans, see *The African American Almanac* (1994), 6th ed., edited by Kenneth Estell.

Access to the Polls and the Protection of Voting Rights

***Nixon v. Herndon* (1927)** Dr. L. A. Nixon, an African American, was refused the right to vote in a primary election because of a State law that banned blacks from participating in Democratic Party elections in Texas. Nixon filed suit against the election officials and his case ultimately reached the U.S. Supreme Court.

> **SPECIAL FOCUS**
>
> Thurgood Marshall on Clarence Thomas:
>
> "I don't know how he will affect the court. And I will not criticize him. But when things change on issues like civil rights they tend to swing far to the other side. That scares the hell out of me."
>
> Source: Todd Brewster, "One Man One Vote," Life, January 1992, p. 72.

Justice Oliver Wendell Holmes, in deciding the case, wrote: "It is too clear for extended argument that color cannot be made the basis of a statutory classification affecting the right set up in this case." As a result of *Nixon* v. *Herndon,* the Texas law was declared unconstitutional.

Nixon v. Condon (1932) As a result of the U.S. Supreme Court ruling in *Nixon* v. *Herndon,* the Texas legislature passed a new law, empowering the state Democratic executive committee to set up its own rules regarding the primary election. The party promptly adopted a resolution allowing only white Democrats to participate in the primary. Nixon again filed suit, and his right to vote was again upheld by the U.S. Supreme Court.

Education

Missouri ex rel. Lloyd Gaines v. Canada (1938) *Gaines* v. *Canada* was brought before the Supreme Court by Lloyd Lionel Gaines, an African American who was refused admission to the School of Law of the State University of Missouri. Gaines charged that the University of Missouri's actions violated his rights under the Fourteenth Amendment.

The University of Missouri defended its decision by claiming that Lincoln University, a chiefly black institution, would eventually establish its own law school. The Supreme Court of Missouri dismissed Gaines's petition and upheld the university's decision to reject his application. The U.S. Supreme Court, however, reversed this decision, maintaining that the state of Missouri needed to provide equal facilities for blacks or, in the absence of such facilities, would be required to admit blacks to existing facilities.

Sipuel v. Board of Regents of the University of Oklahoma (1948) Ada Lois Sipuel, an African American, was denied admission to the law school of the University of Oklahoma in 1948. Sipuel requested legal assistance from the NAACP, which filed a petition in the Oklahoma courts requesting an order directing her admission. The petition was denied on the grounds that the *Gaines* decision did not require states with segregation laws to admit black students to its white schools.

In addition, the Oklahoma court maintained that states are not obligated to set up separate schools unless they were first requested to do so by blacks who were seeking a legal education. The Supreme Court of Oklahoma affirmed the Oklahoma court's decision. The U.S. Supreme Court, however, reversed this decision, maintaining that the state was required to provide African Americans with equal educational opportunities.

LAW

Lloyd Gaines

***Sweatt* v. *Painter* (1950)** Herman Marion Sweatt, the African American petitioner in this case, was refused admission to the University of Texas Law School on the grounds that equivalent facilities were already available in another Texas State law school open only to black students.

The U.S. Supreme Court ruled that Sweatt should be admitted to the University of Texas Law School. Chief Justice Fred M. Vinson wrote that "in terms of number of the faculty, variety of courses and opportunity for specialization, size of the student body, scope of the library, availability of law review and similar activities, the University of Texas Law School is superior" to those in the state law school for blacks. The refusal to admit Sweatt to the University of Texas Law School, Vinson concluded, was therefore unconstitutional.

***McLaurin* v. *Oklahoma State Regents for Higher Education* (1950)** G. W. McLaurin,

Linda Brown Smith returns to Sumner School ten years after winning her Supreme Court case, *Brown* v. *Board of Education of Topeka*

an African American, was admitted to the University of Oklahoma. Because of his race, school officials required him to occupy a special seat in each classroom and a segregated table in both the library and the cafeteria.

The U.S. Supreme Court declared unanimously that the black student must receive the same treatment at the hands of the state as other students and could not be segregated.

***Brown* v. *Board of Education of Topeka* (1954)** This case (which was really five separate but similar suits filed by the NAACP) involved the practice of denying black children equal access to state public schools. The case was named for Linda Brown, an African American student in the Topeka, Kansas, public school system.

The U.S. Supreme Court unanimously held that segregation deprived children of equal protection under the Fourteenth Amendment to the U.S. Constitution. The "separate but equal" doctrine of *Plessy* v. *Ferguson* was overturned.

***Cooper* v. *Aaron* (1958)** The impact of *Brown* v. *Board of Education* was minimal until the Justice Department began to initiate its own desegregation lawsuits. Arkansas state officials had, in fact, passed laws contrary to *Brown* v. *Board of Education*.

In *Cooper* v. *Aaron,* the Attorney General of the United States filed a petition on behalf of the U.S. government to bar the governor of Arkansas and officers of the National Guard from interfering with the admission of nine black children into Central High School in Little Rock in 1957. A law was passed relieving school children from compulsory attendance at racially mixed schools. The Supreme Court declared that the Fourteenth Amendment outlined in the *Brown* case is the supreme law of the land and cannot be ignored.

Employment

***Griggs* v. *Duke Power Company* (1971)** In this case, black workers challenged the Duke Power Company's employee requirement. Jobs at the plant that—prior to the Civil Rights Act of 1964—had been held exclusively by whites were awarded only to employees who either held a high school diploma or had passed intelligence tests.

Before that time, blacks were employed only in the Labor Department, where the highest paying jobs paid less than the lowest jobs in the other departments. The company abandoned its policy restricting black employees in 1965; however, it required employees to complete high school and to earn median scores on two aptitude tests before transferring from Labor to another department.

The Supreme Court found that the Civil Rights Act was intended to achieve equality of employment opportunities and to remove barriers that had previously favored an identifiable group of whites over other employees.

The justices determined that neither the high school diploma nor the intelligence tests were related to successful job performance and that the employment policies were discriminatory against black employees.

Justice Wins Out: The Medgar Evers Murder Case

On June 12, 1963, civil rights leader Medgar Evers was assassinated outside his home. He was returning from an NAACP strategy session and was carrying a stack of sweatshirts bearing the words "Jim Crow Must Go."

In 1964 a white **supremacist** named Byron de la Beckwith was tried two times for the Evers's murder. In both cases, however, the all-white juries could not reach a verdict.

After reopening the case in 1989, Mississippi authorities discovered enough new evidence to arrest and charge Beckwith again. Finally, in February 1994, a jury of eight blacks and four whites found Beckwith guilty. He was sentenced to life in prison.

10
Politics

The Voter and Elected Officeholder

"Laws will not eliminate prejudice from the hearts of human beings. But that is no reason to allow prejudice to continue to be enshrined in our laws to perpetuate injustice through inaction."—Shirley Chisholm, Congressional Record, Joint Resolution 264, 91st Congress, 2nd Session (August 10, 1970)

"Our time has come. We must leave racial battleground and come to economic common ground and moral higher ground. America, our time has come."—Jesse Jackson, address to the Democratic National Convention in San Francisco (July 17, 1984)

In May 1993 *Ebony* published its list of "The 100 Most Influential Black Americans." The largest single group by occupation were politicians and government officials—61 in all. Clearly, the arena of politics is of vital importance to African Americans. This is especially true since the 1992 election year, when a record 39 black lawmakers (or 40, if we include nonvoting Washington, D.C., delegate Eleanor Holmes Norton) were elected to the 103rd U.S. Congress.

Throughout the twentieth century, black politics has almost always been tied to the civil rights struggle. Although such civil rights leaders as A. Philip Randolph and

> **WORDS TO KNOW**
>
> **alliance:** a close partnership or association
>
> **constituency:** the group of voters an elected official serves
>
> **flamboyant:** flashy and exciting
>
> **impeached:** brought before a hearing on charges of wrongdoing
>
> **inaugurated:** formally sworn into office
>
> **incumbent:** the current office-holder
>
> **Jim Crow:** a term (taken from an early minstrel song) that describes the systematic discrimination and segregation of blacks
>
> **resolutions:** statements of intent

Martin Luther King, Jr., never held elective office, they helped pave the way for countless black political leaders, from Ralph Bunche (winner of the Nobel Peace Prize and the highest-ranking American ever to serve in the United Nations) to Carol Moseley Braun (the first African American woman senator in the United States).

POLITICS

Black Politics during the Years of Slavery

The true origins of black American politics stem all the way back to 1787 and the creation of the first black organization, the Free African Society. Founded by Methodist ministers Richard Allen and Absalom Jones, the Free African Society raised political consciousness among blacks while promoting their economic and social welfare.

Numerous black religious, social, and political organizations followed the exam-

---

1836 Alexander Lucius Twilight joins the Vermont legislature, becoming the first African American to be elected to public office.

1870 Hiram Rhodes Revels is elected by the Mississippi legislature as the first black U.S. senator.

1872 P. B. S. Pinchback becomes the first black governor when Governor H. C. Warmoth of Louisiana is **impeached.** Pinchback serves for roughly five weeks, until a new governor is **inaugurated.**

1874 Blanche K. Bruce of Mississippi begins the first full Senate term by an African American.

1877 Frederick Douglass becomes the first black to win a major government appointment when he is named U.S. Marshal of the District of Columbia.

1944 Adam Clayton Powell, Jr., is elected to the U.S. House of Representatives, beginning his 22-year career in Congress. He will become the first black Congressman since Reconstruction to have legislation passed by both houses of Congress.

1965 Fewer than 500 blacks hold elective office in the United States. No city, of any size, has a black mayor.

1966 Edward W. Brooke, from Massachusetts, becomes the first black to win a U.S. Senate seat by popular vote. Robert C. Weaver becomes the first black Cabinet member when he is named Secretary of Housing and Urban Development (HUD).

1968 At the Democratic National Convention in Chicago, Channing E. Phillips becomes the first African American to be nominated for the office of President of the United States.

1969 Shirley Chisholm becomes the first African American woman to serve in the U.S. House of Representatives.

1988 Jesse Jackson completes his second presidential campaign race.

1989 Blacks who hold elective office now number 7,370; this number includes one black governor (L. Douglas Wilder of Virginia, the first black governor since Reconstruction) and 310 black mayors.

1993 A record 39 black politicians take their seats in the 103rd U.S. Congress. Among the 17 newcomers is Carol Moseley Braun, the first black woman senator.

Shirley Chisholm on the steps of the U.S. Capitol in 1969

ple of the Free African Society. In the nineteenth century, most of these groups focused especially on ending slavery and establishing equal rights for blacks. A few groups, despairing of an immediate solution to the race problem in America, focused on creating a separate black nation to which all African Americans could return. This goal was highly controversial and was championed primarily by whites with the support of a few black leaders. Most blacks preferred to remain in America to fight for what was rightfully theirs.

The Convention Movement

On September 15, 1830, at Bethel Church in Philadelphia, Pennsylvania, the first national convention for free blacks was held. Richard Allen, now bishop of the African Methodist Episcopal (AME) Church, delivered the opening prayer. A constitution was drafted, officers were elected, and an address to the general public was composed. This group of a few dozen men from Connecticut, Delaware, Maryland, New York, Pennsylvania, Rhode Island, and Virginia named themselves The American Society of Free Persons of Color.

Their pioneering efforts led to a full-blown convention movement that extended to the end of the Civil War. In all, 11 national conventions were held. As Deirdre Mullane writes in *Crossing the Danger Water* (1993): "Through debates on the assembly floor, adopted **resolutions,** public addresses, and petitions to state legislatures and to Congress,

Richard Allen, cofounder of the Free African Society

POLITICS

Frederick Douglass

convention men sought to make their voices heard." (Black women were invited to attend these conventions beginning in 1848.)

Those who favored a separate black nation during this period, and who eventually immigrated to Africa, included scholar Alexander Crummell, doctor and writer Martin R. Delany, pastor and activist Henry Highland Garnet, and *Freedom's Journal* publisher John Russwurm. Of those who favored abolition, former slave Frederick Douglass was the most eloquent and outspoken. Through his numerous lectures, as well as through his *North Star* paper, Douglass commanded attention among both blacks and whites.

Douglass was among those who took part in the drafting of the address for the Cleveland, Ohio, convention of 1848, considered perhaps the high point of the whole convention movement. The mood of the address was both hopeful (for the strides already taken by blacks) and serious (in recognition of the tremendous battles yet to be fought). A portion of the address follows:

> Every one of us should be ashamed to consider himself free, while his brother is a slave. The wrongs of our brethren, should be our constant theme. There should be no time too precious, no calling too holy, no place too sacred, to make room for this cause. We should not only feel it to be the cause of humanity, but the cause of Christianity, and fit work for men and angels. We ask you to devote yourselves to this cause, as one of the first, and most successful means of self improvement.

Harriet Tubman

POLITICS

Sojourner Truth

A Nation Goes to War

Eventually, because of the untiring antislavery efforts of Douglass, Harriet Tubman, Sojourner Truth, and a host of others both black and white, the nation arrived at civil war. The possibility of war had been brewing at least since the time of the 1850 Missouri Compromise, a hotly debated Act of Congress that allowed slavery to continue in the South and gave slaveowners the right to retrieve runaway slaves who had found refuge in the free states of the North.

The harshness of the Compromise was made evident in 1857 when the U.S. Supreme Court decided the case of *Dred Scott* v. *Sandford*. This decision effectively denied all blacks, slave or free, their U.S. citizenship (at least in a court of law). Until the Civil War, free black men were permitted to vote on a par with white men in only five states: Maine, Massachusetts, New Hampshire, Rhode Island, and Vermont.

Reconstruction and Backlash

Within a few years this changed abruptly. Although the Civil War grew out of Abraham Lincoln's desire to preserve the Union, it concluded with an emphasis on a new dawn for African Americans. Suddenly some four million slaves were transformed into citizens who had the right to vote.

The radical wing of the Republican party, led by Senator Charles Sumner of Massachusetts and Representative Thaddeus Stevens of Georgia, was committed to black empowerment and to a strict program for reshaping the South. Northern white Republicans (and those in the South who believed in equal rights for blacks) literally took over the Southern seats of power, backed by the national military. Resentful Southerners branded these transplanted Northerners as "carpetbaggers"; the term referred to the fact that everything these reformers brought with them could be carried in a carpetbag, or suitcase.

During this period, not surprisingly, Southern blacks began voting in large numbers. (What was surprising, though, was that for a time black registered voters outnumbered white registered voters in five states: Alabama, Florida, Louisiana, Mississippi, and South Carolina.) Several were elected to high office, including Hiram Rhodes Revels, the first black to serve in the U.S. Senate. In 1870 Revels took the seat held by Jefferson Davis, the former president of the Confederacy. He quickly won the respect of

POLITICS

The first African American members of the U.S. Senate and House of Representatives (Hiram Revels is at far left)

many of his constituents for his grasp of important state issues and for his courageous support of legislation which would have restored voting and office holding privileges to disenfranchised Southerners. He believed that blacks would gain their rightful place in American society not through violence but by cultivating education, courage, and moral conviction.

Later historians would discredit the skill of such early black politicians. However, according to W. E. B. Du Bois, this reflected a fear among many whites that blacks might earn a reputation for effective leadership. As Du Bois once said, "If there was one thing South Carolina feared more than bad Negro government it was good Negro government."

With the withdrawal of federal troops from the South, and a compromise among the Democratic and Republican parties that returned control of the South to Southerners, Reconstruction failed. Thereafter, lynchings and a number of lesser punishments became a common means of keeping Southern blacks from obtaining their rightful position in society. The greatest force working against blacks was the Southern Democratic Party, which feared a political **alliance** between the Populist Party and the Republicans. Blacks, the party feared, would hold

Accepting Booker T. Washington's (center) invitation, Theodore Roosevelt addresses the National Negro Business League

conference in London, England, and declared: "The problem of the twentieth century is the problem of the color line." Du Bois was especially opposed to Washington's idea that black economic success should come before black political and social equality. In order to put his own beliefs into action, Du Bois helped found a group that eventually became the National Association for the Advancement of Colored People (NAACP).

By the time the NAACP was fully underway, **Jim Crow** laws had spread throughout the South. According to Lerone Bennett, Jr., in *Before the Mayflower: A History of Black America* (1987), "Only Georgia before 1900

W. E. B. Du Bois

the balance of power in such an alliance. Because of this, most Southern states chose to keep blacks away from the voting polls.

The Twentieth Century and Jim Crow

In 1900 Booker T. Washington helped found the National Negro Business League in Boston, Massachusetts. Since 1881, when he opened the Tuskegee Institute, Washington had championed the economic development of African Americans. However, by the turn of the century it was becoming apparent that Washington's sponsorship of black vocations, black business, and black self-help was not enough to bring about broader justice and racial harmony in a segregated society.

Washington's chief rival was W. E. B. Du Bois, who in 1900 attended an important

POLITICS

Mary McLeod Bethune

had required Jim Crow seating on streetcars, but in the first decade of the twentieth century the following states joined the procession: North Carolina and Virginia (1901); Louisiana (1902); Arkansas, South Carolina, and Tennessee (1903); Mississippi and Maryland (1904), and Florida (1905)."

The Great Depression and Changing Political Tides

Not until 1954 and the legal and political victory of *Brown* v. *Board of Education* would blacks control public opinion enough to overturn the ruinous political and social system of Jim Crowism. In the tragic Great Depression, however, a new source of power for blacks would soon emerge.

In 1932, during a dark period of high unemployment, bank failures, and economic uncertainty, the American public voted Republican president Herbert Hoover out of office in favor of Democratic Party candidate Franklin D. Roosevelt. For the first time since emancipation, black voters had abandoned the party that had supported Abraham Lincoln. Grateful for such support, Roosevelt established a group called the Black Cabinet, which was composed of such leaders as educator Mary McLeod Bethune and lawyer (and later federal judge) William H. Hastie. More importantly, Roosevelt authored the New Deal, a vari-

BLACKS AND THE DEMOCRATIC PARTY

From 1940 on blacks have consistently supported Democratic candidates for president. Prior to 1940 blacks tended to vote Republican. The turning point came with the election of Franklin D. Roosevelt in 1932. Black Democratic support became an overwhelming majority in 1964, when blacks gave Lyndon Johnson 94 percent of their votes.

Since then, blacks have cast at least 85 percent of their votes for Democratic presidential candidates. This consistent support for one party is unique among voting groups and has made blacks a vital **constituency.**

274

POLITICS

Adam Clayton Powell, Jr.

ety of federal programs designed to create new jobs, stimulate the economy, and help all Americans achieve financial security.

World War II and the Election of Adam Clayton Powell, Jr.

Nonetheless, the new administration was slow to address injustices against blacks. In 1941, several months prior to the Japanese attack on Pearl Harbor, civil rights leader A. Philip Randolph threatened a huge march on Washington to protest discrimination in the national defense program. Randolph and others met with Roosevelt, who urged that the march be canceled. However, when Randolph refused to back down, Roosevelt issued an executive order banning racial and religious discrimination in defense industries and government training programs.

Near the end of World War II, a **flamboyant** minister from Harlem was elected to the U.S. House of Representatives. Although few suspected it at the time, Adam Clayton Powell, Jr., would exert an

275

enormous influence on the shape of American politics during his more than two decades of service in Congress.

From the beginning, Powell challenged the unwritten rules that barred him from entering certain dining rooms and other public places. He met these rebuffs head on by making use of all such facilities and insisting that his entire staff follow his lead.

As a freshman legislator, Powell engaged in fiery debates with segregationists, fought for the end of discrimination at U.S. military installations, and sought—through the Powell amendment—to deny federal funds to any project where discrimination existed. This amendment eventually became part of the Flanagan School Lunch Bill, making Powell the first black Congressman since

THE INS AND OUTS OF BLACK MAYORSHIPS

There have been a number of high points for African Americans in politics since the 1960s, but most astonishing has been the steady rise in black mayorships of large cities. In roughly a 20-year period, blacks went from holding zero mayorships to more than 300. Most importantly, these included the halls of some of the largest cities in the country: Atlanta, Baltimore, Birmingham, Chicago, Cleveland, Detroit, Los Angeles, New Orleans, New York City, Newark, Oakland, Philadelphia, Seattle, and Washington.

However, a *Business Week* article dated October 18, 1993 reported that this trend may be changing. "In recent contests, white candidates have recaptured city halls in Los Angeles, Chicago, and Philadelphia. And in Houston, a white businessman edged out a legislator who was trying to become the city's first black mayor," a reporter wrote. A month following the article, New York mayor David Dinkins lost his seat to white Republican challenger Rudolph Giuliani.

The reasons for such changes may be as much tied to voters fed up with big government spending and urban decay as voters who cast their ballot automatically along racial lines. In any event, the article also notes that blacks "are still making political breakthroughs.... A host of white-majority cities, among them Seattle, Kansas City, Mo., and Denver, chose black mayors. Cleveland's Michael White and Baltimore's Kurt Schmoke lead a wave of new-generation African-American politicians who have built broad support across racial lines." And in November 1993, in Minneapolis, Sharon Sayles Belton was elected the first black and first female mayor ever in the city's history.

Reconstruction to have legislation passed by both houses.

More than any other black politician in American history, Powell was able to command stunning political power, which he used to benefit his fellow African Americans. The secret to his numerous legislative successes (nearly 50 in all) was his ability to rise to the chairmanship of the House Committee on Education and Labor, which he controlled from 1960 to 1967. These were the very same years during which first President John F. Kennedy and then President Lyndon Johnson helped oversee the long-awaited fulfillment of political rights for African Americans.

Johnson's "War on Poverty" led to the Economic Opportunity Act, which Powell helped push through Congress in 1964. This Act created many programs that have been helpful to blacks, including Head Start for preschoolers, Upward Bound for high school students, and college work-study financial aid.

The Civil Rights Movement Leads to Breakthrough Gains for African Americans

Interestingly, Powell often found himself at odds with the civil rights leadership outside Congress. However, it is clear that without the mass demonstrations and pressure applied by such leaders as Martin Luther King, Jr., the political victories of the 1960s (such as the Civil Rights Act of 1964 and the Voting Rights Act of 1965, for example) would have been impossible.

The enthusiasm the civil rights movement inspired and the community organization that spread through the cities as part of the war on poverty led to a sharp rise in political consciousness among blacks. It was this new political mood that led blacks to seek political office in ever larger numbers. The first major victories came in 1967 when Carl Stokes was elected mayor of Cleveland, Ohio, and Richard Hatcher took over City Hall in Gary, Indiana, as the nation's first black elected mayors of major cities. In both cases, it was organized black political strength that made victory possible.

In the early 1970s black political participation advanced. The Voter Education Project was formed in Atlanta, Georgia, with the express purpose of registering more blacks and assisting black candidates elected to political office in the South. In addition, the Congressional Black Caucus was formed to lobby the view of blacks elected to the House of Representatives.

A growing black political maturity was evident in 1980. During this election year, the Black Leadership Forum organized a National Conference on a Black Agenda for the Eighties. Other groups that participated included the National Council of Negro Women, the National Conference of Black Mayors, the National Black Caucus of State Legislators, and the Congressional Black Caucus. In all, more than 1,000 blacks representing over 300 organizations gathered to frame an agenda on domestic and international issues of special concern to blacks.

The agenda went far beyond the traditional civil rights concerns and advocated:

1) domestic and foreign economic policies aimed at providing full employment and development of black entrepreneurship

POLITICS

Jesse Jackson and supporters

2) federal programs to improve the quality of education available to minorities, and provision of adequate financial assistance and health care for the needy

3) the halt of U.S. interaction with South Africa and a better program of economic aid to Caribbean countries

4) steps by the government and political parties to increase opportunities for full minority participation in the political process.

The End of the "Second Reconstruction"

However, for the most part, the 1970s and 1980s cast a shadow over the dreams of black Americans for racial justice and equality. With the exception of Jimmy Carter's presidency from 1976 to 1980, it was a time when blacks first felt neglected,

BLACK CONSERVATIVES— A MINORITY MINORITY

Since the early 1980s black conservatives have become a growing "minority within a minority." Led by economist Thomas Sowell, this group (not so much a unified group as a number of individuals who share many of the same views) opposes long-held opinions of traditional black leaders and many black Americans.

For example, black conservatives reject the view that white racism in the post-civil rights era is the main cause of black problems. They also doubt that more and bigger federal programs are needed to help solve black problems, viewing such programs as dependency-producing. Solutions to crime, teenage pregnancy, drug addiction, and unemployment are the responsibility of blacks, they say, who should concern themselves with healing their communities and pushing themselves to achieve higher standards of living.

Black conservative goals and values remain unpopular with the traditional black leadership, especially the Congressional Black Caucus (whose only conservative is Republican Representative Gary Franks). However, they have found support in the growing number of middle-class and wealthy blacks. In addition to Sowell, the list of notable black conservatives includes economists Glen Loury and Walter E. Williams; foundation executive Kay James; writers Shelby Steele and Charles Johnson; Washington official Claudia Butts; publisher and editor Elizabeth Wright; and self-help expert Robert L. Woodson.

---

then threatened. The marches and court decisions that had been so effective during the 1950s and 1960s did not have the same impact during later decades.

Many blacks seemed resigned to the fact that America was still a nation of two societies—one black, one white—separate and unequal. Some blacks decided that the only way to make progress on issues of importance to African Americans was to reject traditional politics. A few looked into alternative movements, including the Nation of Islam and Afrocentrism, which stressed the value of black culture and the black experience (especially its African roots).

One who chose a different path was Jesse Jackson, a minister and veteran civil rights activist who had become the most popular national black leader since King. In 1984 he campaigned for the Democratic nomination for president of the United States. Even though he lost a bitter fight to former vice-president Walter Mondale (who later lost the presidential election to Ronald Reagan), Jackson inspired thousands of blacks at a time when they had just about given up on politics. His candidacy proved that it was possible for an African American to seek the nomination of a major party.

Politics in the 1990s

Since the 1960s, despite various setbacks, African Americans have been selected for political offices in ever-increasing numbers. The presidential election year 1992 was no exception. One of the most significant political developments of 1992 was the election of the first black woman, Carol Moseley Braun, to the United States Senate.

Braun, a native of Chicago, Illinois, shocked political observers by scoring a stunning upset over **incumbent** senator Alan Dixon in the Democratic primary on March 17, 1992. In the November 1992 election, she defeated her Republican challenger, Richard Williamson, by a wide margin. Braun is only the fifth African American to serve in the Senate and only the second since Reconstruction.

Overall, the 1992 national elections increased by 14 the number of African American representatives in Congress. There are now 39 African Americans who occupy seats in the House of Representatives. Many of the gains in representation are probably due to an increasing acceptance of blacks as good political candidates. Also, the process of redistricting has benefitted minority office-seekers. (Redistricting occurs every 10 years and involves the redrawing of district lines for all 435 seats in the U.S. House of Representatives according to population shifts among the 50 states.)

Ron Brown opening the 1992 Democratic National Convention

Blacks and the Clinton Administration

On November 3, 1992, Americans elected Bill Clinton as their new president. President Clinton's Cabinet includes five African Americans. Ron Brown, former Democratic National Committee chairman, was chosen as Secretary of Commerce; he is the first African American to hold this post.

Mike Espy was chosen as Secretary of Agriculture. A Congressman from Mississippi, Espy was elected in 1986 and was the first African American from Mississippi to serve in Congress since Reconstruction.

President Bill Clinton and Vice President Al Gore meet with Representative Kweisi Mfume and Senator Carol Moseley Braun

Jesse Brown was selected to serve as head of the Veterans Affairs Department. Brown, a former director of the Disabled Veterans of America, is the first African American to hold the post.

Hazel R. O'Leary, one of two African American women selected for cabinet-level positions, was chosen as Secretary of Energy. The position of Surgeon General was awarded to Joycelyn Elders. Elders is a talented physician known for her innovative research on diabetes. She is also a controversial figure who has clashed with conservatives over her pro-abortion views and support of contraception in school health clinics.

Another important appointment was that of Clifton R. Wharton, Jr., as the highest ranking black in the State department. Wharton resigned his deputy position, however, on November 9, 1993.

[A number of other chapters in the *African American Almanac* are closely tied to the subject of politics and may provide the reader with additional helpful information. Especially recommended are Ch. 7: "Civil Rights"; Ch. 8: "Black Nationalism"; Ch. 9: "Law"; and Ch. 11: "National Organizations," all in this volume.]

11
National Organizations

In Unity There Is Strength

> **FACT FOCUS**
>
> - African Lodge No. 459 was founded in 1787 by Prince Hall. The oldest black **Masonic** organization in the United States, it is now known as the Conference of Prince Hall Grand Masters and has more than 250,000 members.
> - The Free African Society is regarded as the first independent black organization in the country. Founded in 1787 by Richard Allen and Absalom Jones, it led directly to the formation of the African Methodist Episcopal (AME) Church.

"Keep on going, keep on pushing, keep on fighting injustice."—Mary Church Terrell

The 1994-95 edition of *Black Americans Information Directory* covers nearly 500 national organizations and more than 1,200 regional, state, and local organizations. If one were to include every church, school, charity, club, program, and business—each of these groups merits the term "organization" as well—the number would be staggering. In fact, any group, any association, is by definition an organization. Imagine a civilization that might exist without organizations. It's virtually impossible to do so. (Aren't governments organizations, too? And doesn't every civilization require some form of government?)

We study organizations to learn not only about the people who created them but about the reasons for their creation; for whatever the name, whatever the group, organizations serve specific purposes. They can be as serious and issue-oriented as the Congressional Black Caucus (see Vol. 2, Ch. 10: "Politics," for a full discussion of this group) or as informal and fun-oriented as the Friends of Johnny Mathis. For African Americans, organizations have been especially crucial in developing and providing information, protecting rights and interests, and promoting a host of short- and long-term goals.

Although public and private associations of all kinds have formed and developed

NATIONAL ORGANIZATIONS

Grand Lodge No. 1, Greensville, Mississippi, 1887

without incident during the history of this country, this has not always been true of black and other minority organizations.

Before the eighteenth century only the most casual and limited black gatherings were permitted. African Americans were thus forced to meet secretly and in small numbers for their organizations to survive. This even applied to religious worship. Sadly, records of the earliest black organizations do not exist.

Early Black Organizations

The Free African Society, founded in Philadelphia in 1787, has been generally accepted as the first African American organization in the United States. (Prince Hall's Masonic lodge was granted an English **charter** that same year, however, and individual African American churches were very likely founded between the years 1750 and 1775.) The importance of the Free African Society cannot be overestimated, for out of it grew the African Methodist Episcopal (AME) and AME Zion Churches (see Vol. 2, Ch. 17: "Religion," for a discussion of these and related organizations), not to mention pro-active traditions that gave rise to such modern-day groups as the National Association for the Advancement of Colored People (NAACP), the National Urban League, and the Southern Christian Leadership Conference (SCLC).

Founded by Methodist ministers Richard Allen and Absalom Jones, the Free African Society combined economic and medical aid for poor blacks with support of abolition, including secret communication with blacks in the South.

283

NATIONAL ORGANIZATIONS

Mary Church Terrell established the National Association of Colored Women in 1896

The abolitionist movement of the nineteenth century produced many organizations concerned with African American issues. These included the American Colonization Society (founded in 1816), the New England Anti-Slavery Society (founded in 1832), and the American Anti-Slavery Society (founded in 1833). Although most of these organizations were dominated by whites, such black leaders as Paul Cuffe, Frederick Douglass, and Harriet Tubman symbolized the antislavery movement in their own outstanding ways.

During the late nineteenth and early twentieth centuries a great many black organizations came into existence. The thrust of most of these groups was toward education, betterment, and religious training. In 1895 the National Medical Association was founded to further the interests of black physicians, pharmacists, and nurses; Mary Church Terrell organized the National Association of Colored Women in 1896; and in 1900 the National Negro Business League was formed to promote commercial development.

Twentieth-Century Organizations

The Niagara Movement

Organizers: W. E. B. Du Bois, William Monroe Trotter

Founding date: 1905

The Niagara Movement marked a turning point in African American history. This new organization, founded by a group of black intellectuals and headed by historian W. E. B. Du Bois, met in July 1905 in Buffalo, New York. The organization represented a formal rejection of Booker T. Washington's emphasis on manual and industrial training for blacks as a means of gaining economic security and social equality.

The Niagara Movement, however, suffered from weak finances and a policy that restricted membership to black intellectuals. In 1909 the Niagara Movement was succeeded by a new organization that became the National Association for the Advancement of Colored People (NAACP).

National Association for the Advancement of Colored People (NAACP)

Organizers: William English Walling, Mary White Ovington, Henry Moskowitz

Founding date: 1909 (as the National Negro Committee; present name adopted in 1910)

NATIONAL ORGANIZATIONS

An NAACP office, 1945

The NAACP came into being on February 12, 1909, the one-hundredth anniversary of the birth of Abraham Lincoln. It was largely the brainchild of three people: a white Southerner named William English Walling, who feared that racists would soon carry "the race war to the North"; a wealthy young white woman named Mary White Ovington, who had attended the 1905 meeting of the Niagara Movement as a reporter and also had experienced the conditions in the black ghettos of New York City; and Henry Moskowitz, a New York social worker.

This trio, after enlisting the support of such black leaders as William Henry Brooks and Alexander Walters, proposed that a conference be called "for the discussion of present evils, the voicing of protests, and the renewal of the struggle for civil and political liberty." Following the conference, additional meetings were held and an official name for the group was chosen, the National Negro Committee. The name was changed the following year to the National Association for the Advancement of Colored People.

NATIONAL ORGANIZATIONS

> ### WORDS TO KNOW
>
> **apartheid:** a policy of racial separation
>
> **charter:** a document that outlines the goals of a group
>
> **coalitions:** groups united in purpose
>
> **confrontations:** bold face-to-face meetings
>
> **exonerated:** declared not guilty
>
> **infringement:** the act of overstepping boundaries and intruding on another's
>
> **litigation:** the process of filing and pursuing a lawsuit
>
> **Masonic:** having to do with Masons or Freemasons, an international organization dedicated to universal brotherhood, charity, and mutual aid
>
> **retaliation:** to respond in kind, as in "an eye for an eye"
>
> **rhetoric:** especially effective speaking or writing; alternately, language that is flashy but insincere
>
> **subservient:** inferior or subject to rule by another

Margaret Bush Wilson, former chairwoman of the NAACP

The NAACP is best known for its unswerving attempts to better the condition of African Americans through **litigation,** legislation, and education. During its early years, *Crisis* magazine, edited by W. E. B. Du Bois, became its chief vehicle for communication. Perhaps the NAACP's greatest victory was won in 1954 when the historic *Brown* v. *Board of Education of Topeka, Kansas* case threw out the "separate but equal" doctrine and eliminated segregation in public education. The organization's chief legal counsel in the case was Thurgood Marshall, who went on to become a Supreme Court justice.

During the late 1950s the state of Alabama set out to ban the NAACP from conducting activities within the state, claiming that the association had failed to observe statutes governing corporations operating within the state. The dispute, *NAACP* v. *Alabama,* was finally resolved by the United States Supreme Court in 1958 in favor of the association. However, the association was forced to defend itself in similar cases for several more years.

In the post-civil rights era, the NAACP has focused its attention on a number of growing problems within the black community, including teenage pregnancy, drug abuse, infant mortality, and unemployment. The organization is also known for its annual awarding of the Spingarn Medal, an honor bestowed for "the highest and noblest achievement of an American Negro."

Other key figures: Benjamin Hooks, Benjamin Franklin Chavis, Jr., Roy Wilkins, Walter White, Margaret Bush Wilson, Joel E. Spingarn, James Weldon Johnson.

National Urban League

Organizers: Ruth Standish Baldwin, George Edmond Haynes

Founding date: 1910 (as the Committee on Urban Conditions Among Negroes; in 1911 the organization merged with the Committee for the Improvement of Industrial Conditions Among Negroes in New York and the National League for the Protection of Colored Women to form the National League on Urban Conditions Among Negroes; name later shortened to its present form).

During the early part of the twentieth century several organizations concerned with the plight of urban blacks emerged. In 1906, at the urging of Long Island Railroad president William H. Baldwin, a group of blacks and whites met for the purpose of studying the employment needs of African Americans. This group, known as the Committee for Improving the Industrial Conditions Among Negroes in New York, studied the racial aspects of the labor market (particularly the attitudes and policies of employers and unions) and sought to find openings for qualified African Americans.

At the same time, the League for the Protection of Colored Women was established to provide similar services for black women relocating from the South to New York and Philadelphia. These women, who often had no friends or relatives in the North, often fell prey to corrupt employment agencies which led them into low wage jobs.

A third organization, the Committee on Urban Conditions Among Negroes, was organized in 1910 by Ruth Standish Baldwin, widow of the former Long Island Railroad president. She was joined by George Edmond Haynes, one of only three trained black social workers in the country and the first black person to receive a doctorate from Columbia University. Haynes was named as the first executive secretary of the new agency. A year later the organization merged with the Committee for the Improvement of Industrial Conditions Among Negroes in New York and the National League for the Protection of Colored Women to form the National Urban League (NUL).

From the outset, the organization focused on the social and economic needs of blacks, such as training, improved housing, health, recreation, and job assistance. However, it was not until the 1960s, when Whitney M. Young, Jr., became its new leader that the League began to emerge as a force in the civil rights struggle.

Other key figures: John E. Jacob, Vernon E. Jordan, Jr., Charles S. Johnson, Lester B. Granger, Eugene Kinckle Jones, T. Arnold Hill.

Universal Negro Improvement Association

Organizer: Marcus Garvey

Founding date: 1911 (in Jamaica; 1916 in United States)

During the nineteenth and early part of the twentieth century, a number of individu-

NATIONAL ORGANIZATIONS

Marcus Garvey

als arose to unite Africans throughout the world. Most notable was Marcus Garvey, a black nationalist who founded the Universal Negro Improvement Association (UNIA) in 1911 and championed the "Back to Africa" movement, or the relocation of blacks to Africa.

Garvey's organization attracted thousands worldwide by emphasizing black pride, black economic and political power, and black unity. Although Garvey succeeded in forming the Black Star Line, a steamship company for the cause, he was pursued by the federal government for mail fraud. The UNIA leader served two years of a five-year jail term before being deported to Jamaica in 1927. By 1935 Garvey had retired to England, where he died five years later.

In 1987 New York congressman Charles Rangel introduced two bills to have Garvey **exonerated** of the mail fraud charges. Rangel's efforts came after Robert Hill, editor of a Garvey research project at the University of California at Los Angeles, discovered evidence that pointed to impure political motivations for Garvey's conviction.

Malcolm X was among later black nationalists who looked to the example of Garvey and the UNIA for inspiration.

NAACP Legal Defense and Educational Fund, Inc.

Organizers: Members of the NAACP

Founding date: 1939

Although for its first 20 years, the NAACP Legal Defense and Educational Fund (LDF) maintained its own board, program, staff, office, and budget, it remained tied to its parent. In 1959 it became completely independent. Following the separation of the organizations, a dispute over identity and the use of the parent organization's name erupted. The NAACP sued the LDF for name **infringement.** However, after several months of legal battles, a federal court ruled that the LDF could keep NAACP in its name, since the NAACP was its parent organization.

The LDF has served in the forefront of legal assaults against discrimination and segregation and has amassed an outstanding record of victories. In addition to its litigation, the LDF provides scholarships and training for young lawyers, advises lawyers on legal trends and decisions, and monitors federal programs.

Congress of Racial Equality (CORE)

Organizer: James Farmer

Founding date: 1942

NATIONAL ORGANIZATIONS

The Congress of Racial Equality (CORE) was the first protest organization in the United States to use the techniques of nonviolence and passive resistance championed by Indian nationalist Mohandas K. Gandhi (1869-1948). An interracial organization organized to confront racism and discrimination, CORE was founded in 1942 by James Farmer as the result of a campaign protesting discrimination at a Chicago restaurant. From Chicago the organization spread to other cities and other causes; one of its chief activities was organizing sit-ins and freedom rides throughout the South.

By the mid-1960s CORE had changed direction and Farmer turned leadership of the organization over to Floyd McKissick, a North Carolina lawyer. With McKissick as national director, the organization moved toward an all-black membership and staff. (In 1967 CORE eliminated the word "multiracial" from its constitution.) McKissick left the organization in 1968 and was replaced by the present national director, Roy Innis, former chairman of the Harlem chapter. Farmer broke all ties with CORE in 1976, criticizing Innis for attempting to recruit black Vietnam veterans to fight in Angola's civil war. The organization is now considered largely inactive.

Leadership Conference on Civil Rights

Organizers: A. Philip Randolph, Roy Wilkins, Arnold Aronson

Founding date: 1950

The Leadership Conference on Civil Rights (LCCR) was begun in 1950 in Washington, D.C., to implement the historic report of President Harry S Truman's Committee on Civil Rights, "To Secure These Rights." Beginning with only 30 organizations, the conference has grown in number, scope, and effectiveness, and has been responsible for coordinating the campaigns that have resulted in the passage of important legislation, including the Civil Rights Acts of 1957, 1960, and 1964, the Voting Rights Act of 1965, and the Fair Housing Act of 1968.

The LCCR currently consists of approximately 157 national organizations representing minorities, women, major religious groups, the handicapped, the aged, labor, and minority businesses and professions. These organizations speak for a large portion of the population and together form one of the most broad-based **coalitions** in the nation.

Southern Christian Leadership Conference (SCLC)

Organizers: Ralph Abernathy, Martin Luther King, Jr., Bayard Rustin, Joseph E. Lowery

Founding date: 1957 (as the Southern Negro Leaders Conference; name later changed to Southern Leadership Conference before present name was adopted)

Following the arrest of Rosa Parks, who had refused to give up her seat on a public bus, Martin Luther King, Jr., and Ralph Abernathy organized the Montgomery Improvement Association in 1955 to coordinate a citywide bus boycott. The success of the boycott led to the creation of a new organization, the SCLC.

In January 1957 the group, consisting mainly of black ministers, met at the Ebenezer Baptist Church and elected King as its first president. The time was ripe for such a group, for the civil rights movement

NATIONAL ORGANIZATIONS

The March on Washington was the result of one of the greatest examples of cooperation among black organizations. Organizers of the march include: (left to right) Bayard Rustin (of the Brotherhood of Sleeping Car Porters); Jack Greenburgh; Whitney Young, Jr. (NUL); James Farmer (CORE); Roy Wilkins (NAACP); Martin Luther King, Jr. (SCLC); John Lewis (SNCC); and A. Philip Randolph (Brotherhood of Sleeping Car Porters)

in the South was about to explode. In some areas of the South the NAACP was prohibited from operating and the National Urban League, generally opposed to direct action, was in no position to provide guidance for the growing movement.

The SCLC appealed to blacks "to assert their human dignity by refusing further cooperation with evil." Specifically, the SCLC stressed the moral obligation of blacks to support the legal fight for rights with direct nonviolent action. Under King, the SCLC was a driving force. Its **confrontations** with the forces of bigotry in such cities as Birmingham and Selma, Alabama, helped to arouse the conscience of a nation.

The assassination of King in 1968 dealt the SCLC a severe blow, and there was real concern that without his charismatic leadership the organization would fall apart. Ralph Abernathy, King's closest associate, was elected by the SCLC to succeed the slain leader. On May 11, 1968, shortly after King's death, Abernathy led the "Poor People's Campaign" for jobs and freedom in Washington, D.C. Abernathy resigned from the SCLC in 1977.

One of the many outgrowths of the SCLC is the Martin Luther King, Jr. Center for Nonviolent Social Change, headed by Coretta Scott King.

Other key figures: Jesse Jackson.

Student National Coordinating Committee (SNCC)

Organizers: Black and white college students

NATIONAL ORGANIZATIONS

Ralph Abernathy of the SCLC also played a major role in the March

Founding date: 1960 (as Student Nonviolent Coordinating Committee)

In 1960 a group of black and white college students founded the Student Nonviolent Coordinating Committee (SNCC or "Snick") to engage in civil rights protests, naming future District of Columbia mayor Marion Barry as the first national chairman. SNCC achieved tremendous success in desegregating public facilities and earned respect from the country for its determination to act peacefully in the face of violence.

However, by 1966 the organization's newest, youngest, and most radical leader, Stokely Carmichael (Kwame Toure), had become convinced that the American system could not be turned around without the threat of violent **retaliation.** Carmichael began preaching "black power" and in 1967 left the organization to join the more militant Black Panther Party. In 1969 Carmichael and his wife, South African singer Miriam Makeba, left the United States for Africa, eventually becoming citizens of Uganda.

H. Rap Brown (Jamil Abdullah Al-Amin), the former minister of justice in the old organization, took over leadership of the group and symbolically renamed it the Student National Coordinating Committee. Under his leadership, violence was to be used in situations that demanded it. The organization gradually declined in membership and is now inactive.

Other key figures: Julian Bond, John Lewis.

Black Panther Party

Organizers: Huey P. Newton, Bobby Seale

Stokely Carmichael and H. Rap Brown

NATIONAL ORGANIZATIONS

Bobby Seale speaks at a Black Panther Rally, 1971

Founding date: 1966

The Black Panther Party differed greatly from other civil rights organizations. Its leaders rejected established authority and many middle-class values, reasoning that such outside controls led to indifference toward, or contempt for, disadvantaged black urban youth.

The party armed itself as a defensive measure and imposed strict discipline on its members. Such a military atmosphere, combined with aggressive **rhetoric,** appealed especially to many young black males. However, by 1970 most of the organization's leaders were either imprisoned, exiled, or dead.

Newton was jailed in 1968 on manslaughter charges; Seale had been jailed on charges stemming from the 1968 Chicago convention riot; minister of information, Eldridge Cleaver, fled in 1969 to Algeria to avoid a prison sentence; and in 1970 Mark Clark and Fred Hampton were killed during a police raid.

Other key figures: Stokely Carmichael.

Operation PUSH

Organizer: Jesse Jackson

Founding date: 1971

Operation PUSH (People United to Save Humanity) traces its origin to the civil rights movement of the 1960s. During that decade, the Southern Christian Leadership Conference (SCLC) played a vital role in bettering the lives of African Americans, especially

NATIONAL ORGANIZATIONS

Operation PUSH dinner in 1972; (left to right) Manhattan Borough President Percy Sutton, Jesse Jackson, and presidential candidate George McGovern

basket by concerning itself with all aspects of African American life. It also displayed a special concern for young people through its PUSH-EXCEL program, which is designed to motivate high school students by instilling pride, building confidence, and restoring self-discipline and academic excellence.

In 1984 Jackson left Operation PUSH to organize another group, the National Rainbow Coalition, which he used to support his 1984 and 1988 runs for the presidency and to raise awareness of the underprivileged.

The Operation PUSH platform reads as follows:

> We, the People United to Save Humanity, believe that humanity will be saved and served only when justice is

through numerous nonviolent marches and demonstrations that resulted in major new civil rights laws.

Jesse Jackson joined the SCLC in 1963. Within a few years he became involved with SCLC's Operation Breadbasket, a program designed to lift blacks out of poverty and protect their social and business interests. In 1967 Jackson was asked by Martin Luther King, Jr., to become the executive director of Breadbasket. He served in this position until 1971, when he left SCLC after a serious disagreement with the group's new leader, Ralph Abernathy.

Almost immediately, Jackson established Operation PUSH. This new organization expanded the traditions of Operation Bread-

Randall Robinson meets with Nelson Mandela, 1991

done for all people. We believe that we must challenge the economic, political, and social forces that make us **subservient** to others; and that we must assume the power (of being) given us by the Power of God. We believe that our worth as humane people is expressed in our united efforts to secure justice for all persons.

Other key figures: Willie B. Barrow.

TransAfrica

Organizer: Randall Robinson

Founding date: 1977

Since the civil rights era, organizations have formed to address the concerns of Africans around the world. Founded in 1977 by Randall Robinson, TransAfrica has worked to influence American foreign policy regarding political and human rights in Africa and the Caribbean by informing the public of violations of social, political, and civil rights.

Responding to the continued policy of **apartheid** in South Africa, TransAfrica has supported sanctions against South Africa and has organized demonstrations in front of the South African embassy in Washington, D.C. During one such demonstration, Robinson and numerous others were arrested. Other organizations have also taken a stand on policies affecting Africans around the world.

12
Population

The Growth and Settlement of a Race

> **FACT FOCUS**
>
> - Reports from 1991 indicate that the African American population was approaching more than 31 million, or some 12.4 percent of the nation's total resident population.
> - Since the 1980 **census**, the African American population has grown faster than the white population or the overall U.S. population.
> - From 1790 until 1900, 90 percent or more of the African American population lived in the South.
> - New York has the largest black population of any city in the United States.
> - One of every four metropolitan blacks lives in the suburbs.
> - The **median** age of blacks is 28 years; the median age of whites is 34 years.

"I see, now near at hand, the opening day of the darker races of mankind in which / Americans of African descent stand forth / Among the first Americans."—Reverdy Cassius Ransom, in Prophesy *(c. 1915)*

A New Land, a New People

The beginning of an African American population may be traced to 1619, when a Dutch ship with 20 blacks aboard arrived at Jamestown, Virginia. These first blacks were indentured servants. Unlike slaves, who were considered the property of their owners, indentured servants generally worked for someone for seven years. At the end of that time, they gained their freedom.

The practice of indentured servitude began dying out within a few decades as the slave trade expanded and spread throughout the colonies. By 1630 there were some 60 slaves in the American colonies. Thirty years later the number had increased to 2,920.

Because of a rapidly emerging **agrarian** society, there was a steady demand for an ever-larger labor force. This labor was supplied by constant new shipments of slaves. By 1690 the total slave population in the Ameri-

POPULATION

> ### WORDS TO KNOW
>
> **agrarian:** relating to farming, agriculture, or agribusiness
>
> **census:** an official count of the population that also includes information about age, sex, race, economic status, etc.
>
> **demographics:** the **census** characteristics of a population, broken down by geographic regions
>
> **equity:** value or worth, as in money, property, stocks, etc.
>
> **exodus:** literally, a going out; a massive migration or departure of a people
>
> **fertility:** the state of being able to produce children, determined by age and other factors
>
> **median:** the midway point in a series of numbers

BLACK POPULATION BY STATE, 1790

State	Slaves	Free
Connecticut	2,759	2,801
Delaware	8,887	3,889
Georgia	29,264	398
Kentucky	11,830	114
Maryland	103,036	8,043
New Hampshire	158	630
New Jersey	11,423	2,762
New York	21,324	4,654
North Carolina	100,572	4,975
Pennsylvania	3,737	6,537
Rhode Island	952	3,469
South Carolina	107,094	1,801
Vermont	17	255
Virginia	293,427	12,766
Ohio Territory	3,417	5,463
Maine	None	538

can colonies had grown to 16,729. By 1740 the slave population had reached 150,000. By 1780 it had grown well beyond half a million. Although a free black population did exist, it grew at a slower rate than the slave population. In 1780 there was only one free black for every nine slaves, or around 60,000 who lived unfettered by slavery.

Census-taking Begins

The first official census of the United States was taken in 1790. At that time 757,208 blacks were counted. This figure represented almost one-fifth of the nation's population.

The movement to abolish slavery, which would gain great popularity in the North during the nineteenth century, was already underway. Pennsylvania, Massachusetts, Connecticut, Rhode Island, New York, New Jersey, and the Northwest Territory had passed laws providing for the gradual freeing of slaves. The slave trade itself, according to the U.S. Constitution, was supposed to end in 1808. (No slaves could legally be brought into the country after that date, though illegal trafficking, as well as the legal bartering of slaves within the country, continued.)

POPULATION

The Vicksburg Wharf from which many blacks departed for the West in the Exodus of 1879-81

Emancipation and Migration

By the beginning of the Civil War, there were almost four million blacks in the United States. Over 90 percent of them lived in the South. In fact, from 1790 until 1900, this high percentage hardly varied.

Even the abolition of slavery following the Civil War had only a brief and minor impact on the Southern, rural character of the black population. In other words, most newly freed blacks, for several reasons, chose to remain in the South.

Occasional migration from the South, however, did occur during this period. One early **exodus** took place from 1879 to 1881, when some 60,000 blacks moved into Kansas. The reason for this initial migration was the need for social and economic freedom. The immigration to Kansas strained the resources of the state, and several cities became black refugee camps. One of the towns created by this exodus was Nicodemus, Kansas, which still exists as a small, all-black community.

Although other relocations by Southern blacks to the Midwest or Northeast have been recorded, the effect on the regional distribution of the total black population was minor. When the Emancipation Proclamation was signed, less than 8 percent of all blacks lived in the Northeast or Midwest. After the Civil War, the black population in the Northeast fell slightly, while the percentage rose in the Midwest. By 1900 only 10 percent of all blacks lived in these two Northern regions.

Down and Then Up

During the late nineteenth and early twentieth centuries, the white population grew faster than the black population. The primary reasons for this were large-scale European immigration and the ending of the slave trade.

In 1900 there were 8.8 million blacks in the United States, representing 11.6 percent of the total population. Between 1910 and 1930 the black percentage of the overall population declined. Finally, a low was reached in 1930 when blacks made up only 9.7 percent of the total U.S. population. This marked a turning point, for ever since the African American population has grown at a faster rate than the national average.

The Great Migration

In 1900 nine out of ten African Americans still lived in the South. Between 1910 and 1920, however, the percentage of blacks living in the South began to fall. By 1930 more than one in five blacks resided outside of the South.

For the next four decades, the percentage of African Americans living in the South fell steadily. In 1970 about four in ten blacks were Northerners, a little more than five in ten were Southerners, and the remainder lived in the West.

Historians and social scientists have long debated why blacks failed to leave the South in larger numbers at the end of the Civil War. Did the benefits of living in the South outweigh the drawbacks? Maybe. Or maybe the opportunities and incentives for moving to the North were extremely limited for decades following emancipation.

Migration usually results from both "push" and "pull" forces. "Push" forces are typically negative, while "pull" forces are typically positive. Prejudice, discrimination, and poor job prospects in the South obviously provided the strong push factors. And a somewhat more open society and a far better employment picture in the industrializing North should have provided the pull for a strong South-to-North migration stream.

Some blacks did leave the South during the last decades of the nineteenth century. However, the number of blacks moving North has always been smaller than what might be expected.

European immigration may be one explanation for the slow start of the Southern exodus. As the North industrialized in the late nineteenth and early twentieth centuries, it generated a huge demand for labor. This demand was met in large part by massive immigration of Europeans. A great many of the urban factory jobs were filled first by Irish and German laborers, and later by immigrants from southern and eastern Europe, especially Italy. Had Northern factories not been able to meet their labor needs through immigration, they might have relied more on domestic sources, including Southern blacks.

Eventually, World War I would reduce immigration to the United States. Then, in the 1920s, more restrictive immigration laws were passed, leaving the way open for blacks to leave the South in larger numbers. Consequently, the proportion of the nation's

POPULATION

A black family living in rural Georgia

black population living in the South fell more rapidly during the decade beginning in 1910 than it had during the entire period since emancipation.

Although black migration from the South decreased somewhat during the Great Depression, when jobs were scarce everywhere, the proportion of blacks living in the South continued to decrease. The greatest migration of Southern blacks came between 1940 and 1950. World War II, even more than World War I, had a tremendous impact on American business and the economy. During and following World War II a virtual boom occurred, causing a great northward migration of blacks.

Through the 1960s the net migration of blacks from the South totalled about 4.3

million persons. Mechanization of Southern agriculture after World War II decreased the demand for low-wage labor and gave further cause to leave agricultural areas. The continued exodus of rural blacks decreased the supply of farm labor, thereby motivating Southern farmers to mechanize further and adopt labor-saving methods.

The exodus of blacks from the South during the 30 years between 1940 and 1970 is one of the major migrations in American history. In volume, it equals the total Italian immigration to the United States during its peak a half century earlier. For most blacks, this journey out of the South meant exchanging a rural, agricultural existence for an urban life based on factory jobs.

Migration since 1970

By the 1970s the black migration to the North from the South had ended. Although blacks continued to leave the South, many returned. A few Northern-born blacks, the children of earlier migrants, moved to the South in response to the availability of jobs and a change in the political and social climate. In the early 1970s just as many blacks were moving to the region as were leaving it.

By the mid-1980s, due to reduced economic growth in some areas of the South, black migration to the South had leveled off. The percentage of African Americans living in the western United States has increased from 0.5 percent in 1910 to 9.4 percent in 1990. In the year 2000, about 37 percent of blacks are likely to live in the North, 53 percent in the South, and 10 percent in the West.

Population Growth since 1980

The growth of the black population since the 1980 census is largely due to natural increase and net immigration. Natural increase has been the major source of growth. This increase in the number of births over deaths was due mainly to two factors: 1) a young age structure for blacks, meaning large numbers were in the childbearing years and smaller numbers were approaching the final, high-risk years and 2) a high **fertility** rate for black women under 25 years of age.

The African American population has also grown through both legal and illegal immigration. Along with the stream of Asian and Hispanic migrants to the United States, black immigration has also increased. The Caribbean basin is one source of black immigration. Jamaican and Haitian immigrants, in particular, have been entering the United States to look for work.

The *Mariel* boatlift in 1980 also brought some blacks from Cuba. Political and economic conditions in Africa itself, in addition, have provided many with push and pull incentives. African students who have overstayed their student visas and found work in the United States are associated with this trend.

The Present and Future

The African American population is likely to continue to grow faster than the national average. The black population as a percentage of the total U.S. population is also likely to continue to increase, though probably at a lesser rate than other minorities, including the Asian and Hispanic populations.

One reason for this growth has been the higher than average fertility rates of African Americans. Blacks have—and for at least the next decade or two are likely to continue to have—higher fertility rates than whites, even when differences in median age are taken into account. The median age of the black population, at 28 years, is decidedly younger than the white population, at nearly 34 years.

Reports from 1991 show that the black population is approaching 31,164,000, or approximately 12.4 percent of the nation's total population. This figure is higher than the total populations for many nations. The black population in the United States, for example, is slightly larger than the entire population of Canada. The only nations with black populations that clearly exceed the U.S. total are Nigeria (with an estimated 1993 population of 130 million), Ethiopia (56 million), and Zaire (40 million). South Africa, a country with an overall estimated population of 43 million, has a black population roughly equivalent to the U.S. figure.

Current Demographics

The Black Population by State

Blacks are most prevalent in the South. This region contains 53 percent of the nation's total black population. In 1990, of the ten states with the largest black populations (New York, California, Texas, Florida, Georgia, Illinois, North Carolina, Louisiana, Michigan, and Maryland), six were in the South. Fifty-eight percent of the black population resided in these states. Six other states had black populations of one million or more in 1990: Virginia, Ohio, Pennsylvania, South Carolina, New Jersey, and Alabama.

The Black Urban Population

In 1960 two-thirds of the black popula-

STATES WITH THE LARGEST BLACK POPULATIONS, BY NUMBERS

Rank	State	In Millions
1	New York	2.86
2	California	2.21
3	Texas	2.02
4	Florida	1.76
5	Georgia	1.75
6	Illinois	1.69
7	North Carolina	1.46
8	Louisiana	1.30
9	Michigan	1.29
10	Maryland	1.19

STATES WITH THE LARGEST BLACK POPULATIONS, BY PERCENTAGES

Rank	By Numbers	In Millions
1	District of Columbia	65.8
2	Mississippi	35.6
3	Louisiana	30.8
4	South Carolina	29.8
5	Georgia	27.0
6	Alabama	25.3
7	Maryland	24.9
8	North Carolina	22.0
9	Virginia	18.8
10	Delaware	16.9

POPULATION

BLACK POPULATION CHANGE IN TEN CENTRAL CITIES, 1970 TO 1990

Central Cities	Black Population			Percent Black		
	1990	1980	1970	1990	1980	1970
New York	2,102,512	1,784,337	1,668,115	28.7	25.2	21.2
Chicago	1,087,711	1,197,000	1,102,620	39.1	39.8	32.7
Detroit	777,916	758,939	660,428	75.7	63.1	43.7
Philadelphia	631,936	638,878	653,791	39.9	37.8	33.6
Los Angeles	487,674	505,210	503,606	14.0	17.0	17.9
Houston	457,990	440,346	316,551	28.1	27.6	25.7
Baltimore	435,768	431,151	420,210	59.2	54.8	46.4
Washington, DC	399,604	448,906	537,712	65.8	70.3	71.1
Memphis	334,737	307,702	242,513	54.8	47.6	38.9
New Orleans	307,728	308,149	267,308	61.9	55.3	45.0

tion lived in metropolitan areas. Most of these urban dwellers resided in central cities, as opposed to suburban and close-in rural areas. In 1970 three-fourths of the black population resided in metro areas, and the proportion of blacks living in central cities remained high. By 1990 more than eight of ten blacks resided in metro areas, but the proportion residing in central cities was beginning to decline.

In 1960 blacks comprised 16.7 percent of all central city residents. By 1970 blacks comprised 20.6 percent. One reason for this increase was the continued growth of the black population. Another reason for this change was the migration of whites out of the central cities to suburban and rural areas.

In 1980 African Americans made up 22.5 percent of the total central city population. However, by 1990 this number fell to 22.1 percent. Like the white population, though in smaller numbers, the black population was migrating out of central cities to suburban and rural areas.

The city of New York, the most populous city in the United States, also has the largest black population in the nation. In 1990 more than 2.1 million African Americans resided in Greater New York City. Chicago, Detroit, Philadelphia, and Los Angeles follow, in that order, are cities with the largest black populations.

Among the fifteen cities with the largest black concentrations, Washington, D.C., and Atlanta had black majorities by 1970. By 1990 four additional cities (Detroit, Baltimore, Memphis, and New Orleans) had black majorities, and five of the eleven largest cities in the nation were more than 50 percent black.

Harlem in the early 1930s

The Black Suburban and Rural Populations

The 1970s marked a turning point in the percentage of African Americans living outside of central cities. Between 1980 and 1990, the black population living in suburbs grew faster than did the white suburban population. The white suburban population grew by 9.1 percent, whereas the black suburban population increased by 9.9 percent. In 1980 African Americans comprised 6.1 percent of the suburban population, and by 1990 they comprised 6.9 percent.

In 1960 only 13.3 percent of African Americans residing in metro areas lived in suburban areas. By 1980 this number had increased to 23.3 percent. In 1990, 26.6 percent of the black metro population resided in suburban areas.

Access to suburban residences is important to African Americans for many reasons. One reason is that black suburbanization may permit an open housing market, freedom of movement, and the ability to choose a neighborhood that balances a family's income and its preferences and needs, such as the availability of quality public schools for children.

Black suburbanization may be beneficial in other ways as well. Since so many jobs have been moving from cities to suburbs, the greater share of blacks living in suburbs might eventually garner improved employment opportunities. Finally, for many Americans, moving to the suburbs has meant purchasing a home, which represents a major form of wealth accumulation for middle-class families.

African American households have been less likely than white households to own their own home, even when income and other social and economic characteristics are taken into account. A trend toward suburbanization might offer more blacks the opportunity to build **equity** in a home and thus help to secure middle-class status for current and later generations.

The movement itself has been made possible by open housing legislation and changing attitudes that have helped break down racial barriers. In addition, there has been an increase in the number of middle-income black families who can afford the safety, good schools, acreage, and other conveniences often sought by those who have chosen to move from cities to suburbs.

The Future of the Black Population

The African American population is projected to be one of the fastest growing population groups in the nation during the next 60 years. In fact, the black population is expected to increase by over 4 million by 2000, almost 9 million by 2010, and over 19 million by 2030. By around 2050, the black population will likely reach 62 million, a nearly 100 percent increase in the course of a generation. African Americans will then represent approximately 16 percent of the overall U.S. population.

Although Reverdy Ransom (quoted at the head of this chapter) was a black church leader rather than a population expert, his prediction for the black race was accurate and continues to come true. African Americans, both in numbers and accomplishments, "stand forth among the first Americans."

13

Jobs and Money

The African American Labor Force and Economic Outlook

"Development for any people begins with the belief that development is possible."—Robert L. Woodson, in On the Road to Economic Freedom: An Agenda for Black Progress *(1987)*

*"At the bottom of education, at the bottom of politics, even at the bottom of religion itself, there must be for our race ... economic foundation, economic **prosperity,** economic independence."*—Booker T. Washington, in an address to the National Negro Business League *(1915)*

Never before in American history have so many blacks held so many top positions in so many high-income fields, from film, television, and music to sports, literature, and politics. Their names are known and respected everywhere: Oprah Winfrey, Shaquille O'Neal, Bill Cosby, Jackie Joyner-Kersee, Michael Jordan, Toni Morrison, Quincy Jones, Queen Latifah, Chuck D., Carol Moseley Braun, Prince, Whoopi Goldberg, Spike Lee. All have achieved the American Dream through talent, hard work, and determination, and all have served as role models for younger African Americans.

But what about the average black American, whose name may never be in the national spotlight? Can he or she still attain the American Dream as well? The answer depends on a variety of factors, but perhaps most importantly the individual's background and outlook.

Middle Class and Underclass

There are two very different chapters to the African American story of jobs and money in the 1990s. The first is one of a growing black middle class that is enjoying greater occupational and economic opportunities than ever before, an indication that the American Dream is still alive for educated, motivated African Americans.

The second chapter is more somber. It tells of an increasing number of blacks who are disadvantaged and disconnected from the mainstream of American life. The "complicated truth," according to scholar Henry Louis Gates, Jr., is that "these are the worst of times ... and the best of times" for black America.

Despite the increase in opportunities for

JOBS AND MONEY

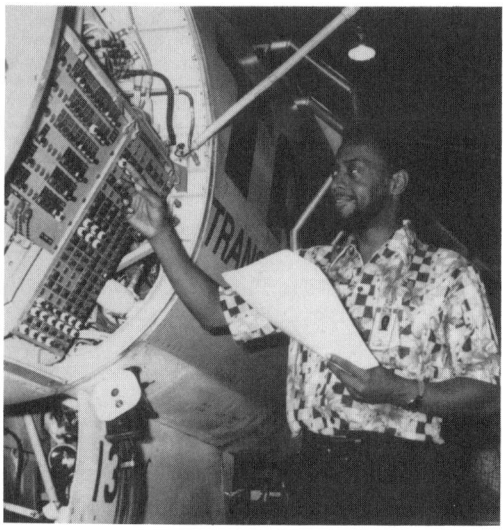

Blacks are holding more higher-status jobs and earning higher incomes than ever before

the black upper and middle classes, blacks as a whole trail whites in wealth, income, and all other measures of social and financial status. Blacks continue to be overwhelmingly employed in lower-paying, blue-collar jobs and are often subject to the unwritten rule of "last hired, first fired" in times of corporate **downsizing.** It comes as little surprise, then, that the **poverty** rate for African Americans has been three times that of whites for over 30 years.

Unemployment

Unemployment is a major problem in the African American community. Despite affirmative action and other favorable government policies and programs, high levels of unemployment among blacks have continued for several decades. In 1980 the unemployment rate for blacks was 14.3 percent. The rate among whites for that year was just 6.3 percent. Through the early 1990s the black rate never dropped below 11 percent, always remaining roughly two and one-half times higher than the rate for whites.

> **WORDS TO KNOW**
>
> **American Dream:** the concept that all Americans, given equal opportunities, may strive for personal and financial success
>
> **derive:** come from
>
> **downsizing:** trimming, through plant closings, layoffs, etc., to make a business healthier and more profitable
>
> **median:** the middle number in a series (half of the numbers being above and half below); not to be confused with average
>
> **poverty:** the condition of being poor; the government determines poverty according to a poverty index based on monetary income alone; in 1990 a family of four was considered to be in poverty if the household income was less than $13,359
>
> **prosperity:** wealth
>
> **ratio:** the relationship of one quantity to another, expressed in a fraction or percentage
>
> **recession:** a general decline in business activity that translates into more layoffs, fewer new jobs, and decreases in household spending power
>
> **stigmatizes:** marks or brands unfavorably

Yet many blacks continue to hold lower-paying, blue-collar jobs

Inequality in Income

African American households have yet to gain equality in income with whites. Recent studies have found that blacks with similar levels of education, occupation, and experience tend to earn less than their white counterparts.

Data on household income from the U.S. Department of Commerce confirm those findings. In 1988 the **median** income for black families was $19,823, compared to $34,222 for whites. In other words, black families had a median income that was around 58 percent of that for whites. By 1990, median family income for blacks was still only 59 percent of that for whites, despite an increase in income for black families over the three years. The corresponding increase for white families countered any gains made by blacks during the period.

Family Structure and Family Income

Family structure has a bearing on the income of African American families and how they compare to white families. For instance, black married-couple families had a median income in 1988 of $30,424. This represents 82 percent of the $36,883 median income reported for white married-couple families that year. This figure declined to 78 percent in 1989, but rose again to 84 percent in 1990.

JOBS AND MONEY

It is important to note that the **ratio** of black/white income in this category is the highest among the various family types. Single black men made only 64 percent as much as single white males in 1988, compared to 62 percent in 1989, and 73 percent in 1990.

Single black women fared the worst. In 1988 this group made only 59 percent as much as single white women, and only 60 percent as much in 1990.

Regional Differences

Income for African American families is likely to vary among different regions of the country. Data from 1990 show that the median family income for blacks was highest in the West, at $27,947, and lowest in the Midwest, at $20,512. These two regions also reported the highest and lowest percentages of black-to-white median family income, respectively. These differences re-

MONEY EARNED

Trends in distribution of family income ranges and receiving income, in percent, 1970-1990.

	1970		1990	
	Black	White	Black	White
Under $5,000	6.8	2.3	11.5	2.5
$5,000-9,999	14.1	5.1	14.1	4.7
Less than $10,000	20.9	7.4	25.6	7.2
$10,000-14,999	13.6	6.9	11.3	7.0
$10,000-34,999	55.1	44.4	44.8	39.5
$35,000-100,000 and over	23.8	48.2	29.5	53.3
$50,000-100,000 and over	9.9	24.1	14.5	32.5
$100,000 and over	.3	2.7	1.3	5.9

Source: "Percentage of Families Receiving Income Selected Ranges and Years by Race: 1990, 1989, 1988, 1970," *The State of Black America 1992,* 1992, p. 80. Primary source: U.S. Department of Commerce, Bureau of the Census, *Money Income and Poverty Status in 1990,* September 1991, Table B-3. Note: Total will not equal 100.0 due to overlap of categories. Data is 1990 CPI-U adjusted dollars.

The highest category of employment for both black and white females was the technical/sales and administrative area

flect the variations in regional economies and job opportunities for blacks and whites.

Age

Age is one of the most important factors to consider when studying income within the African American community, since it tends to be a fairly good measure of work experience.

Generally speaking, income increases as the age of the wage-earner increases. Black householders in the 15- to 24-year-old category had a median family income of $7,218. For those in the 25- to 34-year-old category, the median family income was $17,130. Family income gradually rises for blacks until it peaks in the 45- to 54-year-old category at $30,847. However, in no age category do blacks equal whites in median family income.

Poverty

Government statistics on poverty show that, in total numbers, there were nearly as many blacks in poverty in 1990 as there were 30 years ago. In 1959 there were 9.9 million blacks living below the poverty line; in 1990 that figure was 9.8 million.

Poverty rates represent the major difference between the two periods. In 1959 the poverty rate was 55.2 percent compared to the 1990 rate of 31.9 percent. However, there were important differences in rates of

Family structure has a bearing on the incomes of black families and how they compare to white families

poverty across family types. For instance, black married-couple families had the lowest level of poverty. Black married-couple families without children had a poverty rate of 12.6 percent; those with children had a poverty rate of 14.3 percent. The highest rates were those for female-headed households. Female-headed households without children had a poverty rate of 48.1 percent. For those with children, the poverty rate was 56.1 percent.

Teenage Pregnancy

Whatever the causes of black teenage pregnancy, the results are dramatic for the African American community. Generally speaking, teenage mothers are more likely to be poor and are less likely to finish high school. In more cases than not, the fathers are either nonsupportive or absent. Thus, it is not unusual for teenage mothers to be dependent on welfare as a means of support.

Youth Unemployment

In recent decades, the employment situation for young blacks between the ages of 16 and 24 hit its lowest point in the 1981-82 **recession.** Yet in poverty areas throughout the United States, heavy black teen unemployment continued to loom throughout the decade, approaching a figure of 40 percent.

JOBS AND MONEY

Poverty is not confined to inner cities, but is found in many rural areas as well

Several reasons have been offered for the persistent problem of black teen unemployment. These include economic changes (which have reduced the need for unskilled and semiskilled workers) and rising minimum wages (which discourage certain employers from hiring new workers).

In 1986 a study titled "The Black Youth Employment Crisis" was released. It was based on a survey of young black men living in poverty areas of major American cities and edited by professors Richard Freeman and Henry Holzer. The study showed that there was no single cause for joblessness in young black men. Instead, factors such as crime, drug and alcohol abuse, and performance on the job played major roles.

Crime was singled out as perhaps the most important negative factor. Some 32 percent of the youths interviewed in the survey believed they could earn more from criminal "street" activity than from lawful work.

Growing up in a welfare family was also a significant factor. The study found that

JOBS AND MONEY

> ## THOMAS SOWELL ON BLACK VERSUS WHITE INCOME
>
> For more than a decade, young black husband-wife families outside the South have had incomes virtually identical to those of young white husband-wife families outside the South. In some years black families of this description have had incomes a few percentage points higher than their white counterparts. Today, where husbands and wives are both college-educated, and both working, black families of this description earn slightly *more* than white families of this description—nationwide and without regard to age.
>
> The implication of all this is not, of course, that blacks as a group are doing as well as whites as a group—or are even close to doing as well. On the contrary. The average income of blacks as a group remains far behind the average income of whites as a group. What we are trying to find out is the extent to which this is due to cultural differences rather than color differences that call forth racism and discrimination.
>
> *Source:* Thomas Sowell, *Civil Rights, Rhetoric or Reality?* (1984).

Thomas Sowell

unemployment among 19- to 24-year-olds whose families did not receive public assistance or live in public housing was 28 percent in 1979. Unemployment among those from the same age group who came from families on welfare rose to 43.8 percent. Youths from families who lived both on welfare and in public housing experienced a jobless rate of 52 percent. The problem, Freeman and Holzer wrote, was that "the current welfare system, lacking programs or incentives to promote employment, is doing nothing to correct joblessness."

The Role of the Government

Many of the government programs that address the needs of the poor were developed during the Great Society era of the 1960s. Headstart, Medicaid and Medicare, the Food Stamp Program, and several other forms of assistance were part of a massive effort referred to as the "War on Poverty." Critics of the Great Society programs argue that these programs were expensive, wasteful, and ineffective. Supporters claim that the programs have not failed; instead, America's determination to build a Great Society has.

The most controversial program to date is affirmative action. Launched during the late 1960s by the Nixon administration, affirmative action programs call for guidelines and goals in the hiring of racial and ethnic minorities, the handicapped, and women. They have been effective in promoting change in hiring practices because they have the weight of the federal government behind them. As a direct result, a broader range of opportunities have become available for blacks in government, the corporate world, and colleges and universities.

Critics argue that affirmative action programs do not promote job opportunities in general. Recent studies have shown that while whites support the principle of equality for all, most do not support the idea of

HENRY LOUIS GATES, JR., ON SUCCESS, FAILURE, AND THE BLACK MIDDLE CLASS

First of all, it's time for the black middle class to stop feeling guilty about its own success while fellow blacks languish in the inner city of despair. Black prosperity does not **derive** from black poverty. Those who succeed are those whose community, whose families, *prepared* them to be successful....

Second, we don't have to fail in order to be black. As crazy as this sounds, recent surveys of young black kids reveal a distressing pattern. Far too many say that succeeding is "white," education is "white," aspiring and dreaming are "white," believing that you can make it is "white." Had any of us said this sort of thing when we were growing up, our families and friends would have checked us into a mental institution. We need *more success* individually and collectively, not less.

Third, we don't have to pretend any longer that 30 million people can ever possibly be members of the same social class. After all, the entire population of Canada is 26 million. Canadians are not all members of one economic class. Nor do they speak with one single voice of one single leader. We have *never* been members of a single social or economic class, and never will be.

Source: Henry Louis Gates, Jr., "Two Nations ... Both Black," *Forbes,* September 14, 1992, p. 138.

preferential treatment on the basis of color or other factors unrelated to job experience and performance.

Affirmative action programs have their share of black critics as well. Many black conservatives, including Thomas Sowell and Walter Williams, argue that affirmative action programs do not help the black disadvantaged. They claim that these programs primarily help the black middle class, a group that is already advantaged, if not prospering. In addition, critics of affirmative action argue that it unfairly **stigmatizes** all blacks. Therefore, the success of African Americans in any field is often explained as being due to affirmative action rather than ability and ambition.

The future of affirmative action and other public policies to promote equality is uncertain. At this writing, there are no clear signs from the Clinton administration other than President Bill Clinton's pledge to reform welfare, make government more efficient, and put people back to work.

Current Trends

Major changes have occurred within the black community as a result of the civil rights movement and civil rights laws. Blacks are now holding more higher-status jobs and earning higher incomes than ever before. Yet, the number of African Americans who are poor is nearly as high as it was 30 years ago. The lifestyles and life chances of these two groups, needless to say, are vastly different.

Faced with government ineffectiveness, many African Americans are championing

High unemployment among black youth continues to be a problem. Available jobs are usually at minimum wage in such places as fast food restaurants

self-help programs, individual responsibility, and internal community development. In particular, leaders of the National Association for the Advancement of Colored People (NAACP), the National Urban League, and other major black organizations have called for more black-owned businesses in order to help sustain the black community at large.

Finally, we should remember that strong traditions of hard work, saving, and betterment are widespread in the black community. In his *Climbing Jacob's Ladder,* Andrew Billingsley reports that "There are more than three times as many nonpoor blacks as there are poor blacks. Every black community is peopled with them. The underclass is only half of that poor third."

There is no doubt that the future will continue to be filled with obstacles for African Americans. And no doubt, as in the past, African Americans will not only survive but triumph.

14

Entrepreneurship

Risk-taking and the Creation of Wealth

> **FACT FOCUS**
>
> - In 1848 William Alexander Leidesdorff, a California merchant, became the first African American millionaire.
> - In 1971 Johnson Products became the first African American company to trade its shares on a major stock exchange.
> - Between 1982 and 1987 the number of black-owned businesses grew 38 percent, nearly three times the growth rate for all U.S. firms.
> - In 1987 the single largest African American industry was automobile dealerships and service stations, with nearly $2.2 billion in combined revenues.
> - In 1991 sales for the 100 largest African American industrial and service businesses rose by more than three times the rate of sales for *Fortune 500* companies.
> - In 1992 black-owned TLC Beatrice International Holdings Inc. posted sales of nearly $1.6 billion.
> - Some experts estimate that by the year 2000 blacks and Hispanics will together represent 3 percent of the American population and 50 percent of the buying public for certain products.

"I had to make my own opportunity.... Don't sit down and wait for the opportunities to come; you have to get up and make them."—Madame C. J. Walker

"If you can somehow think and dream of success in small steps, every time you make a step, every time you accomplish a small goal, it gives you confidence to go on from there."—John H. Johnson

Most students have a fairly good idea of who the wealthiest African American entertainer is. But probably very few know who the richest black businessperson is, let alone the history behind the term "the real McCoy." [See the box on page 327 for the answers to these questions.] The millions earned by black singers, athletes, and television and film stars generally grab the headlines in the popular media. Yet year after year millions more are earned by less-recognized but equally successful African Americans in industries from food processing and hair care to communications and automobile sales.

Blacks were in business long before the Civil War and continue their entrepreneurial tradition today. Very often, however, the rich history of black **entrepreneurship** has been either overlooked or underestimated.

Entrepreneurship before the Civil War

During the early years of American history, a number of blacks managed to acquire wealth. Anthony Johnson, who amassed substantial property in Jamestown, Virginia, is believed to be the first African American entrepreneur. Jean Baptiste Pointe Du Sable, a wholesaler and merchant who established the first settlement in Chicago in the early 1770s, was another pre-Civil War entrepreneur.

Yet, until well into the nineteenth century, slavery defined the existence of most African Americans. Usually only free blacks, a distinct minority, were able to accumulate and invest sizable sums of money and then devote themselves entirely to their chosen business activity. They developed enterprises in almost every field of opportunity, including merchandising, real estate, manufacturing, construction, transportation, and mining.

However, there were numbers of slaves who—as a result of thrift, ingenuity, industry, and sometimes the aid of their masters—were able to engage in business activity. Although the nature of slavery prevented full-scale entrepreneurship, slaves did, during their limited free time, sell their labor and products.

The fact that a black business culture existed at all during the era of slavery is testimony to the strong entrepreneurial spirit of a people determined to gain economic freedom even under the harshest conditions.

If it was all but impossible for slaves to engage in private enterprise, it was also hazardous for "free" blacks to do so, since they were really only half free. Free blacks lived under a constant fear of being labeled "run-

> **WORDS TO KNOW**
>
> **capital:** money, property, and other valuable assets that are used to start and sustain a business
>
> **CEO: c**hief **e**xecutive **o**fficer; the highest executive of a company or organization
>
> **corporations:** businesses, formed with permission of the state or federal government, that have the power to own property and make contracts
>
> **entrepreneurship:** the business quality of undertaking risk for the sake of earning a profit
>
> **leveraged buyout:** the purchase of a company in which most of the sale price is financed using borrowed money
>
> **niche:** a desirable place; in business terms, typically a safe market not threatened by competitors
>
> **sole proprietorships:** businesses in which the owner is also the chief operator
>
> **viability:** ability to grow and prosper

ENTREPRENEURSHIP

During their limited free time, some slaves were able to profit by the sale of their labor and products

away" slaves and sold into slavery. In addition, laws were often passed to restrict the movement of free blacks and thus their economic freedom as well.

By 1835 Virginia, Maryland, and North Carolina had passed laws forbidding free blacks to carry arms without a license. The right of assembly was also denied blacks throughout the South. In addition to reflecting slaveowners' fears of an African American uprising, such laws made it extremely difficult for free blacks to earn a living.

Predictably, African American business development was strongest in the North. In 1838, for example, the *Register of Trades of Colored People* in the city of Philadelphia listed 8 bakers, 25 blacksmiths, 3 brass founders, 15 cabinetmakers and carpenters, 5 confectioners, 2 caulkers, 2 chair bottomers, 15 tailoring enterprises, 31 tanners, 5 weavers, and 6 wheelwrights.

The Philadelphia business register also listed businesses run by African American women. Among these were 98 hairdressers,

ENTREPRENEURSHIP

Historically, black-owned firms have been concentrated in a narrow range of service businesses, including small restaurants

81 dressmakers and tailors, 6 cloth processors, and 2 glass and paper makers.

Another business controlled by African Americans in Philadelphia during the 1820s and 1830s was sail-making. Nineteen sailmakers were recorded in the business register of 1838. James Forster, who lived between 1766 and 1841, ran a major manufacturing firm that made sails; in 1829, Forster employed 40 workers, both black and white.

The business enterprise that brought prosperity to the largest number of African Americans in Philadelphia was catering. Robert Boyle, a black waiter, is believed to have developed the concept of catering, or providing food and other related services for private gatherings. Catering quickly spread across the developing country, but it was in Philadelphia that it flourished most.

Significantly, most black businesses of this period involved the craft or service trades. They were small enterprises that required only a modest **capital** investment and allowed African Americans to develop a **niche** without threatening larger, white-owned businesses.

Entrepreneurship after the Civil War

Following the Civil War, the promises contained in the Fourteenth and Fifteenth Amendments and other laws designed to protect the rights of blacks were soon broken by racist judicial rulings. In 1878, in *Hall* v. *DeCuir,* the United States Supreme Court ruled that a state could not ban segregation on a common carrier (a train, for example). In 1896, with the *Plessy* v. *Ferguson* ruling, "separate but equal" became the law of the land. Following these decisions, a pattern of rigid separation of the races was established that remained the norm until the middle of the twentieth century.

Nevertheless, African American educator and spokesperson Booker T. Washington saw bright economic possibilities for his race through business development. In 1900 Washington spearheaded the development of the National Negro Business League to encourage black enterprise. During the organization's first meeting, the delegates concluded that:

> A useless class is a menace and a danger to any community, and ... when an individual produces what the world

ENTREPRENEURSHIP

Booker T. Washington

wants, whether it is a product of the hand, heart, or head, the world does not long stop to inquire what is the color of the skin of the producer.

During the early 1900s, although services continued to be the cornerstone of the black business community, blacks found it easier to raise capital and ventured into more entrepreneurial endeavors. In 1905, for example, Madame C. J. Walker developed a hair care system that gave dry hair a soft texture. Millions of women, both black and white, purchased Walker's products. Before her death in 1919, Walker had more than 2,000 salespeople marketing her ever-expanding line of products, which made her America's first black female millionaire.

Black Agriculture: A Story of Decline

By 1910, 240,000 blacks owned their

ENTREPRENEURSHIP

Madame C. J. Walker made a fortune in hair care products at the turn of the century

The Great Depression of the 1930s again brought extreme hardship to black as well as white farmers. In 1934 the federal government began to reorganize the nation's agricultural system by providing cheap credit for farmers. In addition, the government established acreage controls and price supports to help ensure stable incomes for farmers. However, abuse of the system by dishonest white farmers and local politicians prevented many black farmers from receiving such government benefits.

Dramatic shifts in black agriculture occurred after World War II when tobacco became a more important cash crop. By

The numbers of black farmers have been steadily declining. By 1980 blacks who remained as farm residents tended to be wage and salary workers rather than self-employed

farms and comprised one-sixth of all Southern landowners. Another 670,000 blacks were tenant farmers, or 40 percent of the entire tenant farmer population. This was during the boom era of strong cotton prices, when the start of many small black-owned banks went hand in hand with the growth of the black farming industry.

In the early days of World War I, cotton prices plummeted and help for farmers from private and government sources was largely confined to white farmers. Most black banks collapsed as a result of the depression in cotton. A few years later the boll weevil, a small, grayish beetle, took a heavy toll on cotton fields, especially those of blacks, few of whom could afford to purchase insecticides.

1959 one-sixth of all cigarette tobacco in the South came from black-operated farms. However, the decline of black agriculture after 1959 swept away both tobacco and cotton farmers. Between 1969 and 1979 the number of black cotton farms in the South dropped by a stunning 96 percent and black tobacco farms by 77 percent. By 1980, blacks who remained as farm residents tended to be wage and salary workers rather than self-employed.

Durham: A Story of Triumph

Turn-of-the-century Durham, North Carolina, represented a special case of black enterprise. In publications of the time,

TEN LARGEST BLACK-OWNED INDUSTRIAL/SERVICE COMPANIES

	Company/Location CEO	Year Started	Staff	Type of Business	Sales (in millions of dollars)
1	TLC Beatrice International Holdings Inc., New York, NY Loida Lewis[1]	1987	5,000	Food processor/distributor	1,665.000
2	Johnson Publishing Co. Inc., Chicago, IL John H. Johnson	1942	2,785	Media; cosmetics/hair care	274.197
3	Philadelphia Coca-Cola Bottling Co. Inc., Philadelphia, PA J. Bruce Llewellyn	1985	1,000	Soft-drink bottler	266.000
4	H. J. Russell & Co., Atlanta, GA Herman J. Russell	1952	825	Construction; food services	145.610
5	The Anderson-Dubose Co., Solon, OH Warren Anderson	1991	80	Food distributor	110.000
6	RMS Technologies Inc., Marlton, NJ David W. Huggins	1977	1,176	Computer & technical services	103.300
7	Gold Line Refining Ltd., Houston, TX Earl Thomas	1990	51	Oil refining	91.880
8	Soft Sheen Products Inc., Chicago, IL Edward G. Gardner	1964	547	Hair care products	91.700
9	Garden State Cable TV, Cherry Hill, NJ J. Bruce Llewellyn	1989	300	Cable TV operator	91.000
10	Threads 4 Life Corp., Los Angeles, CA Carl Jones	1990	250	Apparel manufacturer	89.000

Note: [1]Chairwoman (new CEO to be hired)

ENTREPRENEURSHIP

Durham was referred to as "The Wall Street of Negro America." By the late 1940s more than 150 businesses owned by African Americans flourished in Durham. Among these businesses were traditional service providers, such as cafes, movie-houses, barbershops, boardinghouses, pressing shops, grocery stores, and funeral parlors. What distinguished Durham, however, was the presence of large black businesses.

One of the largest and most successful black businesses in the nation was the North Carolina Mutual Life Insurance Company. Other African American Durham businesses included the Banker's Fire Insurance Company, the Mutual Building and Loan Association, the Union Insurance and Realty Company, the Durham Realty and Insurance Company, the People's Building and Loan Association, the Royal Knights Savings and Loan Association, T. P. Parham and Associates, and the Mortgage Company of Durham. Such businesses established a "city of enterprise" for African Americans.

Although Durham was a success, outside economic pressure and racial hatred made it impossible for many blacks to develop stores that could compete in the larger economy. As a result of Jim Crow laws and segregation, most black-owned businesses were forced to limit their market to their own community. A partial exception was the Durham textile mill, which, at the time, was the only hosiery mill in the world owned and operated by African Americans. It operated 18 knitting machines and did business in the open market. The salespeople, who traveled mostly in North Carolina, Indiana, Georgia, South Carolina, and Alabama, were white. This manufacturing firm was perhaps the first large-scale, black-owned enterprise to hire whites.

Other black Durham businesses benefitted from serving mainly white customers. For example, in 1940 Smith's Fish Market supplied Durham's largest white-operated hotel, the Washington Duke. Businessman Freeman M. Smith was also the major supplier for smaller white and black-owned businesses. In 1940 Smith grossed more than $90,000 and opened four other outlets throughout the city. Similarly, Rowland and Mitchell established a tailor shop in 1930 where they did work for "exclusive whites and department stores." It was estimated that 80 percent of their customers were white. Among other successful businesses was Thomas Baily & Sons, a meat and grocery store that opened in 1919 and grossed $80,000 a year by 1940. The Home Modernization and Supply Company, founded in 1938 by the brothers U. M. and R. S. George, grossed more than $100,000 in constructing 500 homes in the Durham area and employed 35 people by 1948.

Many people came to Durham to learn the beautician trade by attending the commercial hair care school established by Jacqueline DeShazor. Beginning with three rooms, she expanded in 1945 to 36 rooms.

African American businesses were so stable and looked so promising for the future that, in 1924, Durham was chosen as the location for the headquarters of the National Negro Finance Corporation, which was capitalized at $1 million. The organization was started to provide working capital to individuals, firms, and **corporations** in all parts of the country. Durham, from the turn of the century until the 1950s, remained unrivaled as the black business capital of America.

ENTREPRENEURSHIP

KIDPRENEUR PROGRAMS: CREATING THE NEXT GENERATION OF BLACK ENTREPRENEURS

It takes a special sort of person to become a highly successful entrepreneur, just as it takes a special sort of person to become a highly successful entertainer, athlete, scientist, or writer. However, many believe that good business practices can be taught to virtually anyone. Such an education can have a lasting influence on one's overall success in life.

In 1974 the Southwest Atlanta Youth Business Organization (SWAYBO), a nonprofit concern devoted to providing black teens and pre-teens with hands-on business experience, was established. The original group consisted of eight young members, who used a $25 loan to invest in potato chips and candy, which they quickly sold for a $40 profit. Over the next two decades, SWAYBO members have sold everything from T-shirts to baby-sitting services and have taken in a total $2 million in revenue, not to mention a priceless amount of practical learning.

SWAYBO is just one of several organizations across the country that sponsor young black entrepreneurship. Others include the New Jersey-based Education, Training and Enterprise Center (EDTEC), the Chicago-based Center for Training Entrepreneurship (CTE), and the New York City-based National Foundation for Teaching Entrepreneurship (NFTE).

"No one knows exactly how many programs exist," Adrienne S. Harris writes, "but experts agree that entrepreneurship education for children has blossomed since the mid-1980s." For help in locating a program, she recommends contacting local National Association for the Advancement of Colored People (NAACP), National Urban League, and National Business League chapters, as well as YMCAs, YWCAs, churches, colleges, universities, and various other black professional groups.

Source: Adrienne S. Harris, "Hot Kidpreneur Programs That Are Making a Difference," *Black Enterprise,* February 1994, pp. 177-82.

Present-day Durham

Today, 150 or so black entrepreneurs and professionals are still held together by the Durham Business and Professional Chain. It would be difficult, however, to recreate the entrepreneurial excitement that existed in Durham between 1900 and 1950. Indeed, scholars have noted that grassroots entrepreneurship tends to develop quickly by groups who newly enter the economy; this was true of African Americans after the end of slavery. However, from generation to generation, there is typically a decrease in the number or rate of entrepreneurs. In the case of African Americans, it took a full-blown civil rights movement to create another surge in the entrepreneurial spirit through increased opportunities.

Black Entrepreneurs in the Post-Civil Rights Era

The civil rights movement led to the creation of laws and agencies that ensured the social, political, and economic rights of African Americans. Perhaps the greatest boost to black entrepreneurship came in 1967 with the establishment of the Small Business Administration (SBA) Section 8 (a) program.

The SBA is authorized to enter into contract with federal agencies on behalf of small and minority businesses. The total dollar value of contracts processed through Section 8 (a) has grown from $8.9 million in 1969 to $2.7 billion in 1985. Through the program, many small and black-owned businesses have been able to stabilize and grow.

The basic idea of set-aside minority assistance programs was called into question during the height of the Reagan-Bush era. In 1989 the U.S. Supreme Court decided the case of *City of Richmond* v. *Croson*. The outcome was unfavorable to minorities, for it struck down as unconstitutional a Richmond, Virginia, city ordinance requiring that 30 percent of public construction contracts be set aside for minority businesses. Although the decision did not apply to federally sponsored programs, it did severely decrease contracts awarded to minorities throughout the country.

Growth Industries

Historically, black-owned firms have

Reginald F. Lewis

Freedom National Bank, Harlem's first black commercial bank, was founded in 1965

ENTREPRENEURSHIP

REGINALD F. LEWIS

Reginald Lewis may have been the most important African American businessman of the twentieth century. His successes were unparalleled, and his food company, TLC Beatrice International Holdings Inc., was the largest corporation ever to be owned by a black American. (TLC stands for "The Lewis Company.")

After developing a successful law firm during the 1970s, Lewis entered the larger business world in 1984 when he purchased the down-and-out McCall's Pattern Company through a newly formed investment firm. The risky purchase ($1 million plus the assumption of $24 million in debt) paid off. By the time of his bid for TLC Beatrice in 1987, Lewis had sold McCall's at a $70 million profit. The Beatrice purchase price was a staggering $985 million, which Lewis financed through a **leveraged buyout**, the largest deal of its kind at the time.

When Lewis died unexpectedly in January 1993, he left his family with more than 50 percent ownership of the $1.6 billion corporation. Although the company now has an uncertain future, Lewis's legacy of superb entrepreneurship lives on. Despite his status as the country's leading black businessman, Lewis always downplayed the importance of race in his career. He preferred to be judged by his performance, and he refused to consider race as a crutch or an obstacle. "It's understandable that [my race] is something people focus on," he once remarked. "But what I focus on and what others focus on are two different things.... I focus on doing a first-rate job on a consistent basis."

---

been concentrated in a narrow range of service businesses including small restaurants, cleaning establishments, funeral parlors, shoe shops, hair salons, and gas stations. The trend, by and large, continued throughout the late 1980s.

However, there have been signs of increasing variety among new black businesses. The growth in corporate and government administration has created a corresponding growth in advertising, accounting, computer, legal, secretarial, and maintenance businesses. Employment in such firms owned by African Americans grew by 224 percent between 1972 and 1987. The number of firms increased nearly five times, and sales grew by 700 percent.

Gross Receipts and Legal Organization

According to the Bureau of the Census, nearly 95 percent of black-owned firms operated as **sole proprietorships** in 1987.

ENTREPRENEURSHIP

Most African American businesses are small enterprises that require hard work and long hours. These businesses are usually in black neighborhoods, such as the Reliable Shoe Repair Shop in Harlem

This high figure was roughly the same as that ten years earlier. Unfortunately, sole proprietorships are usually small businesses with few, if any, employees other than the owner. Still, they contributed a little over one-half of all black business revenue in 1987.

In contrast, Subchapter S corporations (corporations with fewer than 35 stockholders that are taxed differently from regular corporations) accounted for only 3 percent of the total number of firms but 39.2 percent of overall revenue. The remaining 10 percent of revenue was made up by partnerships.

From 1982 to 1987 the total revenue or gross receipts (the total amount of money received before deductions for expenses and taxes) for African American businesses increased 105 percent, from $9.6 billion to $19.8 billion. Only 0.5 percent of the total number of black-owned firms grossed $1 million or more. Slightly more than one-third (35 percent) of the firms had gross receipts of less than $5,000. The average annual gross receipt for a black-owned business was approximately $47,000.

Recent Trends

Since 1962 the Bureau of the Census has published a survey of minority-owned businesses every five years. The survey from 1987 shows that African Americans owned 427,165 businesses, a 37.6 percent increase from the 1982 total, and nearly an 85 percent increase from the 1977 total. The 37.6 percent increase between 1982 and 1987 is greater than the 26.2 percent increase for all United States firms for this time period. These numbers indicate that African Ameri-

Johnson Publishing Company Chairman John H. Johnson pictured with his daughter, Linda Johnson Rice (president and chief operating officer)

ENTREPRENEURSHIP

TRIVIA ANSWERS

If you guessed Bill Cosby is the wealthiest African American entertainer, you were right. In 1993 he had an estimated net worth, according to *Forbes,* of $315 million. It should be noted that Cosby is, of course, a brilliant black American businessmen as well. Syndicated reruns of *The Cosby Show,* in which he has a one-third interest, earn $1 billion annually.

Congratulations if you guessed that the richest African American businessperson is Reginald F. Lewis, the man behind the buyout of international food giant TLC Beatrice International Holdings. At the time of his death on January 19, 1993, Lewis was believed to have a net worth of $415 million. Congratulations, too, if you guessed John H. Johnson, publisher of *Ebony* and *Jet.* According to *Children of the Dream: The Psychology of Black Success* (1992), he "may or may not be the richest black in America."

"The real McCoy," according to Carole Marsh, author of *Black Trivia,* has to do with black businessman and inventor Elijah McCoy. During his 40-year career McCoy obtained some 57 patents related to automatic lubrication.

---

cans are starting business enterprises at a greater rate than Americans in general.

Modern-Day Milestones: A Look Back and a Look Forward

Since the mid-1980s several important milestones in the world of African American business have occurred. One involved the death, on October 26, 1988, of S. B. Fuller. The founder and president of Fuller Products Company, Fuller was long considered one of the deans of black entrepreneurs. He began a career in cosmetics sales when he was 17, eventually building his business into a national company employing more than 5,000 people.

During the 1960s Fuller expanded his company into newspapers, appliance and department stores as well as farming and beef cattle production. He is credited with teaching business skills to John H. Johnson and George Johnson, two of the most notable black entrepreneurs of the modern era.

John H. Johnson founded Johnson Publishing Company in 1942 with a $500 loan and an idea for a single monthly magazine, the *Negro Digest.* By its 50-year anniversary in 1992, Johnson Publishing had become the second largest black company in America, with annual sales of $275 million. Just as importantly, through *Ebony, Jet,* and its other enterprises, the company had created a legacy of helping to promote self-esteem among African Americans.

ENTREPRENEURSHIP

Berry Gordy, Jr., waves his trophy after being inducted into the Rock 'n' Roll Hall of Fame, 1988

George Johnson actually worked for Fuller Products from 1945 to 1948. While there he developed a hair straightener for men and began marketing it himself in 1954, eventually founding the Johnson Products Company and the Ultra-Sheen, Classy Curl, and Afro Sheen product lines. Like Johnson Publishing, Johnson Products became a symbol of pride among African Americans. One of the company's major contributions to African American culture and business was its pioneering sponsorship of the television dance show *Soul Train,* which in turn generated scores of advertising, modeling, and entertainment-related jobs for blacks.

Beginning in the 1980s, however, the company became plagued with problems of rising debt and falling sales and earnings. A 1989 divorce settlement left Johnson's ex-wife, Joan B. Johnson, in charge. In 1993 Joan Johnson decided to accept a purchase offer for the company from Ivax Corporation, a white-owned, Miami-based company. Her decision to sell caused great controversy in the black community, but before completing the deal she sought and won the support of Operation PUSH **CEO** Willie Barrow, who had threatened a boycott of the company's products.

The sale (for a premium price of $67 million) came five years after Berry Gordy, Jr., completed a similarly controversial sale of his Motown Records. Although there will always be those who will argue that historically black companies should remain in black hands, there are some black business leaders who view such deals—which promise to arise more often in the future—in a positive light. "It's a recognition of the black consumer market and its future **viability**," said Earl G. Graves, editor and publisher of *Black Enterprise* magazine. When a black company becomes a candidate for acquisition by mainstream industry, "it shows that the company has matured and proven itself" (Brett Pulley, "Profit over Pride," *Emerge,* December/January 1994, pp. 63-5).

15

The Family and Health

The Backbone of the Community

FACT FOCUS

The Family

- Although one-third of black families were prospering in 1993, another one-third were functioning below the poverty line.
- In 1991 only 36 percent of African American children lived with both parents.
- The increase in families headed by single mothers is more typical of the black population than of any other American racial or ethnic group today.
- African American families headed by single moms number 3 million, as opposed to 239,000 headed by single dads.
- In 1990, 12 percent of black children lived with their grandparents, 6.5 percent of black children lived with other relatives, and 1 percent lived with non-relatives.

Health

- The infant mortality rate in the United States is higher than rates in 21 other industrialized countries.
- Black women are more likely than white women to give birth to low-weight babies.
- Although African Americans represent only 12 percent of the U.S. population, 31 percent of all new AIDS cases in 1989 were black.

"The purity of the family is the purity of the race"—John Wesley Edward Bowen, in a sermon delivered to Asbury Methodist Episcopal Church in Washington, D.C., January 31, 1892

THE FAMILY

Hopeful Appraisals

Perhaps no other subject in African American studies is as widely discussed and

THE FAMILY AND HEALTH

In recent years there has been significant growth in the number of middle-class and wealthy African American families

crucial to the future of blacks as the black family. The editors of *Ebony* considered the topic so important that they devoted their entire August 1993 issue to articles focused on the family. Their approach, however, was somewhat unusual in that it was primarily positive. In his publisher's statement, John H. Johnson wrote:

> It is an issue on the Black family nobody knows, the Black family nobody notices or interviews or even talks about.
>
> *That* family, the invisible Black family, has always been the backbone of the Black community. And today, as in the days of segregation and sorrow, it is made up of tens of thousands of heroic fathers and mothers who are paying bills, raising and educating children, holding family reunions and loving one another, often in the face of almost **insurmountable** odds.

Johnson's message is one that runs counter to that of many scholars, journalists, politicians, and Hollywood producers. The lead *Ebony* article goes on to state that:

> Social scientists habitually cite drug abuse, gang crime, teenage pregnancy and other problems that plague the Black community as proof positive that the Black family is disintegrating and beyond repair. Yet, nothing could be farther from the truth.

At least one leading black **sociologist** who shares this view is Andrew Billingsley.

THE FAMILY AND HEALTH

Yet many black families remain poor and constantly struggle to stay together

> **WORDS TO KNOW**
>
> **abstinence:** voluntary avoidance of a certain behavior
>
> **aspirations:** ambitions
>
> **cardiovascular:** the system that links the heart and blood vessels
>
> **generative:** capable of continuing, through reproduction, etc.
>
> **insurmountable:** not able to be overcome
>
> **intravenous:** directly into a vein
>
> **maligned:** spoken ill of
>
> **pathology:** the condition and results of a disease
>
> **prenatal:** taking place before birth
>
> **sociologist:** one who studies human society
>
> **vulnerable:** open to attack or injury

Beginning with his landmark study titled *Black Families in White America* (1968), Billingsley has corrected a number of myths regarding the black family, including one that held that blacks have not historically valued the traditional married-couple family.

Billingsley's most recent work, *Climbing Jacob's Ladder* (1992), begins with the announcement that:

> The African-American family is neither dead nor dying, nor vanishing. Instead, the family remains a resilient and adaptive institution reflecting the most basic values, hopes, and **aspirations** of the descendants of African people in America. But to say that black families are alive is not to say that they are all faring well.

It would be naive in the extreme to ignore the many pressures bearing down and compromising the ability of many to meet the basic needs of their members. But there is another side to the story. And we argue in this book that this other side—enduring, positive, and powerful—is more important because it is more **generative.** It can continually renew and sustain this vital sector of American society in the years ahead.

Billingsley shares this balanced, positive, broad-based approach to studying black families with such pioneering black scholars as W. E. B. Du Bois, Charles S. Johnson, and E. Franklin Frazier. Yet however posi-

THE FAMILY AND HEALTH

THE CHARLENE CARROLL FAMILY— FROM UNDERCLASS TO UPPER CLASS

Following is an uncommon and inspiring success story from Billingsley's *Climbing Jacob's Ladder:*

Charlene Carroll grew up in a female-headed family. Her mother and father separated when she was a year old. When she was eleven, her mother became disabled and she was placed in a foster home. Like so many other such children, she was moved from one foster home to another until she was eighteen. At nineteen, she dropped out of high school. Like many other young women, she became an unwed teenage parent. The long arm of the extended family reached out to her and an aunt took her in, even though she herself was poor and lived in a public housing project.... By the time Carroll was thirty-five, she owned three beauty salons, earned more than $100,000 a year, and was a pillar of her community.

Carroll's rise from the bottom to the top of the socioeconomic structure, from the underclass to the upper class in a single generation was partly due to her own personal attributes—her intelligence, curiosity, and determination—as well as the strong work orientation received from her mother. It was partially due to the care and guidance she received in foster care, a service which is as often **maligned** as single-parent families. But her success also had to do with the guiding hand of her aunt, who took her in when she became pregnant. She always liked fixing hair, so with the encouragement and support of her aunt she went to cosmetology school. She was bright, learned fast, and became proficient at her trade. Pretty soon she was doing the hair for all her aunt's friends in the housing project. Later, she got a job in Olive Benson's salon in Boston. There she was encouraged to do further study in some of the leading cosmetology schools in San Francisco, London, New York, and Montreal. After six years she was ready to branch out on her own.

There is still another feature of Carroll's experience not generally included in descriptions of women who get pregnant out of wedlock. She got married and had another child. With the help of her husband and $5,000 of family savings, she applied for and received a government loan of $15,000 from the Small Business Administration in order to set up her own business. Thus in 1976, this young mother, wife, and hairdresser became an entrepreneur....

Now with her firefighter husband and three children, Carroll enjoys the benefit of a strong, stable, modern family.

Source: Andrew Billingsley, "And Still We Rise: Single-Parent Families in Helping Communities," *Climbing Jacob's Ladder: The Enduring Legacy of African-American Families* (1992), pp. 335-36. *Primary source:* Herschel Johnson, "We're in the Money," *Black Enterprise,* August 1984, pp. 40-6.

THE FAMILY AND HEALTH

Extended families have long been a strong support system with the African American community

tive Billingsley's approach is, it is also necessarily concerned with "the many pressures bearing down" on the black family.

Many of the statistics Billingsley cites are discouraging. However, what most elevates his work is the attention it gives to real-life success stories and his final call for a "society more responsive to, and supportive of, all its members."

Different Shapes, Different Sizes

Families are society's building blocks. Healthy, well-educated families with stable incomes make for healthy societies. The family, of course, comes in all shapes and sizes. There are nuclear (parents and children), extended (parents, children, and relatives), single-parent, biracial, adoptive, and foster families. There are families in which the parents are married, divorced, separated, remarried, or never married. There are upper class, middle class, and working class families. There are also underclass families. Called the "poorest of the poor," these families are especially **vulnerable** to the breakdown of social institutions.

Each family has its own structure, its own way of operating. Such structures can and do change over time. A death of a family member, a divorce, a new job, or the loss of a job are examples of personal changes that can affect how individual families operate. Some of these changes help strengthen families. Others tend to damage them. Still oth-

333

ers are neither good nor bad in and of themselves.

Changes can also be seen as part of a larger picture. Black families across the United States change as a group over time, both because of changes at the personal level and because of developments in American society. The same is true of white, Hispanic, and other family groups.

Extended and Augmented Families

One family pattern that has historically been common among African Americans is the extended family. This family grouping includes other relatives such as grandparents, aunts, uncles, cousins, nieces, nephews, or other relatives, formally or informally adopted, who share the household temporarily or for a longer time period with a nuclear family. Extended families have long been a strong support system within the African American community. Today, members of extended families may not all live in the same household, because of the migratory patterns of family members, but they still function as a supportive unit.

Augmented families, identified by Billingsley in his *Black Families in White America* (1968), include unrelated persons who form supportive, family-like relationships. Another classification, "fictive kin" (as Carol Stack calls them), includes "play" mothers, brothers, sisters, and so on, who usually do not live together. In some communities, these friendship networks resemble and substitute for extended family networks that may no longer exist. Foster families are also a growing phenomenon in the African American community, and the increase of female-headed households is more characteristic of the black population than of any other American racial or ethnic group today.

In 1991 married-couple families were only 48 percent of all African American families

African American households presently fall into the following categories: 1) married couples with children; 2) married couples without children; 3) extended families (usually those including grandparents); 4) blended families; 5) single-parent families (usually but not always headed by women); 6) adults living together (with or without children); and 7) single-person households (chiefly female).

Families and Money

The Upper Class

During the early 1990s differences in income among America's black families continued to widen. Approximately one-third of

THE FAMILY AND HEALTH

EIGHTH GRADERS' HOUSEHOLDS

Eighth graders, and the types of households in which they live, 1988.

Race/ethnicity	Single parent household[1]	Single parent/other relative			Two parent		
		Mother/female guardian only in household	Father/male guardian only in household	Other relative or non-relative only in household	Mother and father in household	Mother and guardian in household	Father and guardian in household
Black	46.5	36.1	2.1	8.3	38.4	13.3	1.9
White	17.7	12.9	2.7	2.1	67.9	11.6	2.9
Hispanic	23.4	17.7	2.2	3.5	63.5	11.2	1.9
Total	22.3	16.5	2.6	3.2	63.6	11.5	2.6

Source: "Percentage of Eighth Graders from Different Types of Households, by Selected Background Characteristics," *A Profile of the American Eighth Grader,* 1990, p. 6. *Primary source:* U.S. Department of Education, National Center for Education Statistics. "National Education Longitudinal Study of 1988: Base Year Student Survey." *Notes:* [1]This column is the sum of mother only, father only, and other relative or non-relative columns.

black families were prospering, with annual incomes above $50,000. These families were primarily headed by married, well-educated, double-income couples. They also tended to live in suburban areas, were nuclear or blended in nature, and possibly were part of supportive friendship networks.

In addition, these affluent black families were generally headed by second-, third-, and even fourth-generation college graduates, the heirs of a family tradition of education, motivation, and hard work.

The Middle Class

Another one-third of black families had entered the ranks of the middle class, with incomes from $25,000 to $50,000. The extended or augmented family structure was central to many of these homes. "Fictive kin," too, were often part of these family relationships.

This often unsung group, championed by publisher John H. Johnson and other black business leaders and economists, experienced enormous gains during the 1980s. According to the November 9, 1992 issue of *Forbes,* black income as a whole rose faster than white income as a whole from 1981 to 1991. The successes and contributions of the middle class were central to this rise.

The Working Class and Lower Class

The final one-third includes the nation's neediest black families. This grouping includes the 1) working class nonpoor, with incomes of $10,000 to $25,000; 2) former working-class families who have fallen on hard times; 3) the "working poor," who are employed daily but at minimum wages (less than $10,000) that do not permit secure or dependable livelihoods; and (4) families of the "underclass" (or "outerclass," a term used by President Bill Clinton in 1993), most of which are headed by single women.

Single Mothers. In 1991 married-couple families (those with and without children) represented only 48 percent of all African American families. Forty-six percent of African American families were headed by a female householder with no husband present. Overwhelmingly, the nation's poor black families fell into this latter category.

Low-income African American families, in fact, are plagued by the growth of their numbers headed by poor, never-married black females; teenage pregnancies; the shortage of marriageable, employed black males; disparities between black and white earning power; poor housing and social services; chronic unemployment and underemployment; and rising welfare dependency.

Family Structure and Stability

In 1991 only 36 percent of African American children lived with both parents, compared to 58.5 percent in 1970 and 67 percent in 1960. This dramatic decline roughly parallels the changes in living arrangements of African American adults resulting from increased divorce and separation rates as well as increases in births to never-married women.

In 1991, 67 percent of black female-headed families had one or more children under 18 years old present in the household;

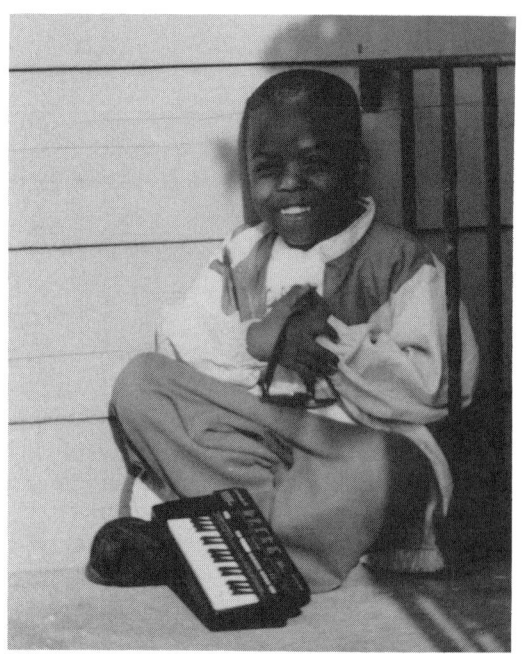

In 1991 only 36 percent of African American children lived with both parents

56 percent had two or more. These families were more likely to be poor than were married-couple families. They were also more likely to live in inner cities. About 30 percent lived in public housing.

Violence and Other Problems of the Inner-City Family

Unprecedented levels of crime and gang violence have also undermined African American families. With drug trafficking rampant in most inner-city areas, drug-related killings have reached record levels among African Americans. These activities continue to have a negative impact on black families and communities.

Robert B. Hill, in his article "Economic Forces, Structural Discrimination, and

VIOLENCE AMONG THE YOUNG

Violence among the young, a growing problem in American society as a whole, has become especially pronounced in the African American community in recent years. The statistics are nothing short of staggering. The Department of Justice estimates that 100,000 children carry guns to school every day. The American Psychological Association reports that 45 percent of first- and second-graders in Washington, D.C., have seen muggings; 31 percent have witnessed shootings; 39 percent have viewed dead bodies. According to the Children's Defense Fund, black children are the most likely victims of violent crimes. The National Crime Survey shows that nearly one-half of all violent crimes against 12- to 19-year-olds take place either in or near schools.

A major part of the problem is the alarming spread of gangs, which are present in every major American city and draw from every cultural community. Many experts believe that the growth of gangs is directly related to the breakdown of families. Gangs, by their very structure, serve some of the same functions as families, providing support and a sense of belonging to those with little or no home life. And schools, despite their best efforts, cannot completely fill these needs. As Michael Green, a former member of the Crips, said in a 1990 interview:

> I went almost all the way through high school. I got good grades, I was in the band—I played the drums—but I never got the attention I wanted, so I left it all and joined the gang. There I got a little attention—from the other gang members. I felt they loved me and they were a family. I'd die for them, I'd kill for them, I'd go to jail for them.

Once the violence begins—because of gangbanging or otherwise—it tends to become an inescapable cycle, especially in poorer black communities where black on black violence is becoming commonplace. Even gang leaders have recognized the need to curb the violence; during 1993 a number of gang summits were held in key cities across the nation. Rival gang leaders came together pledging peace and inviting the help and cooperation of civic and political leaders. Although many criticized the summits for "legitimizing," or justifying, gangs, many others viewed the talks as a positive and necessary development.

Acting as head of the National Association for the Advancement of Colored People (NAACP), Benjamin Chavis embraced leaders at a gang peace summit in Chicago. According to Ann LoLordo, Chavis has said that the NAACP plans to commit itself to seeking solutions to the violence. To those naysayers "who call the truce movement a sham because the gangs still tote guns and sell drugs," Chavis responds: "'God has given us everything we need. If the peace is to be maintained, it has to be the responsibility of each one of us.'" But everyone agrees that an end to the violence will not come easily or quickly, for the factors that contribute to violence in American society are many and the resources that might curb it—strong families, safe neighborhoods, teen jobs, and after-school programs—are becoming increasingly rare.

Sources: Léon Bing, *Do or Die,* New York: HarperCollins Publishers, 1991; James Alan Fox and Glenn Pierce, "American Killers Are Getting Younger," *USA Today,* January 1994, pp. 24-6; Michael B. Green (in an interview with Kristina Rebelo), "'You See a Red Rag, Shoot,'" *Sports Illustrated,* May 14, 1990, p. 46; Ann LoLordo (*Baltimore Sun*), "NAACP Tackles Life or Death Issue: Director Commits Resources to Ending Gang Violence," *Star Tribune,* November 7, 1993, p. 10A; Lori S. Robinson and Jimmie Briggs, "Kids and Violence," *Emerge,* November 1993, pp. 45-50; Ronald D. Stephens, "Gangs, Guns, and School Violence," *USA Today,* January 1994, pp. 29-32.

Black Family Instability" (1990), points to government as one of the forces that perpetuate the inner-city problem. Hill sees as particularly crippling the absence of public policy to provide affordable housing for moderate and low-income families. He also says this absence has a greater impact on African American families because of their unique employment and income problems.

One result of the housing shortage is a return to traditional black extended or augmented family arrangements; deprived family members seek temporary housing with relatives and friends share their homes with those less fortunate. Another consequence is that increasing numbers of black families are homeless.

The Great Society: A Failure?

Sociologist K. Sue Jewell, in her 1988 book *Survival of the Black Family: The Institutional Impact of U.S. Social Policy*, maintains that "policies, procedures, and assumptions underlying social and economic programs in the 1960s and 1970s, the 'Great Society' years, contributed to the disintegration of black two-parent and extended families and to an increase in black families headed by women." In Jewell's view, the liberal social policy of the Great Society era resulted in modest, not substantial, gains for middle-class African American families.

Senator Daniel Patrick Moynihan, in "How the Great Society Destroyed the American Family," an article in *The Public Interest* (No. 108, 1992), claims that "Great Society" programs destroyed the inner-city black family structure largely through welfare policies and argues that social scientists still do not know what public policies will reverse the downward spiral of life conditions of inner-city black families. Moynihan forecasted the crisis in the social structure of inner-city black families in March 1965 in "The Negro Family: The Case for National Action."

EIGHTH GRADERS: LATCHKEY KIDS

Percentage of eighth graders who usually have no one home when they return home from school, 1988.

Race/ethnicity	Usually no one home when returns home from school
Black	17.6
White	18.6
Hispanic	12.4
Total	17.6

Source: "Percentage of Eighth Graders Who Usually Have No One Home When They Return Home From School, by Selected Background Characteristics," *A Profile of the American Eighth Grader,* 1990, p. 52. *Primary source:* U.S. Department of Education, National Center for Education Statistics. "National Education Longitudinal Study of 1988: Base Year Student Survey."

FAMILIES IN POVERTY

Families below poverty level by race and type of family, 1990.

Race and family type	Number of families (in thousands)	Number below poverty level (in thousands)	Percent below poverty level
All families	66,322	7,098	10.7
Black	7,471	2,193	29.3
Married couple-families	3,569	448	12.6
Male householder, no wife present	472	97	20.6
Female householder, no husband present	3,430	1,648	48.1
White	56,803	4,622	8.1
Married couple-families	47,014	2,386	5.1
Male householder, no wife present	2,277	226	9.9
Female householder, no husband present	7,512	2,010	26.8

Source: "Families Below Poverty Level by Race and Type of Family, 1990," *The State of Black America 1992,* 1992, p. 320. *Primary source:* Bureau of the Census, *Current Population Survey,* March 1990.

In this Department of Labor paper, Moynihan argued that the black community had become immersed in "a tangle of **pathology**" that included family breakdown. Many prominent African Americans disputed Moynihan's conclusions and accused him of "blaming the victims" of social conditions rather than looking at the causes of their problems.

Number and Size of Families

In 1991 the number of African American families increased to 7.5 million, up from 3.4 million in 1950. This increase was most evident in the number of married-couple families and female-headed families with no husband present. In 1991, married-couple families comprised only 48 percent of all African American families, contrasted with 1950 when they comprised 78 percent. Forty-six percent of African American families in 1991 were headed by a female householder with no husband present, a staggering increase from the 1950 proportion of 18 percent.

This proportion is moving swiftly toward being equal with the percentage of married-couple families. The increase in black female-headed families can be assigned to a number of factors: 1) the shortage of eligible black males; 2) the shorter life expectancy of black males; 3) increasing separation

THE LARRY TOLSON FAMILY—LOWER CLASS AND FULL OF LOVE AND SUPPORT

Following is another success story from Billingsley's *Climbing Jacob's Ladder:*

In 1991 at age twenty-seven, Tolson was already father of nine children, whom he was raising alone. It all began when he was twenty-one and decided to get married and settle down. He did and in rapid-fire order three children were born: Lawrence, now aged seven, plus twins Perry and Larry, Jr., now six. Then the mother moved out. He soon struck up a relationship with another woman who was eager to help him make a family. Together for five years, they produced six additional children, including two sets of twins: Lance and Leonard, Latise and Lakita, Lisa, and LaShawn. Then she left.

While numerous local authorities and others who do not know him frequently question whether he can possibly raise these nine children well, Tolson continues to do what seems impossible.

Who is this determined young man? He works part-time as an auto mechanic. He is a full-time student at a local technical institute. In addition, he finds time to do volunteer work for the local senior citizens group and the neighborhood council. An observer has confirmed that Tolson's children are always clean, well fed, and well dressed. Those old enough to attend school always test in the top levels of their class.

A local community leader and member of the city council, Wilhelmina J. Rolark, who helped Tolson find housing for his family has described him as "an exceptional father. He's determined to make something of himself and he is totally dedicated to his children." Tolson has described his own source of strength. "My saving grace," he told reporter Courtland Malloy, "is that I took home economics from seventh grade through high school. Even changing diapers is not so bad," he said, "when you get used to it."

Their five-bedroom public housing apartment is well kept. He has taught the children to help him with the cooking and cleaning and other chores. Tolson also gets a hand from the neighbors. His volunteer work pays off. "There are many elderly women out here, and they help me a lot," he said. "They baby-sit, braid hair, and sew. So my volunteering is one way to say thanks."

He also gets strong moral support from his mother. When asked if he feels burdened by such responsibility at such a young age, Tolson responded as though these responsibilities have saved his very life. "A lot of my friends are either in prison, strung out on drugs, or dead," he said. "And I was heading along the same path until these babies started coming. I no longer get high, unless it's on my kids. Through them, I've experienced the joy of true devotion, and now I know what love really means. I can't give that up."

Source: Andrew Billingsley, "Climbing Jacob's Ladder: Self-Help Redefined," *Climbing Jacob's Ladder: The Enduring Legacy of African-American Families* (1992), pp. 380-81. *Primary source:* Courtland Malloy, "Single Father and His Nine Children Have a House Full of Love," *Washington Post,* January 27, 1991, p. B3.

THE FAMILY AND HEALTH

Households led by single fathers represented just 6 percent of all black families in 1991

and divorce rates among African Americans; 4) the rising rate of out-of-wedlock parenthood; 5) increasing permissiveness regarding sex; and 6) the wider availability of welfare assistance to aid father-absent families with dependent children.

Families in Poverty

Proportionally many more black than white families were in poverty in 1990: 29.3 percent of African American families lived in poverty, compared with 8.1 percent of white families. African American families were more than 3½ times more likely to be poor than were white families, a situation which has not changed measurably since 1967 (figures are from the United States Bureau of the Census). Of 7,471,000 black families in 1990, 2,193,000 were below the poverty level, whereas only 4,622,000 of 56,803,000 white families were in similar circumstances. In absolute numbers, more white families than black ones were poor, but the proportions of poor families were racially lopsided.

Seventy-five percent of the African American families in poverty in 1990 were maintained by women alone, 20 percent were maintained by married couples, and the remainder by men alone. For the past 23 years, the poverty rate for female-headed black families has been consistently higher than the rate for other black family types.

Thirty-seven percent of all black families with related children under 18 years old were poor in 1990. This was not statistically different from the 1967 level of 39 percent or the 1982 level of 41 percent. Fifty-six percent of black families maintained by women with children under 18 years old were poor in 1990, less than the 64 percent in 1982 at the end of the 1981-82 recession (figures are from the United States Bureau of the Census).

The Elderly

In 1990, 34 percent of elderly black individuals (65 years old and over) were poor. While this marks an improvement over the 1967 figure of 53 percent, proportionally more elderly blacks than whites were poor in both comparison years. Despite the presence of policies such as Social Security, Medicare, and Supplemental Security Income (SSI), designed to help all elderly Americans, black seniors were twice as likely as elderly whites to be poor in 1967, and in 1990 they were three times more likely to be poor (United States Bureau of the Census).

Marriage and the Shortage of Black Men

In 1991 only 38.4 percent of African American women 15 years of age and over were married, compared to 60.3 percent in 1960. The corresponding percentages for African American men were 44.8 percent in 1991 and 63.3 percent in 1960. More research must be done to reveal the causes for this very drastic change in marriage patterns among African Americans in the last 30 years.

The population of black males aged 15 years old and over in 1990 stood at 10,074,000, compared to 12,124,000 black females in the same age grouping. The resulting ratio of approximately 83 males to every 100 females makes the matching of every black female with a same-race male for the traditionally valued lifetime monogamous marriage a numerical impossibility. There simply are not enough African American men alive.

Further, when one counts the number of black males who are poorly educated and therefore educationally mismatched in relation to their more highly educated black female counterparts, the pool of eligible men shrinks even lower.

High black male unemployment rates further compound the problem. Reportedly, many of today's young black men delay marriage or never marry because of their unemployment or underemployment status, the rationale being that lack of a job or small earnings will not enable them to support families. These factors also help to explain the increasing numbers of never-married black females. However, well-educated black men who are employed at good salaries are also less likely to be married than their white counterparts (David T. Ellwood & Johnathan Crane, 1990.)

Black Men in Prison

Incarcerated single black men are also unavailable as marriage partners, and black men in prison who are married are unavailable to be at home with their families and/or provide for them. Among inmates of state prisons (sentenced to a maximum term of at least one year) there were nearly 200,000 black men in 1986, or more than 40 percent of the total state prison population. In 1990 there were more than 150,000 black male jail inmates (sentenced to one year or less).

Interracial Marriage

Marriage outside the race further reduces the number of black men available for marriage to black women. In 1991 there were 156,000 marriages of black men to white women, compared to 75,000 marriages of white men to black women. This represented a "loss" of another 81,000 marriageable black men.

Fertility and Births

Fertility Rates

In 1989 there were 90.4 live births per 1,000 black women aged 15 to 44 years old while there were 64.7 live births to comparable white women. That year, there were 673,124 live births to black females, or approximately 17 percent of all births nationwide. Black women have had higher fertility rates than white women for the past two centuries. However, birth rates are similar for black and white women with the same level of educational attainment (figures from William P. O'Hare, et al., "African Americans in the 1990s," *Population Bulletin:* 46[1], 1991).

Teenage Pregnancy

For a number of years Marian Wright Edelman of the Children's Defense Fund has stressed that teenage pregnancy is a special problem among poor and minority groups ("Address to the National Conference on Educating Black Children," *Education Black Children: America's Challenge*, 1987). Joyce Ladner has explained that the causes of teenage pregnancy range from attempts to find emotional fulfillment to the desire to achieve "womanhood" to ignorance of contraceptives ("Black Teenage Pregnancy: A Challenge for Educators," *The Journal of Negro Education*, 56[1], 1987, pp. 53-63). Political conservatives maintain that poor teenagers view welfare programs such as Aid to Families with Dependent Children (AFDC) as a workable source of economic support and consequently view pregnancy as a means of tapping into the welfare system at an early age (Irving Kristol, 1992).

Teenage pregnancy is both a national problem and an African American problem. Data from the National Center for Health Statistics reveal that in 1989 the birth rate for all teenagers aged 15 to 17 years old was 36.5 live births per 1,000. African American girls in that age group were almost three times more likely than white girls to give birth (80.0 compared to 28.3 per 1,000).

Among girls younger than 15 years old, the birth rate was seven times higher among blacks than whites. Furthermore, in 1989 African American girls in the 15- to 17-year-old age group were almost five times more likely to have a second baby and seven times more likely to have a third baby as white girls in this age group. This has caused great concern in the African American community and in the larger society. Teenage childbearing intensifies such social problems as high infant mortality, low educational achievement, poor physical and mental health, long-term welfare dependency, and poverty.

Many teenage mothers do not complete high school, the basic educational expectation in this country. As a result, they are often seriously undereducated and lack marketable skills. Others do not know how to care adequately for their children. By and large, their children will not have the same opportunities and life-chances as more advantaged children.

CHILDREN OF INTER-RACIAL MARRIAGES

According to the Population Reference Bureau's December 1992 report, the proportion of mixed-race births for which the race of both parents was known more than tripled between 1968 and 1989. In actual numbers, the births of children with a black and a white parent increased from 8,700 in 1968 to 45,000 in 1989. This increase was described as "a striking sign of social change" with respect to attitudes about interracial marriage.

Source: Susan Krafft, "Black Death the Demographic Difference," *American Demographics* 13(12), 1991, pp. 12-13.

Various efforts have been aimed at stemming the tide of teenage pregnancy. Some states have reduced welfare payments for girls and women on public assistance who have more than one out-of-wedlock birth. Black sororities, fraternities, churches, and civil groups have initiated programs to work directly with African American teenagers. The Children's Defense Fund continues to enlighten the public through a multimedia campaign that urges black males as well as females to be more responsible for their sexual behavior.

HEALTH

Birth

Infant Mortality

Infant mortality rates for African Americans remain more than double that of whites. In 1989, 17.7 deaths per 1,000 live births were reported for black infants, compared to 8.2 deaths per 1,000 live births for whites. The black/white infant death ratios have not changed appreciably since 1950, when the black infant mortality rate was 43.9 deaths per 1,000 live births, and the white rate was 26.8 deaths per 1,000. Some progress has been made since 1950, however, as the infant mortality statistics have improved for both races. Nonetheless, the infant mortality rate in the United States is higher than rates in 21 other industrialized countries.

African American women are more likely than whites to give birth to low-weight babies, many of whom either fall victim to serious health problems or die during their first year. These babies are very prone to Sudden Infant Death Syndrome (SIDS), respiratory distress syndrome, infections, and injuries. This phenomenon occurs because unusually large numbers of babies are born to low-income, under-educated, mothers (many of whom are teenagers) who have poor **prenatal** care and poor nutrition and who smoke, use drugs, or otherwise fail to take care of themselves properly during their pregnancies.

Drug- and Alcohol-Related Births

Mothers who used drugs (including alcohol) during their pregnancies have given birth to a new and growing population of children. Many of these children experience after-birth withdrawal problems from drugs that affected them in the womb; they are later more prone to physical and mental disabilities, followed by behavioral problems and learning impairments when they arrive in the nation's schools. Infants whose mothers drink large amounts of alcoholic beverages during pregnancy are at risk of fetal alcohol syndrome, a group of birth defects including mental retardation, deficient growth, and defects of the skull, face, and brain.

Child Health

Immunization

Thousands of children are not being immunized, though our society knows that immunization can prevent the spread of communicable diseases. In 1990 only about one-half of inner-city young children had been immunized against measles, mumps, and rubella. Measles outbreaks have erupted in many American cities in the 1990s; most were among poor, inner-city children. Nearly 100 deaths from measles were reported in 1990 (figures are from National Commission on Children, 1991).

Lead Poisoning

Urban children who live in old and/or poor housing also remain at risk of being exposed to high levels of lead. It has been estimated that 12 million American children, primarily those who are poor, are at risk of lead poisoning and potentially will have their intellectual growth stunted because of this exposure (National Commission on Children, 1991). Like black adults, black children are also at greater risk of accidents, physical abuse, and other violence that may result in disability or death.

Sickle Cell Anemia

Sickle Cell Anemia (SCA) is a chronic inherited affliction caused by a defect in the hemoglobin component of the blood. It can be passed on to the children of two people who carry the gene for the defective trait. The presence of this abnormal hemoglobin trait can cause distortion (sickling) of the red blood cells and a decrease in their number. The source of SCA seems to be malarial countries; people with sickle cell disease are almost always immune to malaria, so it appears that the sickle cell is a defense mechanism against malaria.

Sickled red blood cells have been found in 1 of every 12 American blacks. However, the active disease occurs about once in 600 American blacks and once in every 1,200 American whites. It is estimated that about 50,000 persons in the United States suffer from the disease. Persons of other races and nationalities are affected by the trait and the anemia, including people from Southern India, Greece, Italy, Syria, Turkey, the Caribbean, and South and Central America.

African American couples who intend to have children are advised to undergo blood tests to determine whether they are carriers of the sickle cell gene. Two such carriers should agree not to produce children, since one in two children will have the trait and one in four the anemia. There is only one chance in four that their child will be free of the disease. Some areas (Washington, D.C., for example) have enacted laws requiring that newborns be screened for sickle cell anemia, along with other diseases. As a result of such legislation, newborns found to be afflicted with SCA can be cared for from birth.

AIDS

An unusually high percentage of African Americans suffer from Acquired Immune Deficiency Syndrome (AIDS), the final stage of a disease caused by the Human Immunodeficiency Virus (HIV). The HIV virus severely weakens the body's immune system, leaving HIV-infected people vulnerable to a number of other infections. At this writing, there is no cure for AIDS and the disease is 100 percent fatal.

Although African Americans represent only 12 percent of the United States population, 31 percent of all new AIDS cases in 1989 were black. The 1993 report "The Challenge of HIV/AIDS in Communities of Color" states that blacks and Hispanics, representing 21 percent of the population, accounted for 46 percent of all AIDS cases in September 1992 ("AIDS and Race," *Washington Post,* January 25, 1993). Unknown is the number of such persons infected with HIV who have not as yet experienced symptoms of the disease. The saddest news is that the disease is expected to spread even faster among African Americans in the future.

AIDS is spread during unprotected sexual intercourse, **intravenous** drug use, or unscreened blood transfusions. It can also be transmitted from mother to child during pregnancy or the birth process. It is estimated that 52 percent of the AIDS cases among African Americans in 1989 resulted from intravenous drug use.

While AIDS is fatal, it is preventable. Practicing sexual **abstinence** will greatly limit the risk. Adults and teenagers who are sexually active may reduce the risk if they engage in such "safe sex" practices as using condoms and avoiding behaviors that put them at risk of AIDS infection, such as having multiple sex partners or having sex with an intravenous drug user. And intravenous drug users should never share needles. The African American community and the larger society are saturating the public with information about AIDS in the hope that education will cause people to behave differently and thereby slow the progress of the disease.

Cigarette, Alcohol, and Drug Use

The African American community and the larger society are also bringing to the fore information about the dangers of cigarette, alcohol, and drug use. The abuse of or addiction to cigarettes, alcohol, marijuana, cocaine, and other drugs is a serious social problem in contemporary American society.

The National Center for Health Statistics reports that, in a given month in 1991, 4 percent of black youth age 12 to 17 years smoked cigarettes, compared with 13 percent of whites and 9 percent of Hispanics of the same age. Twenty percent of blacks, 20 percent of whites, and 23 percent of Hispanics in this same age group had used alcohol. Five percent of African Americans and Hispanics but 4 percent of whites had used marijuana. And 0.5 percent of blacks, 0.3 percent of whites, and 1.3 percent of Hispanic youths had used cocaine.

In the 18 to 25-year-old group in the given month, 22 percent of blacks had smoked cigarettes, compared to 36 percent of whites and 25 percent of Hispanics. Fifty-six percent of blacks had used alcohol, compared to 67 percent of whites and 53 percent of Hispanics. Fifteen percent of blacks, compared to 14 percent of whites and 9 percent of Hispanics had used marijuana; and 3.1 percent of blacks had used cocaine, compared to 1.7 percent of whites and 2.7 percent of Hispanics.

These percentages represent large numbers of young people. It is clear that youths are using cigarettes, alcohol, and drugs as early as age 12 and that usage increases through the young adult period. Recently, activist groups have taken cigarette and alcohol companies to task for targeting African Americans and youths in their advertising campaigns for their products. Cigarette smoking has been identified as a major risk factor in lung cancer, **cardiovascular** disease, and chronic lung disease. Alcohol and drug abuse is often associated with gangs and violent crime.

Life Expectancy

Life expectancy at birth increased substantially during the first 90 years of this century, from 33 years for African Americans of both sexes in 1900 to 70.3 years in 1990. Corresponding figures for both sexes of all races are 47.3 years in 1900 and 75.4 years in 1990. Provisional data of the National Vital Statistics System project a life expectancy of 66 years for black males born in 1990 and 74.5 years for black females born that year, an average of 70.3 years for both sexes. Corresponding life expectancy projections for white males and females born in 1990 are 72.6 and 79.3 years, averaged at 76.0 years.

At the other end of the age spectrum, black males aged 65 in 1990 are projected to live 14.2 more years, and black females 17.6 additional years, averaged for both sexes at 16.1 years. This compares with 15.3 more years for white males, and 19 additional years for white females, averaged for both sexes at 17.3 years. Thus the same pattern holds: white people in the United States continue to have longer life expectancy than African Americans.

These black/white differences can be attributed to a number of factors. African Americans have higher death rates due to the following major causes: accidents, homicides, suicides, heart disease, strokes, liver disease, cancer, diabetes, and AIDS. It is also true that whites, more than blacks, have health insurance coverage of some kind and sufficient personal income to purchase higher-quality health care.

Higher education and income levels among whites also assure them the greater likelihood of eating nutritionally balanced, healthy meals. Dietary patterns and food choices of low-income blacks include too many fats and sweets, factors that contribute to obesity and high blood pressure, which carry their own sets of health risks.

Homicide and Death by Accident

Homicide among African American men is a primary cause for the drop in their life expectancy. In 1989, 61.1 percent of all black male deaths and 12.9 percent of all black female deaths from accidents and violence were due to homicide. Some social theorists claim that the increasing numbers of African Americans who are poor and homeless, added to those who are involved in drugs or other substance abuses, account for the higher homicide rates among African Americans. Motor vehicle deaths and other accidents also accounted for many deaths among black males since 1970.

Suicide

Suicide rates are lower among African Americans than whites, but black suicide rates are on the rise. In 1985 the suicide rate for white males exceeded that for black males by 70 percent; by 1989, the difference had narrowed to 40 percent. Data from the National Center for Health Statistics show that more than 30,000 lives are lost through suicide annually.

Among all Americans, the age-adjusted death rate by suicide in 1989 was 11.3 deaths per 100,000. For black males, the rate was 12.5 per 100,000, and for black females, it was 2.4 per 100,000. Among black adolescents and young adults aged 15 to 24 years old, the suicide rate for males was 16.7 per 100,000, and 2.8 per 100,000 for females, increases of 49 percent (from 1984 to 1989) and 40 percent (from 1986 to 1989), respectively.

THE FAMILY AND HEALTH

Health Care

Medicaid

Many American families, including a high percentage of black families, receive health care through the federally funded Medicaid program. The total number of Medicaid recipients in the United States increased from 17.6 million in 1972 to 25.3 million in 1990. 7,800,000 black persons were covered by Medicaid; 5,686,000 of these had incomes below the poverty line and 2,123,000 had incomes above it.

Solutions

What do African American families need to improve their overall condition? Like other American families, they need federal, state, and local policies that are designed to strengthen all families regardless of race, class, or composition.

Law enforcement improvements related to drugs and alcohol is one of the most urgent priorities. Low-income blacks and other Americans also need universal health care policies, jobs that pay cost-of-living wages, and affordable housing in safer neighborhoods. The children and adults in many of these families are in dire need of quality education. Recreational and other leisure-time outlets must also be made available to the youth and children in cities. Middle-and upper-income black families would benefit from an end to discriminatory employment and promotion policies designed to limit their upward mobility.

In the *African American Almanac*, 6th ed. (1993), Faustine C. Jones-Wilson states:

> Within the African American community itself, certain attitudinal and behavioral changes are essential. For example, more highly educated young black men must decide to marry and to produce and maintain families. Substance abuse must be curtailed; people who have hope for the future and who feel that they have some power and control over their lives are less likely to "escape" through drugs or alcohol. Children and youth need more adult interaction and supervision in their lives, whether it comes from family members or "significant others" such as mentors provided by organizations like Concerned Black Men, Inc., or other community service-minded groups.

Once again, the National Urban League has called for a "Marshall Plan for the Cities" to address all of the current problems. If our society wants to save its cities and a significant portion of its human capital—of which these families comprise a significant part—it must give serious consideration to the formation and execution of such a plan in both the cities and the rural areas. By so doing, the nation can help all its citizens become productive workers, consistent taxpayers, praiseworthy parents, and contributing members of stable families.

16
Education

The Force That Liberates

"There is no shame in not knowing how to read. The shame is in not learning how when you have the chance."—Monster Kody, in Léon Bing's Do or Die *(1991)*

"You've got to give to get. And if you don't plan on givin', then you better not plan on gettin'."—Joe Clark

Many Africans who came to the English colonies as **indentured** servants in 1619 were natives of West Africa, a region noted in ancient times for its brilliant cultural and educational heritage. Education may have taken an important place in the lives of at least some of these settlers. However, it is certain that by the mid-1600s, as slavery began replacing indentured servitude, education was looked upon as the entitlement solely of the ruling classes.

Education through the Church

Aside from the efforts of individuals, early attempts at educating blacks in America can be traced back to efforts by Christian churches. Although the primary goal of missionaries was to convert Africans to Christianity, the process often involved general education.

> **WORDS TO KNOW**
>
> **curriculum:** the standard information, teaching plan, and testing for a course or major field of study; the entire teaching program of a given school or college
>
> **Eurocentric:** concerned primarily with European or Western culture
>
> **illiterate:** a person who cannot read or write; the phrase *functional illiterate* refers to those whose reading and writing abilities are less than adequate
>
> **indentured:** bound by contract to work for another for a certain length of time
>
> **manumission:** liberation from slavery
>
> **multicultural:** concerned with minority as well as majority cultures
>
> **propagation:** expansion from person to person, place to place; reproduction or multiplication

In the early 1600s French Catholics in Louisiana were probably the first to begin providing instruction to black laborers. The

EDUCATION

French *code noire,* a system of laws, required that masters educate their slaves.

Pennsylvania Quakers, who opposed the institution of slavery, organized monthly educational meetings for blacks beginning in the early 1700s. In 1750 Quaker Anthony Benezet established an evening school in his home, which remained successful until 1760. In 1774 Quakers in Philadelphia joined together to open a school for blacks.

The Society for the **Propagation** of the Gospel in Foreign Parts, established by the Church of England in 1701 for the purpose of converting African slaves to Christianity, was another organization that provided educational opportunities for blacks. In 1751 the Society sent Joseph Ottolenghi to convert and educate blacks in Georgia. Ottolenghi "promised to spare no pains to improve the young children."

African Free Schools in New York and Philadelphia

Like various churches, the antislavery movement played an important part in the

---

1634 French Catholics begin providing instruction to black servants and slaves in Louisiana.

1685 Reverend Morgan Goodwyn denounces Virginia laws that prohibit slaves from attending Quaker educational meetings.

1701 The Church of England organizes the Society for the Propagation of the Gospel in Foreign Parts for the purpose of converting and educating black slaves.

1743 A school for black youths opens in Charleston, South Carolina.

1787 The New York African Free School is established by the Manumission Society.

1800-1830 Individual schools for blacks are developed by churches, free blacks, and some slaveholders. Black college attendance begins.

1830-1860 Educational opportunities for blacks are cut short due to a rising fear of the increasing power of slaves. "Black Codes" are passed in several states, denying African Americans a number of rights, including access to educational facilities of any kind.

1861 The Civil War is launched, leading to the mass education of blacks.

1865 The Freedmen's Bureau is founded under General Oliver Otis Howard. By 1870 the Freedmen's Bureau operates more than 2,600 schools in the South, with 3,300 teachers educating 150,000 students.

1954 The *Brown* v. *Board of Education* Supreme Court case declares segregation in public schools unconstitutional.

1960s Black studies programs begin to spread rapidly across American campuses.

1988 Fifteen years after court-ordered busing touched off violent opposition and "white flight" from the city, Boston leaders approve a new plan to save the public school system. The plan will allow parents to select for their children a school closer to home, in order to reduce lengthy bus rides.

EDUCATION

School-aged children in the rural South, c. 1865

creation of schools. In 1787 the **Manumission** Society founded the New York African Free School; by 1820 more than 500 black children were enrolled. Support increased as other African free schools were established in New York, until 1834 when the New York Common Council took over control of the schools.

In 1804 African Episcopalians in Philadelphia organized a school for black children. In 1848 a black industrial training school opened in Philadelphia at the House of Industry. Other schools begun in Philadelphia included the Corn Street Unclassified School (1849), the Holmesburg Unclassified School (1854), and the Home for Colored Children (1859). By the mid-1860s there were 1,031 pupils in the black public schools of Philadelphia and another 1,290 in private or charitable schools.

Freedmen's Organizations and Agencies

At the close of the Civil War hundreds of thousands of free blacks were left without homes and adequate resources. As a means for providing temporary assistance to the

EDUCATION

EDUCATIONAL GOALS

Percentage of eighth graders who plan to either quit or graduate high school and attend either trade school or college after high school graduation.

Education Levels

Race/ethnicity	Won't finish high school	Will finish only high school	Vocational trade business after	Will attend college	Will finish college	Will attend graduate school
Black	1.4	8.2	10.2	16.3	39.4	24.5
White	1.3	10.74	9.2	11.9	45.2	21.9
Hispanic	2.6	14.8	10.7	17.1	33.2	21.5
Total	1.5	10.5	9.4	13.1	42.8	22.7

Source: "Percentage of Eighth Graders Aspiring to Various Education Levels, by Selected Student Characteristics," *A Profile of the American Eighth Grader,* 1990, p. 71. *Primary source:* U.S. Department of Education, National Center for Education Statistics, "National Education Longitudinal Study of 1988: Base Year Student Survey."

newly freed slaves, mutual aid societies were formed.

The New England Freedmen's Aid Society, organized in Boston in 1862, was founded to promote education among free Africans. Supporters of the organization included writer and clergyman Edward Everett Hale, editor and abolitionist leader William Lloyd Garrison, and poet and journalist William Cullen Bryant. That same year in New York the National Freedmen's Relief Association was founded. Other societies, including the Port Royal Relief Committee of Philadelphia, quickly followed. In 1863 several of these organizations merged to form the United States Commission for the Relief of the National Freedmen, which in 1865 became the American Freedmen's Aid Union.

During the 1860s Congress created the Freedmen's Bureau and passed several Freedmen's Bureau Acts. Under the acts, the bureau's chief functions were to provide food, clothing, and medical supplies. Working together with various charities, bureau commissioner general Oliver Otis Howard established and maintained schools and supported teachers in their work. By 1870 the bureau operated over 2,600 schools in the South with 3,300 teachers educating 150,000 students. Almost 4,000 schools were in operation before the agency folded.

EDUCATION

Students at Tuskegee Institute, 1902

Independent Schools in the Late Nineteenth Century

The early education of African Americans was largely a function of private schools founded to meet the needs of African Americans. One of the oldest black independent schools still in existence is the Tuskegee Institute, which was established in 1881 by an act of the Alabama general assembly. Booker T. Washington, the school's organizer and first principal, developed a **curriculum** that would provide black students with the means to become economically self-supporting.

Similarly, in 1883 in a lecture room at the Christ Presbyterian Church, Lucy Laney opened what would become the Haines Normal and Industrial Institute in Savannah, Georgia. In 1901 Charlotte Hawkins Brown founded the Palmer Memorial Institute in Sedalia, North Carolina; Nannie Helen Burroughs founded the National Training School for Women and Girls in Washington, D.C. By the end of the first year, Burroughs's school

EDUCATION

Mary McLeod Bethune dedicated her life to teaching and government service

had enrolled 31 students. Twenty-five years later more than 2,000 women had trained at the school.

Perhaps the best known of all black women educators is Mary McLeod Bethune. In 1904, with only $1.50 and five students, Bethune founded Daytona Normal and Industrial Institute for Girls (now Bethune-Cookman College) in Daytona Beach, Florida. Nineteen years later the institute merged with the Cookman Institute of Jacksonville, Florida, founded in 1872 by D. S. B. Darnell. Some 2,000 students now study at Bethune-Cookman College.

Early Black Institutions of Higher Education

One of the oldest of the historically black institutions of higher education, Wilberforce University (named for English abolitionist William Wilberforce) was founded in 1856 by the African Methodist Episcopal Church. The school awarded its first degree in 1857. The oldest institution in operation today, Cheyney State in Pennsylvania, was founded in 1837.

Between 1865 and 1871 several primarily black institutions of higher learning where founded, including, in 1865, Atlanta University (now Clark-Atlanta University), Shaw University, and Virginia Union University; in 1866, Fisk University and Lincoln Institute (now Lincoln University); in 1867, Talladega College, Augusta Institute (now Morehouse College), Biddle University (now Johnson C. Smith University), Howard University, and Scotia Seminary (now Barber-Scotia College); in 1869, Tougaloo College; and, in 1871, Alcorn College (now Alcorn State University) and Benedict College.

Daniel A. Payne, the first African American president of a black college in the Western world—Wilberforce University in Ohio

ENROLLMENT AT HISTORICALLY BLACK COLLEGES

Enrollment at historically black colleges and universities, 1980 and 1988.

	Total	Public		Private	
		4-year	2-year	4-year	2-year
Number of institutions, fall 1989	106	40	11	49	6
Total enrollment, fall 1980	233,557	155,085	13,132	62,924	2,416
Men, total	106,387	70,236	6,758	28,352	1,041
Men, black	81,818	53,654	2,781	24,412	971
Women, total	127,170	84,849	6,374	34,572	1,375
Women, black	109,171	70,582	4,644	32,589	1,356
Total enrollment, fall 1988	239,755	158,606	15,066	64,644	1,439
Men, total	100,561	66,097	6,772	27,219	473
Men, black	78,268	50,545	3,192	24,081	450
Women, total	139,194	92,509	8,294	37,425	966
Women, black	115,883	73,893	5,894	35,145	951

Source: *Digest of Education Statistics 1991,* November 1991, p. 215. *Primary source:* Department of Education, National Center for Education Statistics.

Religious organizations were instrumental in the founding and support of these early black institutions. Atlanta, Fisk, Talladega, and Tougaloo were founded by the American Missionary Association; Benedict, Shaw, and Virginia Union were founded and supported by the American Baptist Home Mission Society.

By 1900 there were some 34 black institutions in the United States for higher education and more than 2,000 blacks with earned degrees.

Other early scholars of African American studies include sociologist E. Franklin Frazier (1894-1963), historian George Washington Williams (1849-1991), John Edward Bruce (1856-1924) and Arthur Schomburg, founders of the Negro Society for Historical Research (1911), and Alain Locke, founder of the Associates in Negro Folk Education (1934).

EDUCATION

> ### CARTER G. WOODSON: FATHER OF AFRICAN AMERICAN HISTORY
>
> In September 1915 Carter G. Woodson, a Harvard University graduate, organized the Association for the Study of Negro Life and History (now the Association for the Study of Afro-American Life and History). The association's primary goals were to promote research, to encourage the study of African American history, and to publish material on black history. In 1916 the organization began publishing the *Journal of Negro History,* for which Woodson served as editor until his death in 1950.

Carter G. Woodson

Early Promoters of African American Studies

From the beginning, the purpose of African American studies has been to spread knowledge about the social, cultural, political, and historical experiences of Africans. One of the pioneers in the field of black studies, theologian and educator Alexander Crummell, helped found the American Negro Academy in Washington, D.C., in 1897. The purpose of the organization was to foster scholarship and promote literature, science, and art among African Americans.

The organization's members hoped that through the academy, an educated black elite, which would shape and direct society, would be born. Crummell first conceived the idea of an American Negro academy while a student at Cambridge University, in England. The organization's founding members included Paul Laurence Dunbar, William Sanders Scarborough, and W. E. B. Du Bois. Following Crummell's death in 1908, Du Bois was elected president of the academy.

The End of Segregation in Public Education

In the years that followed the United States Supreme Court's 1896 ruling in the case *Plessy* v. *Ferguson,* segregation in public education became general practice. Prior to the Court's decision in *Brown* v. *Board of Education* (1954), black children were very often subjected to inferior educational facilities. However, by the 1930s a string of school desegregation cases reached the Court.

EDUCATION

A black schoolroom in Missouri, c. 1930

When Lloyd Lionel Gaines was refused admission to the law school of the State University of Missouri, he applied to state courts for an order to compel admission on the basis of rights guaranteed under the Fourteenth Amendment. At that time, the state of Missouri maintained a practice of providing funds for blacks to attend graduate and professional schools outside of the state, rather than provide facilities itself.

The university defended its action by maintaining that Lincoln University, a predominantly black institution, would eventually establish its own law school, which Gaines would be able to attend. Until then the state would allow him to pursue his studies outside the state on a scholarship. Ruling in the case *Missouri ex rel. Gaines* v. *Canada* in 1938, the Supreme Court declared that states were required to provide equal educational facilities for blacks within its borders.

Taking an even greater step in 1950, the Supreme Court ruled that a separate law school for blacks provided by the state of

EDUCATION

W. E. B. DU BOIS ON EMANCIPATION AND THE THIRST FOR EDUCATION

One of the greatest champions of education in African American history was W. E. B. Du Bois. Born in Great Barrington, Massachusetts, on February 23, 1868, Du Bois received a bachelor's degree from Fisk University and went on to become the first black to earn a doctorate from Harvard University. A founding member of the National Association for the Advancement of Colored People (NAACP), he served as editor of that organization's *Crisis* magazine until 1934. Tremendously talented and industrious, Du Bois taught Latin, Greek, economics, and history and published books on a wide variety of topics throughout his life. At the time of his death in 1963, Du Bois was at work in his newly adopted country of Ghana on the *Encyclopedia Africana*.

In the following passage, taken from his *Black Reconstruction in America* (1935), Du Bois describes the reaction of African Americans to emancipation:

> They were consumed with desire for schools. The uprising of the black man, and the pouring of himself into organized effort for education, in those years between 1861 and 1871, was one of the marvelous occurrences of the modern world; almost without parallel in the history of civilization. The movement that was started was irresistible. It planted the free common school in a part of the nation, and in a part of the world, where it had never been known, and never been recognized before. Free, then, with a desire for land and a frenzy for schools, the Negro lurched into the new day.

Texas violated the equal protection clause of the Fourteenth Amendment. The case centered on Herman Marion Sweat, who was refused admission to the University of Texas law school because equivalent facilities were already available in another, blacks-only Texas school. The Court allowed Sweat to be admitted to the University of Texas law school, since "in terms of number of the faculty, variety of courses and opportunity for specialization, size of the student body, scope of the library, availability of law review and similar activities, the University of Texas Law School is superior."

EDUCATION

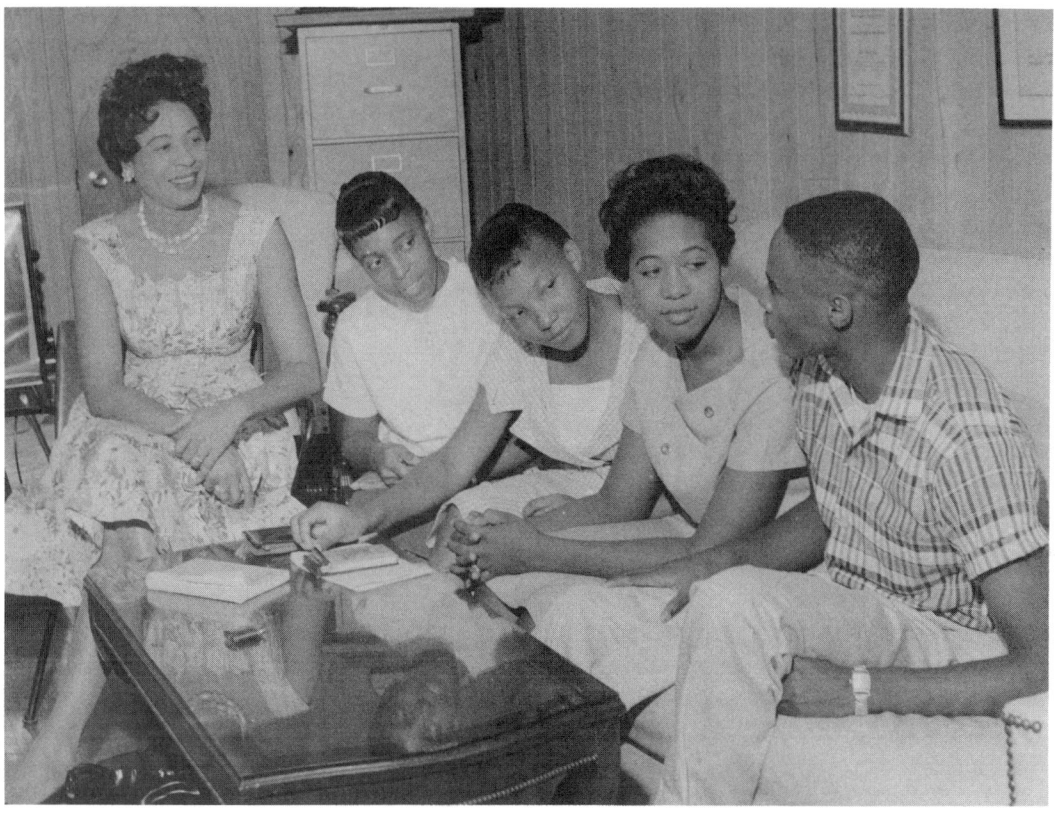

Daisy Bates with four black students who will attend formerly all-white high schools in Little Rock, Arkansas, 1959

In 1952 five different cases, all dealing with segregation in public schools but with different facts and from different places, reached the United States Supreme Court. Four of the cases, *Brown* v. *Board of Education* (out of Kansas), *Briggs* v. *Elliott* (out of South Carolina), *Davis* v. *Prince Edward County School Board* (out of Virginia), and *Gebhart* v. *Belton* (out of Delaware) were considered together; the fifth case, *Bolling* v. *Sharpe,* which came out of the District of Columbia, was considered separately since the district is not a state.

After hearing initial arguments, the Court was unable to reach an agreement. In 1953 the Court heard further arguments. Thurgood Marshall, legal counsel for the NAACP Legal Defense and Education Fund, represented the black students involved. On May 17, 1954, the Court unanimously ruled that segregation in all public education deprived minority children of equal protection under the Fourteenth Amendment. (In the *Bolling* case, the Court determined that segregation violated provisions of the Fifth Amendment, since the Fourteenth Amendment is expressly directed to the states.)

359

Black Colleges in the Twentieth-Century

Predominantly black colleges and universities continue to account for many black graduates. This is especially true in the areas of science, mathematics, and engineering, where 65 percent of African American doctors, 35 percent of African American lawyers, and 50 percent of African American engineers are graduates of historically black colleges and universities. In 1964 over 51 percent of all blacks in college were still enrolled in the historically black colleges and universities. By 1970 the proportion was 28 percent, and by fall 1978, 16.5 percent. As recently as 1977, 38 percent of all black degrees were earned at black institutions. In 1980 some 190,989 African Americans were enrolled at historically black institutions. By 1988 the total black enrollment at these institutions reached 217,462.

Independent Schools in the Late Twentieth Century

For years independent schools have been founded in order to exert greater control, ensure quality in education, and to meet the needs of African American children.

In 1932, in order to promote religious growth in the Muslim community, the Nation of Islam founded the University of Islam, an elementary and secondary school to educate black Muslim children in Detroit. Clara Muhammad, the wife of Elijah Muhammad, served as the school's first instructor. In 1934 a second school was opened in Chicago; by 1965 schools were operating in Atlanta and Washington, D.C. The current system of black Muslim schools named for Clara Muhammad is an outgrowth of the earlier University of Islam. There are currently 38 Sister Clara Muhammad schools in the United States.

In 1966 Gertrude Wilks and other black community leaders in East Palo Alto, California, organized the Nairobi Day School, a Saturday school. In 1969 the school became a full-time school. It closed in 1984.

Also founded as a Saturday school program in 1972, the New Concept Development Center in Chicago set out to create an educational institution that promoted self-respect, cooperation, and an awareness of

---

EIGHTH GRADERS: HOW THEIR TIME IS SPENT

Average number of hours an eighth grader spends per week on outside reading, homework, and watching television.

	Outside reading	Homework	TV total
Black	1.6	5.2	27.6
White	1.9	5.7	20.8
Hispanic	1.6	4.7	22.6

Source: "Average Number of Hours an Eighth Grader Spends per Week on Outside Reading, Homework, and Television Watching, by Selected Background Characteristics," *A Profile of the American Eighth Grader,* 1990, p. 49. Primary source: U.S. Department of Education, National Center for Education Statistics, "National Education Longitudinal Study of 1988: Base Year Student Survey."

EDUCATION

DROPOUTS

Age and race of dropouts, 1980-1989, as of October 1989.

Age and Race	Number of Dropouts (per 1,000)				Percent of Population		
	1980	1985	1987	1989	1980	1985	1989
Black[1]	934	748	706	648	16.0	12.6	11.4
16-17 years	80	70	77	61	6.9	6.5	5.6
18-21 years	486	376	338	363	23.0	17.5	17.4
22-24 years	346	279	273	220	24.0	17.8	14.9
White[1]	4,169	3,583	3,522	3,314	11.3	10.3	10.5
16-17 years	619	424	401	328	9.2	7.1	6.1
18-21 years	2,032	1,678	1,577	1,690	14.7	13.6	14.6
22-24 years	1,416	1,372	1,465	1,236	14.0	13.3	13.4
Hispanic[1,2]	919	820	941	1,168	29.5	23.3	27.9
16-17 years	92	97	76	80	16.6	14.6	12.5
18-21 years	470	335	410	538	40.3	29.3	34.9
22-24 years	323	365	439	524	40.6	33.9	41.1
Total Dropouts[1,3]	5,212	4,456	4,349	4,109	12.0	10.6	10.7
16-17 years	709	505	500	395	8.8	7.0	5.9
18-21 years	2,578	2,095	1,966	2,128	15.8	14.1	15.0
22-24 years	1,798	1,724	1,785	1,516	15.2	14.1	13.7

Source: "High School Dropouts 14 to 24 Years Old, by Age, Race, and Hispanic Origin: 1970 to 1989," *Statistical Abstract of the United States,* 1991, p. 156. Primary source: U.S. Bureau of the Census, *Current Population Reports,* series P-20, No. 443 and earlier reports; and unpublished data. Notes: [1]Includes persons 14-15 years, not shown separately. [2]Persons of Hispanic origin may be of any race. [3]Includes other groups not shown separately.

African American history and culture. In 1975 public school teacher and nurse Marva Collins founded the Westside Preparatory School in Chicago.

Current Problems, Needs, and Trends

Recently the educational and social needs of urban youth, particularly African Ameri-

EDUCATION

Principal Clifford Watson with students of the Malcolm X Academy, Detroit, Michigan

can males, have been given increased attention. Studies show that nearly 40 percent of adult black males are functionally **illiterate,** and that the number of male convicts is far greater than the number of college students. Addressing these issues, such large urban school systems as Baltimore, Detroit, and Milwaukee have attempted to create programs that focus on the problems and needs of African American males.

In *African American Almanac,* 6th ed. (1993), Kwame Kenyatta underscores this educational crisis, stating:

Many African children do not graduate, they simply drop out. They become statistics at juvenile centers, group homes, foster care, adoption agencies, prison yards, and grave yards. They are often referred to by such code names as 'at risk' and 'inner city youth.'

Kenyatta goes on to assert that "They are at risk because they have been targeted for failure," and that "It is virtually impossible to educate African children using the **Eurocentric** teaching style."

LEAN ON ME: THE JOE CLARK STORY

In 1982 Joe Clark was appointed principal of Eastside High, an inner-city school in Paterson, New Jersey. The school, which served mainly black and Hispanic students, had a reputation for poor instruction, poor discipline, and violence. Fighting in hallways and in classrooms was common and weapons had been used against both students and teachers. Drug dealers worked the school daily. Graffiti was everywhere. Broken windows, fencing, doors, and furniture often went unrepaired. The educational process at Eastside was equally run-down. Students and teachers worked in a state of constant fear, truancy and dropout rates were high, and academic test scores were among the lowest in the state.

Clark moved quickly to establish a new order for the school. He replaced officials whom he considered "loafers," and set up a chain-of-command that defined responsibilities and problem-solving channels. He drew up new student policies, including a tough suspension system, student photo I.D. tags, and dress code guidelines. Before school opened in the fall, he oversaw a major restoration of the building itself. On opening day, Clark greeted his students with his bullhorn: "I am your new principal, Joe Clark. Mr. Clark to you. This is the new Eastside High School. What was, exists no more. Go to your classrooms. Please walk to the right."

In his first week Clark suspended 300 students for violations of his new rules. Suspensions and expulsions became Clark's way of ridding the school of what he called "leeches, miscreants and hoodlums." Clark was a high-profile presence at Eastside, giving daily messages over the public address system, tirelessly patrolling the halls, chatting with students and visiting classrooms, berating teachers he felt weren't doing their job, and praising those who were.

By the beginning of 1988 Clark found himself at the center of a national debate on reform in inner-city schools. His tough-fisted approach to discipline was widely criticized, as was his belief that "You can't save everybody," that some problem students need to be let go so that real learning can still take place for others. For the same reasons, Clark was also widely celebrated. In May 1989 he underwent open-heart surgery and resigned two months later from Eastside. Since then he has lectured on school management, education reform, and drug control in inner cities. Clark is the author of *Laying Down the Law: Joe Clark's Strategy for Saving Our Schools* and the subject of the 1989 Warner Bros. film *Lean on Me*.

EDUCATION

In African-based education, the black student becomes the center of the learning environment

In response, some educators have adapted an Afrocentric approach to education. "Some people say all Afrocentrists want to do is celebrate African people," Molefi Asante, the conceiver of this philosophy and the author of the first line of Afrocentric schoolbooks, said in an address to Detroit educators. "No, we want to tell the truth. Our children should know African contributions to all human knowledge" (*The Detroit News,* January 30, 1994).

For example, students should learn that there were black cowboys on the western frontier. But, Asante maintained, students should also learn that these cowboys, like their white counterparts, killed Native Americans.

Many believe that an Afrocentric curriculum will help curb crime and violence among African American youth, for a student's own self esteem is built up by learning of African American contributions to society.

In recent years, efforts at creating alternative schools and **multicultural** curriculums have received increased attention. In 1991 the Institute for Independent Education, an organization providing technical assistance to independent neighborhood schools, reported an estimated 300 such schools serving children of color in the United States (Gail Foster, "New York City's Wealth of Historically Black Independent Schools," *The Journal of Negro Education,* 61, 1992, pp. 186-200). Traditional public and private elementary and secondary schools have also begun embracing multicultural studies.

Perhaps Kenyatta is correct when he writes:

> As we move toward an African-centered education, African children will no longer see the contributions of their people as a footnote of history, but rather as the center and origin of history—African centrism will stand and be celebrated as one of the most progressive educational philosophies in the twenty-first century.

17
Religion

The Tie That Binds

"We make a living by what we get, but we make a life by what we give."—Barbara Harris

There is probably no more truly black institution in the United States than the black church, regardless of **denomination,** location, or size. For centuries, the black church has been the source of hope, relief, support, and salvation for tens of millions of African Americans. Aside from its huge spiritual impact, the black church has played an equally important cultural role. For example, churches tend to be the strongest unifying force in communities and one of the first sources of education and a multitude of social programs.

Themes of suffering, deliverance, and heavenly reward have been central to the faith of many peoples, but this is especially true of blacks, given their long and terrible struggles to end slavery and secure basic civil rights. The Negro spiritual, in many ways, contains the essence of the black struggle and—along with gospel music—is one of the greatest African American contributions to organized religion and to Western culture and music as a whole.

Perhaps the most important dimension of African American religion, though, has been its continual fostering of leaders who have championed the causes of the downtrodden. The civil rights movements of the 1960s would not have been possible without the leadership and facilities of black churches. The same is true of the abolitionist and Underground Railroad movements more than a century earlier. Religion, clearly, is the tie that binds the African American community to its troubled past, its strengthened present, and its hopeful future.

The Old and the New

The first African slaves and servants who arrived on North American shores brought their own religious beliefs and practices with them. Only a small number were Muslims or Christians. The vast majority followed their native African religions. Although there were hundreds of these religions, Africans in general shared the belief that the world was created by an all-powerful God who thereafter removed himself from direct involvement in people's lives.

Because of this belief, Africans chose to worship a number of lesser spirits who busied themselves with human problems. Chief

RELIGION

among these were their African ancestors, or the "living dead." If proper offering were made to an ancestor, the individual would be blessed with good fortune, but if the ancestor were slighted, misfortune would result.

The Fon, Ibo, Nago, Kongo, and other tribes brought their forms of religion to French-speaking Haiti. Blending with Catholicism and other beliefs, the African forms developed into Voodoo. Magic rites and worship of a variety of spirits (or *orishas*) characterizes this religion. Voodoo spirits often possess their worshipers, who then become mediums (or go-betweens) of their gods. Contrary to what many think, the most essential element of Voodoo is neither such possession nor the casting of evil spells; it is the personal healing that is sought by the worshiper. Voodoo still thrives in Haiti and other parts of the Western Hemisphere, most notably New Orleans.

Voodoo's cousin, Santería, originated in Spanish-speaking Cuba among the Yoruba, Bantu, and Kongo people. This religion has spread to large urban areas in America, including Miami and New York.

The type of African spirituality that took root in North America merged elements from many African cultures. Since slave masters mixed Africans from many tribal backgrounds, no "pure" African religion emerged. However, numerous traditions did survive and can be found in modern-day sermons, church music, church organization, funeral practices, and structures and rituals within the religious home.

Christian Missionary Efforts

The first serious effort to convert African Americans to Christianity was made by the Anglican Society for the **Propagation** of the Gospel in Foreign Parts, which sent mis-

---

c. 1750 The first black church in the United States, the Silver Bluff Baptist Church, is formed.

1787 A large number of blacks withdraw from St. George's Church in Philadelphia. Led by Richard Allen and Absalom Jones, they launch the Free African Society.

1794 Absalom Jones founds St. Thomas's Protestant Episcopal Church. Richard Allen founds the Bethel African Methodist Episcopal Church, the first AME Church in the United States

1852 Daniel Alexander Payne is elected bishop of the AME Church.

1906 Pentecostalism emerges as a major religious phenomenon and leads to the growth of the Church of God in Christ and various Holiness churches, among others.

1961 Martin Luther King, Jr., and others form the Progressive National Baptist Convention after breaking with the National Baptist Convention.

1989 Barbara Harris is ordained as the first female bishop in history by the U.S. Episcopal Church. Joan Salmon Campbell becomes the first black woman and the sixth female to head the Presbyterian Church, U.S.A.

sionaries to North America in 1701. The effort had little success, for many Africans mocked those who imitated the whites too closely. In addition, white slave masters often objected to black church attendance and feared that slaves would demand their freedom following **conversion.**

The numerous colonial laws stating that conversion could not entitle slaves to freedom were little comfort to some slave masters, who suspected that Christianity would weaken the slave system. On the other hand, some slave masters believed that because Africans came from a pagan culture the slave system was justified, even after Christian conversion occurred.

By the mid-1700s efforts to convert African Americans to Christianity were becoming more and more successful. In his seven missionary tours throughout North America between 1742 and 1770, the spellbinding speaker George Whitefield (an English Methodist) converted large numbers of both black and white Americans. Traveling ministers such as Francis Asbury (the first Methodist bishop in the United States) were also well received by African Americans at the end of the eighteenth century.

Baptist and Methodist churches, in fact, were the most successful in attracting black members. Since these churches did not require that their ministers be well educated, doors were opened for aspiring African American ministers, many of whom lived in states where teaching African Americans to read and write was forbidden by law. Furthermore, the Baptists and Methodists, unlike more reserved denominations, were not opposed to the passion and energy of black preachers and congregations. Finally, the antislavery stance of notable Methodist and Baptist leaders, such as Asbury, John Wesley, and John Leland, and the greater degree of equality nurtured within many Baptist and Methodist congregations were attractive to African Americans.

Early Black Congregations

Probably the first independent black congregation was the Silver Bluff Baptist Church in South Carolina, which may have

> **WORDS TO KNOW**
>
> **Armageddon:** the place referred to in the Biblical Book of Revelation where the last battle is to be fought between the forces of good and evil; the time of the last battle; also referred to as the *apocalypse*
>
> **consecrated:** made or **ordained** a bishop through a religious ceremony; made or declared sacred
>
> **conversion:** the change from lack of faith to religious faith; the change from one religion to another
>
> **denomination:** a specific religious body or organization
>
> **dioceses:** a religious district presided over by a bishop; large or prominent religious districts are called *archdioceses*
>
> **ecumenical:** anything promoting the unity of Christian churches
>
> **evangelists:** literally, bringers of good news; those fervently devoted to spreading the gospel

RELIGION

THE STORY OF "AMAZING GRACE"

At the age of 11 an English boy named John Newton (1725-1807) decided to follow in his father's footsteps to become a sea captain. However, within a few years he had earned a reputation for wickedness, which ultimately led him to desert the British navy.

Upon his capture, Newton was placed in irons and whipped. He then fled England to live first in Guinea and then Sierra Leone. There he joined forces with a white slaver, standing guard over hundreds of chained Africans during voyages to the New World.

While aboard a vessel bound for Brazil, Newton read about Christianity. He experienced an inner conversion at the age of 23 after surviving a fierce storm at sea; Newton believed that he had been saved so that he could perform important Christian work. In 1742 he married Mary Catlett, a sweet-natured woman who influenced his behavior. To rid himself of the taint of the slave trade, he became an evangelical minister. In 1779 he and English poet William Cowper composed 281 hymns. The most famous of these was "Amazing Grace." Newton began his hymn with these words: "Amazing Grace, how sweet the sound / That saved a wretch like me / I once was lost but now am found / Was blind, but now I see."

---

been formed as early as 1750 and certainly before 1775. David George and seven other men and women helped found the church. George Liele, one of George's associates, often preached at the Silver Bluff Church before emigrating to Jamaica in 1782.

Andrew Bryan, one of Liele's converts, founded the First African Baptist Church in Savannah, Georgia, in 1788. In the early years of his ministry, Bryan was whipped and twice imprisoned by whites who feared him. But he bought his freedom, prospered, and eventually came to own much property, including eight black slaves. His death in 1812 was mourned by blacks and whites alike. While many black churches continued to be served by white ministers until 1865, black pastors and black **laypersons** ministering to black Baptist and Methodist congregations were not at all unusual at this time, either in the South or in the North.

Discrimination in White Churches

While white preachers urged black Americans to convert and many largely white congregations welcomed them into membership, racial prejudice was never absent from the religious scene. Although the level of discrimination varied from region to region and church to church, some problems unfortunately remained constant.

RELIGION

First African Baptist Church, Savannah, Georgia

Chief among these was the shortage of **ordained** African American clergy. For example, some African American ministers were ordained as deacons within the Methodist Episcopal Church prior to 1820, but none in the four decades thereafter. No black American Methodist minister was ordained by the Methodist Episcopal Church to the higher office of elder or **consecrated** as a bishop prior to the Civil War, unless he was willing to emigrate to Liberia.

Other discriminatory practices also formed part of the religious climate. The Methodists and many other denominations tried to restrict such tasks as the administering of sacraments for the white clergy alone. In addition, segregated seating in churches was common in both the North and the South and church discipline was often unevenly applied. Of course, racial discrimination in the churches was only a small part of the much larger political and moral debate over slavery.

Resistance to discrimination took many forms. In the North, Peter Spencer in Wilmington, Delaware, Richard Allen in Philadelphia, and James Varick in New York led their black followers out of white Methodist churches and set up independent black congregations. In Allen's case, his departure was preceded by a dramatic clash over segregated seating in Philadelphia's white Methodist church. Each of these men then used his congregation as the nucleus of a new black Methodist denomination. Spencer formed the African Union Church in 1807; Allen formed the African Methodist Episcopal (AME) Church in 1816 (he established the Bethel

WORDS TO KNOW

laypersons: non**ordained** church members; also referred to as the *laity*

liturgical: having to do with the order and nature of public worship, including the songs, rituals, readings, prayers, and sermon that form a religious service

ordained: established or invested with the title of minister, priest, rabbi, and so forth

propagation: expansion from person to person, place to place; reproduction or multiplication

schism: a split or break within an organization, usually as a result of serious disagreement

speaking in tongues: a gift of the Holy Spirit described in the New Testament (see Acts 2:4 and 1 Corinthians 12-14)

temperance: in general, the quality of self-restraint; historically, movements promoting moderation, total avoidance, or prohibition of alcoholic liquor

RELIGION

Richard Allen

AME Church in 1794, but had to wait more than 20 years for complete independence for his denomination); and Varick founded a denomination that would eventually be called the African Methodist Episcopal Zion (AME Zion or AMEZ) Church in 1821.

Meanwhile, in Charleston, South Carolina, a more explosive situation was taking shape. Morris Brown, a black Methodist minister from Charleston who had helped Allen organize the AME Church, organized an independent black Methodist church in his home city. The authorities harassed Brown's church and sometimes arrested its leaders. Nevertheless, within a year more than three-quarters of Charleston's black Methodists had united with him.

The oppression of African Americans in Charleston was so severe that many members of Brown's congregation, including important lay leaders, joined the revolt planned by Denmark Vesey to take over the Charleston armory and, eventually, the whole Charleston region. The conspirators, captured before they could carry out their plans, testified that Brown had not known of their scheme. The minister was allowed to move to Philadelphia, where Allen made him the second bishop of the AME Church.

The Black Church Responds to the Slavery Question

The mid-nineteenth century saw increased antislavery activity among many black church leaders and members. Some supported the gradual emancipation program sponsored by the American Colonization Society, which encouraged free blacks to emigrate to Africa and Westernize and Christianize the Africans there. Virginia Baptist pastor Lott Cary and Maryland Methodist minister Daniel Coker were the two most prominent black American religious leaders to emigrate to Africa in the 1820s. By the 1850s there were enough black Methodists in Liberia for the Methodist Episcopal Church to consecrate a black bishop, Francis Burns, to serve the Liberian churches. While some black Americans were emigrating to Africa, others emigrated to the West Indies. Episcopalian bishop James T. Holly, for example, settled in Haiti to undertake missionary work.

Because of the extreme repression in the slave states, Southern blacks were unable to express openly their views on political issues. They were, however, often able to make their views clear. When a white minister dwelled too long on the Biblical text that servants should obey their masters, his African American listeners were likely to desert him.

More importantly, black Christians often held secret meetings in "brush arbors" (rude structures made of pine boughs) or in the middle of the woods. There they could sing spirituals and pray openly for the quick advent of freedom. Whites feared slave revolts, which provided a violent outbreak of dissent. The 1831 revolt of Nat Turner, a Baptist preacher in Northampton County, Virginia, did not cease until both blacks and whites had suffered tremendous bloodshed. Frightened whites in the South intensified their watch over black churches in the aftermath of the Turner revolt. Even conservative black preachers such as Presbyterian John Chavis in North Carolina and Baptist "Uncle Jack" in Virginia were banned from preaching.

Northern black American leaders could afford to be more open in their beliefs. Most rejected outright the views of the American Colonization Society and favored instead the immediate abolition of slavery. Presbyterian minister Henry Highland Garnet was a prominent abolitionist, urging African American slaves in 1843 to "let your motto be RESISTANCE! RESISTANCE! RESISTANCE!" AME Bishop Daniel Payne and AME Zion Bishop Christopher Rush, both emigrants from the Carolinas to the North, were outspoken abolitionists who after the mid-1840s became the most prominent leaders in their respective churches. Frederick Douglass was one of the few leading black abolitionists who did not pursue a ministerial career, and even he had briefly served as an AME Zion preacher in New Bedford, Massachusetts.

Evangelist Jarena Lee, the first woman to preach in the African Methodist Episcopal (AME) Church

Black Female Religious Leadership

The contributions of black women ministers were also vital. Women sometimes served as traveling **evangelists,** especially within the black denominations. While Sojourner Truth's speeches have rightly become famous, Maria Stewart, Jarena Lee, Zilpha Elaw, and other early nineteenth-century women also spoke eloquently. None of these women were ordained, but a former slave from Maryland named Elizabeth, whose ministry began in 1796, spoke for many female preachers when she was accused of preaching without a license: "If the Lord has ordained me, I need nothing better." Rebecca Cox Jackson left the AME Church in the 1830s when she felt that men denied her the chance to exercise her ministry, and she eventually became head eldress of a predominantly black Shaker community in Philadelphia.

During the post-Civil War years, some black women sought and obtained formal ordination from their denominations. Sarah Ann Hughes, a successful North Carolina evangelist and pastor, was ordained by Bishop Henry McNeal Turner in 1885, but complaints from male pastors caused her ordination to be revoked two years later. Mary J. Small and Julia A. J. Foote were ordained by AME Zion bishops not long thereafter. Many women exercised their ministry through church-related groups, such as women's **temperance** and missionary societies, while others, such as Anna Cooper and Frances Jackson Coppin, became renowned educators.

Black Churches during Reconstruction

After the Civil War black church membership grew rapidly. This was especially true in the South, where the black clergy played a prominent part in the Reconstruction governments. In 1870 AME minister Hiram Revels became the first African American to serve as a United States Senator. However, Revels was only the groundbreaker; many black ministers went on to serve in the Congress or in their state governments.

African American participation in Reconstruction politics was effective in large part because ministers in the AME and AME Zion Churches, and many black Baptist ministers, carefully and patiently educated their congregation on every civic and political issue (although the newly established black denomination, the Colored Methodist Episcopal Church, largely stayed away from politics during Reconstruction).

After the end of political Reconstruction in the 1870s, African Americans were largely expelled from Southern politics, though many black ministers and laity continued to play an active role on such issues as temperance. Still, the Southern white campaign of terror, lynching, and discrimination virtually erased black political power and participation until the onset of mid-twentieth century civil rights movements.

The Black Church's Response to Segregation

As the Jim Crow system took hold in the South, black ministers responded strongly. First, they directly challenged new segregation laws by engaging in civil disobedience and boycotts. For example, when the city of Nashville, Tennessee, segregated its street cars in 1906, influential Baptist minister R. H. Boyd led a black boycott of the streetcars, even operating his own streetcar line for a time.

Second, black ministers sponsored a separate set of institutions to serve black Americans excluded from white establishments. The Congregationalists, Baptists, and Northern Methodists established schools in

RELIGION

Baptism on the Potomac River, Washington, D.C.

the South for African Americans during Reconstruction, but the AME, AME Zion, and Christian Methodist Episcopal (CME) bishops forged ahead to establish their own network of schools. The black denominations also developed their own publishing houses, which produced books and periodicals that were vital to the black community. Virtually every institution with ties to African American communities received some support from black churches.

Third, some black ministers believed that the civil rights retreats of the late nineteenth century should spur African Americans to leave the United States for a destination where their civil rights would be respected. A "Back to Africa" movement sought to enable black Americans to find a home where they could run governments, banks, and businesses without interference from whites. Thus Turner helped to organize a steamship line to carry black Americans back to Africa,

RELIGION

First Baptist Church, Washington, D.C.

and two shiploads of black immigrants sailed to Liberia in 1895 and 1896 as a result of his efforts.

Some black church leaders, such as CME bishop Lucius Holsey and AME bishop Richard Cain, held views similar to those advocated by Turner, but many more church leaders vigorously opposed Turner's program. Simultaneously, African missionary work continued to occupy the attention of black Americans at the end of the nineteenth century. Under the guidance of bishops Payne and Turner, for example, the AME Church maintained a strong missionary presence in Sierra Leone, Liberia, and South Africa.

Black Churches in the Twentieth Century

In the past 100 years, black religious life has become characterized by increased diversity. At the same time, traditional African American concerns, including the continuing quest for freedom and justice, have been not only maintained but strengthened.

Pentecostalism, which burst on the American scene in 1906, has become a major religious force within the black community. The Church of God in Christ, a Pentecostal denomination, has become the second largest black denomination in the United States. Meanwhile, the charismatic (or

Neo-Pentecostal) movement has revitalized many congregations within mainline black denominations.

The black nationalism of Turner survived in the work of such men as Marcus Garvey, Elijah Muhammad, and Malcolm X. There has been a spectacular rise of storefront churches, some of which were led by flamboyant showmen such as Father Divine and Sweet Daddy Grace. Each of these trends has been significantly aided by the black migrations from the South to the North, which greatly strengthened Northern black communities.

The Social Gospel Movement and Martin Luther King, Jr.

Many twentieth-century black ministers began preaching a "Social Gospel." One of the most famous was Reverdy Ransom of the AME Church, who was popular during the early 1900s. Social Gospellers emphasized societal sin (such as the starvation of children and the denial of human rights) and maintained that Christian repentance of these sins must be followed by concrete action. The Martin Luther King, Jr., was profoundly influenced by this Social Gospel movement.

Many black religious leaders in the 1960s thought that King's brand of social activism was too radical. One of King's most determined critics during the 1960s was Joseph H. Jackson, the conservative president of the National Baptist Convention of the U.S.A., Inc. The attempt by King's minister friends to remove Jackson as president of the Convention in 1960 and 1961 led to a **schism**, with King and his supporters forming a new denomination named the Progressive National Baptist Convention. King came under further criticism when, in 1967 and 1968, he made it clear that his belief in pacifism also led him to oppose American military involvement in Vietnam.

The Black Theology Movement

The "Black Theology" movement, which grew rapidly after King's assassination, attempted to redefine Christianity through the words and deeds of King, Malcolm X, and others. Albert Cleage, pastor of the Shrine of the Black Madonna in Detroit, argued that Jesus is a black messiah and that his congregation should follow the teachings of Jehovah, a black God. Claiming that "almost everything you have heard about Christianity is essentially a lie," Cleage preached that black liberation was at the core of the Christian gospels. In the 1980s black women including Jacquellyn Grant, Delores Williams, and Katie Cannon conceived "womanist" theologies that countered the triple oppression of race, class, and gender suffered by most black women.

Current Trends

While competing interests had weakened the overall influence of the black church by the early 1990s, it nevertheless remained the central institution in the black community. Many black churches are vigorously confronting such problems as drug abuse and homelessness that are visible symptoms of the increasing desperation of the black underclass. The First AME Church of Los Angeles sponsors a "Lock In" program, which on weekends presents anti-drug messages to youth. Similarly, many congregations have taken vigorous action against crack houses.

Parochial schools, feeding centers, and housing for senior citizens are also part of the black church's outreach to the black community.

Many black ministers have noted, however, the growing division of the African American community along lines of social class and have urged middle-class black Americans to give more generously to programs that aid the poor. James Cone, a leading black theologian, has stated that black churches need to devote less time and attention to institutional survival and more to finding ways to deal with such pressing issues as poverty, gang violence, and AIDS.

To meet such goals, black churches participate in a wide variety of **ecumenical** projects. The Congress of National Black Churches, a group of six black churches, continues to sponsor a variety of projects to improve the economic and social situation of the African American community. Partners in Ecumenism, a project of the National Council of Churches, has challenged white denominations to be more responsive to black concerns. At a grassroots level, African American churches are successfully joining forces to combat problems that are too large for any congregation to address alone. In Marks, Mississippi, for example, the Quitman County Development Organization has sponsored a Black Church Community and Economic Development Project. This organization has assisted church leaders in developing programs on teen pregnancy and parenting.

The spirit of cooperation has inspired individual denominations to explore merging or establishing close working relationships with other denominations with similar backgrounds and traditions. Black churches also have found themselves forced to address issues related to the racial tensions of the 1990s.

Leading black pastors in Los Angeles have condemned both the police brutality that was revealed in the Rodney King incident and the violence of inner-city rioters, while urging attention to the problems of inner-city residents. James Lawson of the Holman United Methodist Church stated that those who burned buildings during the 1992 Los Angeles riots were "responding to a society of violence, not simply a society of racism," and he therefore issued "a call to repent."

While many black Methodist and Baptist denominations are showing only limited membership growth, other black denominations are showing marked membership increases. Foremost among these are the Pentecostalist churches, whose lively worship and extensive social ministries are attracting members from all classes within the black community. The largest of these denominations, the Church of God in Christ, is now estimated to have more than three million members. Charismatic congregations within mainline black churches such as the AME Church are also thriving, and for similar reasons.

Other groups that have made large membership gains among African Americans include Roman Catholicism and Islam. More than 1,500,000 African Americans now belong to the Roman Catholic Church, which has worked hard in recent years to be sensitive to their needs. (Before the Civil War, black Catholics were confined largely to Maryland and Louisiana. However, Catholics

More than 1.5 million African Americans belong to the Roman Catholic Church. Pictured is Reverend George Clements giving communion

made greater efforts to convert African Americans after the Civil War. By the end of the nineteenth century, there were about 200,000 black Catholics in the United States.)

In many inner cities, the Roman Catholic Church has maintained parishes and schools in predominantly African American neighborhoods, although closings, mostly for financial reasons, are increasing in such **dioceses** as Detroit. Moreover, the Church has been receptive to some **liturgical** variation, allowing gospel choirs and African vestments (attire) for priests in black churches. Nevertheless, Roman Catholics confront some serious problems in serving black parishioners. Fewer than 300 of the 54,000 priests in the United States are black, meaning that some black congregations must be served by white priests. In 1989 George A. Stallings, Jr., a priest in Washington, D.C., broke away from Catholicism, arguing that the Catholic Church was still racist and did not do enough for its African American members.

Mainstream Islam, despite its own complex problems, has also made large gains in the United States. Of the six million Muslims in this country, one million are believed to be

RELIGION

Barbara Harris, the first female Anglican bishop

black. Most African American Muslims do not distinguish between people of different races and worship side by side with recent Muslim immigrants from Asia and Africa. Louis Farrakhan's Nation of Islam, however, which continues to follow Elijah Muhammad's black separatist teachings, continues to maintain a devoted following. Due to its very conservative stance on gender issues, Islam has proven to be more popular among black men than among black women.

The cause of gender equality continues to progress slowly in black churches. While two predominantly white denominations, the United Methodist and Protestant Episcopal Churches, have elevated black women to the rank of bishop in the past decade, none of the largest historically black denominations have done so. Nevertheless, women in some black churches are achieving ever-more powerful positions in the ministry. Vashti McKenzie, a former model, disc jockey, and radio program director, has recently been appointed pastor of the Payne Memorial AME Church, an "old-line" church in Baltimore. Her creative ministry, she says, is designed to "provide a message of hope for a hurting community." There are presently more than 600 female pastors in the AME Church.

Preaching the gospel faithfully in a way that also touches people's lives is the most

RELIGION

An African Methodist Episcopal (AME) congregation, 1948

important goal of black churches. In a recent survey, 22 percent of black clergy considered the greatest problem of the black church to be "lack of evangelism in fulfilling its religious role." Ministerial training and financial support is another area needing improvement in many black churches. There is no danger, however, that the black churches will lose sight of their many vital functions, both within the black community and in American society as a whole.

Black Denominations

African Methodist Episcopal (AME) Church

The AME Church was founded in 1816 at a conference convened in Philadelphia by Richard Allen, who was elected as its first bishop and who may be regarded as the first major leader of blacks in the United States. In the following years it grew throughout the North and Midwest. After the Civil War, the denomination expanded quickly throughout the South and the West.

The AME Church's 1989 membership was 2.2 million (about 1 million of whom lived in Africa and the Caribbean). The Church oversees about five thousand churches as well as six colleges and two seminaries. Payne Theological Seminary is located at Wilberforce, Ohio, at the site of the Church's oldest school, Wilberforce University. Turner

379

Theological Seminary is one of six schools that have joined to form the Interdenominational Theological Center in Atlanta.

African Methodist Episcopal Zion (AME Zion) Church

Another AME Church was founded in 1821 in New York City. James Varick was elected its first "superintendent"; the title of the presiding officer was later changed to bishop. In 1848 the word "Zion" was added to the name of this church in order to avoid confusion with that founded by Richard Allen. The AME Zion Church grew only slightly prior to 1860, but expanded quickly in such Southern states as North Carolina and Alabama after the Civil War.

As of 1989 the AME Zion Church had 1,300,000 members (100,000 of whom lived in Africa or the Caribbean) and 2,900 churches. The church supports two junior colleges, one regular college, and one seminary. Livingstone College, a four-year institution, and Hood Theological Seminary are both located in Salisbury, North Carolina.

African Orthodox Church

The African Orthodox Church was founded in 1921 by Archbishop George Alexander McGuire, once a priest in the Protestant Episcopal Church. McGuire was the chaplain for Marcus Garvey's United Negro Improvement Association, but Garvey soon rejected his chaplain's efforts to found a new denomination. This church is today an independent body adhering to an "orthodox" confession of faith. Its nearly 6,000 members worship in some 25 to 30 churches.

African Union First Colored Methodist Protestant Church, Inc.

This denomination was formed in 1866 by a merger of the African Union Church and the First Colored Methodist Protestant Church. The African Union Church traced its roots to a Union Church of Africans founded in 1813 by Peter Spencer in Wilmington, Delaware. Today, this denomination has more than 309 churches and a membership of about 8,000.

Apostolic Overcoming Holy Church of God

This Pentecostal denomination, originally known as the Ethiopian Overcoming Holy Church, was incorporated in Alabama in 1919. Evangelistic in purpose, it emphasizes purification, holiness, and the power of divine healing. As of 1975 it claimed 350 churches and about 100,000 members.

Black Jews

Several different groups in the past century have been known by this name. Included among these are the Commandment Keepers, founded in Harlem in 1919 by a Nigerian-born man known as "Rabbi Matthew"; the Church of God and Saints in Christ, founded in 1896 in Lawrence, Kansas, by William Crowdy; and the Church of God founded in Philadelphia by Prophet F. S. Cherry. In terms of doctrine, these groups share little more than a dislike of Christianity and an affection for the Old Testament. Some black Jews claim descent from the Falasha Jews of Ethiopia, who now reside in Israel. However, few black Jews are recognized as such by orthodox rabbis. The Church of God and Saints of Christ is probably the largest of these groups, with more than 200 churches and a membership of 38,000.

RELIGION

A black rabbi stands in front of his Bronx, New York, synagogue

Christian Methodist Episcopal (CME) Church

The CME Church, known until 1954 as the Colored Methodist Church, is the third largest black Methodist body in the United States. After the Civil War some black Methodist churches did not want to join the AME or AME Zion Churches; these churches successfully petitioned the Methodist Episcopal Church, South, for the right to form their own denomination, and the Colored Methodist Church was formed. The first CME General Conference was held at Jackson, Tennessee, in 1870. There the Church's first two bishops, William H. Miles and Richard Vanderhorst, were elected.

In 1989 the CME Church had about 900,000 members (of whom 75,000 were located overseas) and about 3,000 churches. It maintains five colleges as well as the Phillips School of Theology, a seminary which is part of the Interdenominational Theological Center in Atlanta.

Church of Christ (Holiness) Inc.

This denomination was organized by Bishop Charles Price Jones, a renowned and

RELIGION

African American churches remain strong, healthy institutions

prolific gospel song and hymn writer, in 1907. Some 160 churches and 9,300 members belong to this denomination, which upholds the possibility of sanctification and Christian perfection. The Holy Ghost is seen as a fundamental gift for each believer. The church operates Christ Missionary and Industrial College in Jackson, Mississippi.

Churches of God, Holiness

This denomination was organized by K. H. Burruss in Georgia in 1914. Membership in the group's 40-odd churches totals some 25,000.

Church of God in Christ

The Church of God in Christ (COGIC) was organized in 1897 by two former Baptist preachers, Charles H. Mason and C. P. Jones. It was initially strongest in Alabama, Mississippi, and Tennessee. Mason reorganized COGIC in 1907 when he and Jones parted on the issue of **speaking in tongues.** At that time, Mason was appointed "General Overseer and Chief Apostle" of the Church as well as its first bishop. It has subsequently expanded very rapidly throughout the United States, especially in black neighborhoods in the inner cities.

As of 1989 COGIC has about 3,700,000 members, many of whom are located in Africa and the Caribbean, and about 10,000 churches. It maintains bible colleges and a junior college, with plans for a university (All Saints University in Memphis). Its Charles H. Mason Theological Seminary is part of the Interdenominational Theological Center in Atlanta.

Fire Baptized Holiness Church

This church was organized on an interracial basis as the Fire Baptized Holiness Association in Atlanta, Georgia, in 1898. Its African American members formed the Fire Baptized Holiness Church in 1908. The church follows standard Pentecostalist doctrines on divine healing, speaking in tongues, and sanctification. As of 1958 it had about 50 churches and a membership of about 1,000.

Imani Temple African-American Catholic Congregation

The Imani Temple was founded in Washington, D.C., by George Augustus Stallings, Jr., a former Roman Catholic priest, in July 1989. The schism occurred when Stallings, in defiance of his archbishop, performed a mass based on an experimental rite currently being used in Zaire. This was the first schism from the Roman Catholic Church in the United States since 1904.

Stallings also voiced a number of criticisms of the Roman Catholic Church at the time of the schism, declaring: "There are not enough black priests, not enough black church members, and some of the relatively few black churches that exist are being closed and consolidated. The black experience and black needs are addressed minimally in church services and life." He also asserted that "we could no longer afford to worship white gods in black houses." Thirteen black American Catholic bishops issued a statement denouncing Stallings and accused him of expressing "personal disappointment [and] individually felt frustration" under the cover of charges of racism.

Black Catholic reactions to these developments were mixed. Many expressed sympathy for Stallings's concerns but were unwilling to leave the Roman Catholic Church. Stallings assumed the title of archbishop of Imani Temple in 1991, and at the same time ordained a woman to the priesthood of the African-American Catholic Congregation.

In forming his denomination, he has experienced some setbacks. Several formerly close associates split with Stallings in 1991, alleging a lack of fiscal accountability in the church and accusing him of taking his innovations too far. The denomination currently claims 3,500 members in 6 cities.

National Baptist Convention of America, Unincorporated

The National Baptist Convention of America was formed in 1915 as a result of a schism with the National Baptist Convention, U.S.A., Inc., over the issue of control of the denominational publishing house. In 1989 it listed 2,400,000 members and 7,800 churches. It has missions in Jamaica, Panama, and Africa, and supports 10 colleges.

National Baptist Convention of the U.S.A., Inc.

The National Baptist Convention was formed in 1895 through the union of three smaller church organizations, the oldest of

Elijah Muhammad

which had been founded only fifteen years earlier: the Baptist Foreign Mission Convention of the U.S.A.; the American National Baptist Convention; and the National Baptist Educational Convention of the U.S.A. The Convention incorporated itself after a dispute over the publishing house led to a schism in 1915.

The National Baptist Convention, Inc., as of 1989, had 7,500,000 members (100,000 of whom were in foreign countries) and more than 30,000 local churches.

National Primitive Baptist Convention of America

After the Civil War, black and white Primitive Baptists separated. It was not until 1907, however, that black Primitive Baptists formed the National Primitive Baptist Convention. Each congregation is independent and a decision by officials of a local church is final. In 1975 they listed a membership of 1,600,000 in 2,198 churches.

Nation of Islam

After the death of Elijah Muhammad in 1975, his son Warith D. Muhammad assumed leadership of the movement. Warith Muhammad dramatically shifted away from his father's teachings of black nationalism, stating that whites could become members. He sought to bring his movement into accord with Orthodox Islam, and he eventually succeeded, renaming the Nation of Islam as the World Community of Al-Islam in the West and then as the American Muslim Mission before the merger was accomplished.

Not all members of the Nation of Islam followed Warith Muhammad. The largest splinter group was headed by Louis Farrakhan, who had split from Muhammad by 1978 to reestablish the Nation of Islam on the basis of Elijah Muhammad's original black separatist teachings.

Progressive National Baptist Convention, Inc.

The Progressive National Baptist Convention, Inc., was formed in 1961 as a result of a schism in the National Baptist Convention of the U.S.A., Inc. The schism resulted from a dispute over leadership and strategy during the civil rights struggle. Martin Luther King, Jr., and others committed to such tactics as nonviolent civil disobedience left to form the new denomination. The convention's motto is "Unity, Service, Fellowship, and Peace."

The Convention has 1,200,000 members and 1,000 churches.

RELIGION

Haile Salassie

Rastafarians

Rastafarians regard Ethiopian Emperor Haile Selassie (1892-1975) as God. Jamaican-born black nationalist Marcus Garvey and Reggae musician Bob Marley are other historically well-known members of the Rastafarian faith.

Rastas differ on specific teachings, but they basically believe that they are descended from black Hebrews exiled in Babylon and therefore are true Israelites. They also believe that Haile Selassie (whose name before taking the throne was Lij *Ras Tafari* Makonnen) is the direct descendant of King Solomon and the Queen of Sheba, and that God is black.

Most white men, they believe, have been worshipping a dead god and have attempted to teach the blacks to do likewise. They hold that the Bible was distorted by King James and that the black race sinned and was punished by God with slavery. They view Ethiopia as Zion (the promised land), the Western world as Babylon (a corrupt land), and believe that one day they will return to Zion. They preach love, peace, and racial harmony but warn that **Armageddon** is fast approaching.

In addition, Rastas do not vote or drink alcohol; they regard marijuana as the holy herb, tend to be vegetarians, and wear their hair in long, uncombed plaits called dreadlocks. The hair is never cut, since it is considered part of the spirit, nor is it ever combed.

There are an estimated 50,000 Rastas in Britain and almost 1,000,000 in the United States, approximately 80,000 of whom live in New York City.

385

FURTHER READING

Aptheker, Herbert, ed., *A Documentary History of the Negro People in the United States,* New York: Carol Publishing Group, 1990.

Bennett, Lerone, *Before the Mayflower,* 6th ed., Chicago: Johnson Publishing Company, 1987.

Berry, Mary Frances, and John W. Blassingame, *Long Memory: The Black Experience in America,* New York and Oxford: Oxford University Press, 1982.

Billingsley, Andrew, *Climbing Jacob's Ladder: The Enduring Legacy of African-American Families,* New York: Simon & Schuster, 1992.

Bing, Léon, *Do or Die,* New York: HarperCollins Publishers, 1991.

Bogle, Donald, *Toms, Coons, Mulattoes, Mammies, and Bucks: An Interpretive History of Blacks in American Films,* New York: Continuum Publishing Company, 1989.

Clark, Joe, with Joe Picard, *Laying Down the Law: Joe Clark's Strategy for Saving Our Schools,* Washington, D.C.: Regnery Gateway, 1989.

Collins, Charles M., and David Cohen, eds., *The African Americans,* New York: Viking Studio Books, 1993.

Copage, Eric V., *Black Pearls: Daily Meditations, Affirmations, and Inspirations for African Americans,* New York: William Morrow, 1993.

Durham, Michael S., *Powerful Days: The Civil Rights Photography of Charles Moore,* New York: Stewart, Tabori & Chang, 1991.

Edwards, Audrey, and Craig K. Polite, *Children of the Dream: The Psychology of Black Success,* New York: Doubleday, 1992.

Franklin, John Hope, and Alfred A. Moss, Jr., *From Slavery to Freedom: A History of Negro Americans,* New York: McGraw Hill, 1988.

Haber, Louis, *Black Pioneers of Science and Invention,* San Diego: Harcourt Brace Jovanovich, 1987.

Hampton, Henry, and Steve Fayer, *Voices of Freedom: An Oral History of the Civil Rights Movement from the 1950s through the 1960s,* New York: Bantam, 1990.

Hardnett, Carolyn J., and Dawne A. Johnson, "Black Year in Review," *Emerge,* December/January 1994, pp. 55-60.

Harley, Sharon, et al., *The African American Experience: A History,* Englewood Cliffs, New Jersey: Simon & Schuster, 1992.

Haskins, James, *Black Music in America: A History through Its People,* New York: Crowell Junior Books, 1987.

Hughes, Langston, Milton Meltzer, and C. Eric Lincoln, *A Pictorial History of Blackamericans,* New York: Crown Publishers, 1983.

Johnson, John H., with Lerone Bennett, Jr., *Succeeding against the Odds,* New York: Warner Books, 1989.

Kimbro, Dennis, *Daily Motivations for African-American Success,* New York: Fawcett Columbine, 1993.

FURTHER READING

King, Anita, ed., *Quotations in Black,* Westport, Connecticut: Greenwood Press, 1981.

Low, W. Augustus, and Virgil A. Clift, *Encyclopedia of Black America,* New York: McGraw Hill, 1981.

Marsh, Carole S., *Black Trivia: The African-American Experience, A-to-Z!,* Decatur, Georgia: Gallopade Publishing Group, 1992.

Mullane, Deirdre, ed., *Crossing the Danger Water: Three Hundred Years of African-American Writing,* New York: Doubleday, 1993.

Pelz, Ruth, *Black Heroes of the Wild West,* Seattle: Open Hand Publishing, 1990.

Salley, Columbus, *The Black 100: A Ranking of the Most Influential African-Americans, Past and Present,* New York: Carol Publishing Group, 1993.

Shaw, Arnold, *Black Popular Music in America,* New York: Schirmer Books, 1986.

Thum, Marcella, *Hippocrene U.S.A. Guide to Black America: A Directory of Historic and Cultural Sites Relating to Black America,* New York: Hippocrene Books, 1991.

Westridge Young Writers Workshop, *Kids Explore America's African-American Heritage,* Santa Fe, New Mexico: John Muir Publications, 1992.

INDEX

A

Aaron, Hank 542, 544
Abbott, Robert Sengstacke 128, 474, 566
"ABC" 501
Abdalla, Mohammed Ahmed ibn 44
Abdul-Jabbar, Kareem 546
Abernathy, Ralph 13, 159, 289-291, 293
Abiel Smith School and Museum of Afro-American History 139
Abolition Movement 222, 296, 371
Abraham's Oak 531
Abyssinia 433
Abyssinian Baptist Church 144, 145
Acquired Immune Deficiency Syndrome (AIDS) 24, 329, 345
Act to Prohibit the Importation of Slaves (1807) 81
Act to Suppress the Slave Trade in the District of Columbia 85
Acts of Art Gallery 526
Adams, John Quincy 136
Adams Memorial Museum 179

The Addams Family 466
Adelina, Patti 512
Affirmative action 16, 313
Africa 21-54
Africa Bambaataa 503
Africa World Press 489
African American Museums Association 478
African American National Historic Site 139
African Ceremonial 438
African Civilization Society 249
African Free Schools 350
African Grove Theatre 431
African Lodge No. 459 282
African Meeting House 139
African Methodist Episcopal (AME) Church 134, 269, 282-283, 354, 369, 379, 486
African Methodist Episcopal Zion (AME Zion) Church 370, 380, 486
African National Congress 51
African Orthodox Church 380
African Party for the Independence of Guinea-Bissau and Cape Verde 26, 29

African Protestant Episcopal Church 222
African Union Church 369, 380
African Union First Colored Methodist Protestant Church, Inc. 380
Afrikaner 49, 51
Afro-American Historical and Cultural Museum 150
Afro-American Museum of Detroit 129
Afro-American Music Opportunities Association 515
Afro-American Symphony 513, 515
Afrocentrism 279
Agriculture 319
Aida 437
AIDS (Acquired Immune Deficiency Syndrome) 24, 329, 345
Aiello, Danny 460
Ailey, Alvin 438, 442
Ain't Misbehavin' 441
"Ain't That A Shame" 497
Akim Trading Company 250
Al-Amin, Jamil Abdullah (see H. Rap Brown)

389

INDEX

Albert, Donnie Ray 517
Alcoholism 346
Alcorn College 354
Alcorn State University 354
Aldridge, Ira 431
Alexander, Archie Alphonso 170
Alexander, Cheryl 441
Alexander, Erika 472
Alexander, John H. 561
Alexander, Marcellus 483
Alex Haley House 157
Alhambra Theatre 434
Alice Adams 452
Ali, Muhammad 7, 549, 578
Allen, Debbie 441, 443, 463
Allen, Richard 150, 222, 249, 268-269, 282-283, 366, 369-370, 379-380
Allensworth, Allen 171
Allensworth Colony 171
All God's Chillun' Got Wings 435
All in the Family 467-468
The All-Negro Hour 479
"All She Wants To Do Is Rock" 494
Almond, Edward M. 569
Alvin Ailey American Dance Center 442
Alvin Ailey American Dance Theater 429, 442
Alvin Ailey Repertory Ensemble 442
"Amazing Grace" 368
AME Book Concern 486
Amen 470
American Anti-Slavery Society 223, 284
American Baptist Home Mission Society 355
American Colonization Society 30, 222, 246, 249, 284, 370-371
American Freedmen's Aid Union 352

American Missionary Association 355
American Muslim Mission 384
American National Baptist Convention 384
American Negro Academy 170, 356, 488
American Negro Theater 436
American Revolution 218
The American Society of Free Persons of Color 269
American Urban Radio Network 479
American Visions 478
Ames, Alexander 140
AME Sunday School Union and Publishing House 486
AME Zion Book Concern 486
AME Zion Churches 283
Amin Dada, Idi 46
Amistad Murals 153
Amistad 136
Amos Fortune Grave Site 142
Amos, John 467
Amos 'N' Andy 464
Amsterdam News 145, 475
Anderson, Eddie 451-452
Anderson, James H. 145, 475
Anderson, James, Jr. 578
Anderson, Jo 534
Anderson, Marian 169, 490, 513
Anderson, Thomas 436
Andersonville Prison 161
Angelou, Maya 75, 121-123, 418, 427, 439
Anglican Society for the Propagation of the Gospel 366
Angola 23, 35, 39
Anguilla 56, 64
Anjouan 53
Anna Lucasta 436
Annie Allen 417
Ansel Clark Grave Site 135
Antigua 56, 64

Anti-Slavery Record 223
Apartheid 51-52
Apollo Theater 145-146, 438
Apostolic Overcoming Holy Church of God 380
Appo, William 512
Arceneaux, Andrea 485
Argentina 55
Aristide, Jean-Bertrand 56, 63
Armstrong, Henry 549
Armstrong, Louis 148, 450, 505-507, 511
Aronson, Arnold 289
Art Ensemble of Chicago 511
Arthur, Chester 561
Aruba 57, 64
Asbury, Francis 137, 367
Asbury Methodist Episcopal Church 137
Ashantis 29
Ashe, Arthur 542-543, 552, 555
Associates in Negro Folk Education 355, 488
Association for the Advancement of Creative Musicians 511
Association for the Study of Afro-American History and Literature 488
Association for the Study of Afro-American Life and History 356
Association for the Study of Negro Life and History 167, 356, 488
Atlanta University 161, 354
Atlanta University Press 487
The Atlanta Daily World 476
Atlanta Voice 476
"Atlantic Coastal Line" 498
Attucks, Crispus 3, 4, 140, 557
Augin, Charles 441
Augusta Institute 354
"Aunt Clara" Brown's Chair 173

390

INDEX

Autobiography of Miss Jane Pittman 469
Avery, Margaret 458
Ayler, Albert 510

B

Back to Africa movement 288, 373
Bahama Islands 58
Bailey, Deford 498
Bailey, Pearl 435
Baker, David 511, 515
Baker, Josephine 434
Bakongo 35, 39
Baldwin, James 145, 425, 427, 439
Baldwin, Maria 141
Baldwin, Ruth Standish 287
Baldwin, William H. 287
Ballard, Hank 496
Ballou, Charles C. 565
Baltimore Afro-American 474-475
Bambara, Toni Cade 463
Bandanna Land 433
Banker's Fire Insurance Company 322
Bannarn, Henry 522
Banneker, Benjamin 76, 137-138, 165, 533, 534
Banneker-Douglass Museum 137
Banneker's Almanac 533
Bannister, Edward Mitchell 520
Bantu 26, 37-39, 44
Baptist Foreign Mission Convention of the U.S.A. 384
Baraka, Imamu Amiri 15, 145, 426, 439, 460
Barbados 55, 58
Barber-Scotia College 354
Barbuda 56, 64
Barkley, Charles 542, 546
Barnett, Neema 463

Barrow, Willie 294, 328
Barry, Marion 291
"Bars Fight" 417
Barthe, Richmond 522, 530-531
Baseball 543
Basie, Count 493, 507
Basketball 546
Basquiat, Jean-Michel 524
Basutoland 49
Bates, Daisy 356, 359
Battle, Hinton 441, 444
Baylor, Elgin 554
A Bayou Legend 517
Beacon Hill 139
"Beale Street Blues" 159
Beale Street Historic District 158
Beard, Andrew 535
Beard, Matthew (Stymie) 449
Bearden, Romare 523, 528, 531
Beatty, Tally 442
Beauford Delaney 527
Bebop 508
Bechet, Sidney 506
Beckwourth, Jim 172, 174, 178, 180
Beckwourth Pass 172
Beckwourth Trail 178
Bedouin, King 40
Belafonte, Harry 436, 453-454
Belasco Theater 438
Belize 68
Bell, Alexander Graham 538
Bell, Thomas 168
Beloved 418, 421
Belton, Sharon Sayles 276
Benedict College 354
Benezet, Anthony 350
Benin 24, 33, 214
Benjamin Banneker Boundary Stone 165
Benjamin Banneker Marker 138
Benjamin, Eli 573
Benjamin, Fred 444
Benny, Jack 451

Benson, Al 495
Berber 32
Bergon, Flora Baston 512
Bermuda 58
"Bernadette" 501
Berry, Chuck 497
Best, Willie "Sleep 'n Eat" 450
Bethel African Methodist Episcopal Church 222, 269, 366
Bethune-Cookman College 159, 169, 354
Bethune, Mary McLeod 9, 160, 167, 169, 274, 354
Bethune Museum and Archives 167
Bethune, Thomas "Blind Tom" Green 430, 511
BET News 485
Betsimisaraka 53
Beulah M. Davis Collection 138
Beverly Hills Cop 445, 458
Beverly Hills Cop II 458
Bickerstaff, Bernie 554
Biddle University 354
Biggers, John 523
Billingsley, Andrew 314, 330
Billops, Camille 528
"Bird on a Wire" 498
Birth of the Blues 452
The Birth of a Nation 448
Birthright 446
Black Power movement 291
Black Aesthetics Movement 425
Black American 476
Black Arts Movement 425
Black Birds 434
Black Cabinet 9, 274
Black Civil War Veterans' Memorial 166
Black Classic Press 489
Black Codes 228
Black Codes of Mississippi (1865) 92
Black Composers Series 515

391

INDEX

Black Enterprise 328, 473, 478
Black Entertainment Television 473, 485
Black Families in White America 334
Black Family 478
"Black Family Summit" 17
Black Faneuil Hall 139
Black Filmmakers Hall of Fame 449
Black Heritage Trail 139
Black History Month 167
Black Is the Color of My TV Tube 481
Black Jews of Harlem 251
Black Leadership Forum 277
Black Magic 429
Black Muslims 7, 11, 13, 37, 252, 377
Black nationalism 8, 10, 245, 375
Black Nativity 440
Black Panther Manifesto 112
Black Panther Party for Self-Defense 11, 13, 14, 112-113, 236, 291-292
Black Patti 512
Black Perspectives on the News 483
Black Regiment Memorial of the Battle of Rhode Island 151
Black Star Line 288
Black Stars 477
Black Swan 512
Black Theology movement 375
Black Women in American Bands and Orchestras 513
Blackbirds of 1928 434
Blackboard Jungle 453
Blackburn, Robert 522
Black Nationalism movement 245-254
The Blacks 439
Blackwell, David H. 533

Blair, Henry 535
Blair, Mary 435
Blake, Eubie 434
Blanche K. Bruce House 167
Bland, James A. 150, 432
Blanshard, Terence 510
Blanton, Jimmy 508
Bledsoe, Jules 435
Bledsoe, Tempestt 472
Blow, Kurtis 503
"Blueberry Hill" 497
Blue Flames 495
Blues 490
Blues for Mr. Charlie 439
The Bluest Eye 420
Bluff City News 479
Bluford, Guion 538
Blyden, E. W. 249-250, 253
Body and Soul 449
Boer Wars 51
Boley Historic District 179
Bolling v. *Sharpe* 359
Bonaire 57, 64
Bond, Julian 232, 291
Bond, Margaret 515
Bonds, Barry 545
Bonet, Lisa 472
Bontemps, Arna 425
Booker T. Washington Monument 154, 170
Booker T. Washington National Monument 167
Boone, John William 512
Bootee, Duke 503
Bootsy's Rubber Band 502
Borde, Percival 438
Bornu 33
Boston Guardian 474
Boston Massacre 140
Botswana 49
Bowe, Riddick 550, 551
Bowers, Thomas 512
Boxer, David 532
Boxing 549

Boyd, Richard Henry 372, 486
Boyle, Robert 318
Boyz N the Hood 448, 461
Brac, Cayman 60
Braddock, Jim 130
Bradford, Alex 440, 441
Bradford, William 141
Bradley, Ed 482, 484
Bradley, Thomas 16
Bragg Smith Grave Site and Memorial 162
Braun, Carol Moseley 17, 19, 243, 267-268, 280-281, 305
Brazil 25, 70, 72
"Brer Rabbit, Brer Fox, and the Tar Baby" 419
Brides of Funkenstein 502
Bridge, Edmund Pettis 153
Bridgewater, Dee Dee 441
Briggs-Hall, Austin 436
Briggs v. *Elliott* 359
British Togoland 29
British Virgin Islands 56, 59
Brockington, Horace 530
Brokaw, Tom 243
Brooke, Edward W. 112, 268
Brooks, Gwendolyn 417, 425
Brooks, William Henry 285
Brotherhood of Sleeping Car Porters and Maids 290, 566
Brown, Ann 434
Brown, "Aunt Clara" 173
Brown, Buster 444
Brown, Charlotte Hawkins 353
Browne, Roscoe Lee 439, 440
Brown, Henry 429, 431
Brown, H. Rap (Jamil Abdullah Al-Amin) 291, 232, 291
Brown, James 426, 495, 499, 501
Brown, Jesse 281
Brown, Jim 548
Brown, John 133, 143-144, 170, 176-177
Brown, Linda 107, 177, 265

INDEX

Brown, Morris 370
Brown, Morris, Jr. 512
Brown, Ronald H. 17, 19, 280
Brown, Roy 494
Brown, Sterling 488
Brown, Tony 473, 483, 484
Brown v. *Board of Education of Topeka, Kansas* 11, 107, 177, 195, 228, 232, 256-257, 265-266, 274, 286, 350, 356, 359
Brown, William 517
Brown, William Wells 417
Brown, Wilson 156
Bruce, Blanche K. 133, 167, 268
Bruce, John E. 250, 355
Brunson, Dorothy 483
Bryan, Andrew 163, 368
Bryant, Linda 527
Bryant, William Cullen 352
Bubbles, John 435
Buck Benny Rides Again 451
Buffalo Soldiers 560
Buganda 46
Bunche, Ralph J. 9, 131, 149, 267, 488
Bunker Hill Monument 139
Burke, Selma 518
Burke, Solomon 499
Burleigh, Harry T. 149
Burns, Francis 370
Burroughs, Margaret 528
Burroughs, Nannie Helen 353
Burrows, Stephen 526
Burr, Seymour 140
Burruss, K. H. 382
Burton, LeVar 470
Burundi 43
Bush, George 119-120, 261, 565
Business 315-328
Bussey, Charles M. 575
Butler, Jo 527
Butler, Octavia 428
Butterbeans and Susie 438
Butts, Claudia 279

By Any Means Necessary: The Trials and Tribulations of the Making of Malcolm X 447
Bynoe, Peter C. B. 555

C

Cabin in the Sky 435, 452-453
Cabin, Mayhew 177
Cabral, Luis 29
Cadoria, Sherian Grace 557
Cain, Richard 374
Caldwell, James 140
Calloway, Cab 450, 493
Cambridge, Godfrey 439, 444
Cameroon 26
Campbell, Clive 503
Campbell, E. Simms 524
Campbell, Joan Salmon 366
Campbell, Sally 178
Canada 73
Cannon, Katie 375
Capers, Virginia 441
Cape Verde 26, 29
Caribbean 56
Caribbean basin 55
Carmen 442
Carmen Jones 435, 453-454
Carmichael, Stokely 13-14, 232, 236, 291-292
Carney, William H. 140, 560
Carroll, Diahann 458, 464, 466
Carroll, Vinette 440
Carr, Patrick 140
"Carry Me Back to Old Virginny" 150
Carter, Benny 507
Carter G. Woodson House 167
Carter, Jimmy 278
Carter, Nell 441
Carver, George Washington 154, 156, 175, 535, 539
Car Wash 444
Cary, Lott 370

Cary, Mary Ann Shadd 169
The Cascades 157
Casey Jones Railroad Museum 158
Catlett, Elizabeth 528-529
Catlett, Mary 368
Catlett, Sid 507
Cato 3
Cayman Islands 60
Cay, Samana 58
Ceasar, Adolph 440
Cedras, Raoul 63
Center for Black Music Research 516
Center for Training Entrepreneurship (CTE) 323
Central African Republic 36-38
Central City, Colorado 173
Central High School (Little Rock, Arkansas) 108, 154, 155
Chad 36-38
Chamberlain, Wilt 546
Chameleon Street 462
Chance, Cathy 530
Chapelle Administration Building 164
Charismatic movement 374, 376
Charity 430
Charles Alston, Charles 521, 523
Charles H. Mason Theological Seminary 383
Charles, Ray 496, 497
Charles Richard Drew House 165
Charles, Suzette 17
Charlotte Forten Grimké House 168
Charlton, Cornelius H. 575
Chavis, Benjamin 287, 337
Chavis, John 163, 371
Checole, Kassahun 489
Chehalis County Museum 180
Cherry, F. S. 380
Chesnutt, Charles W. 417, 423

393

INDEX

Chicago Defender 128, 474, 476, 479, 564, 566
Chicago South Side Community Art Center 522
Chicago Tribune 476
Childress, Alice 436
Childress, Alvin 436
A Child's Story of Dunbar 488
Chisholm, Shirley 11, 16, 267-269
Chocolate Dandies 434
"Choice of Color" 498
Christ Missionary and Industrial College 382
Christian, Charlie 508
Christian Methodist Episcopal (CME) Church 373, 381
Christophe, Henri 62
Christy Minstrels 432
Chuck, Berry 497
Chuck D 305, 503
Churches of God, Holiness 382
Church of Christ (Holiness) Inc. 381
Church of God and Saints in Christ 380, 486
Church of God in Christ 366, 374, 376, 382
Church of God in Christ Publishing House 486
Cinqué Gallery 528
Cinqué, Joseph 136, 528
City of Richmond v. *Croson* 324
Civil disobedience 13
Civil Rights Act (1866) 93, 228
Civil Rights Act (1875) 227, 257-258
Civil Rights Act (1957) 289
Civil Rights Act (1960) 289
Civil Rights Act (1964) 11, 13, 111-112, 235, 257, 277, 289
Civil Rights Act (1990) 119
Civil Rights Act (1991) 119
Civil Rights Cases 260

Civil Rights Memorial 152
Civil Rights Movement 8, 227-244, 245-254
Civil War 74, 225, 557
The Clansman 448
Clark, Ansel 135
Clark-Atlanta University 161, 354, 441
Clark College 161
Clarke, Kenny 508
Clark, Joe 363
Clark, Mark 236, 292
Clark, William 175, 177, 179
Claude McKay Residence 147
Clay, Henry 246
Cleage, Albert 375
Cleaver, Eldridge 236, 292
Clements, George 376-377
Cleveland Gazette 474
Clifton, Nat "Sweetwater" 546
Climbing Jacob's Ladder 331
Clinton, Bill 19, 121, 243, 280-281, 314, 336, 418
Clinton, George 501
Clorinda: The Origin of the Cakewalk 149, 433
Clotel; or, The President's Daughter 417
CME Publishing House 486
Coachman, Alice 551
Coalition Against Blaxploitation 456
Coates, Paul 489
Coburn, Titus 140
Codrington, Christopher 56
Coffey, Alvin Aaron 172
Cohen, Leonard 498
Coker, Daniel 370
Coker, Gylbert 529
"Cold Sweat" 499
Cole, Bob 432, 433
Cole, Nat "King" 490
Coleman, Ornette 509, 515
Coleridge-Taylor, Samuel 515

Coles, Honi 444
Coles, Kim 472
Collins, Janet 438
Collins, Marva 361
Colombia 72
Colonel Robert Gould Shaw Monument 140
Colorado Pioneers Association 173
Colored Methodist Episcopal Church 372, 486
The Color Purple 458
Coltrane, John 426, 509-511
Columbus, Christopher 1, 2, 56, 58, 65, 67, 70, 72-73, 216
Coming to America 445
Commandment Keepers 380
Committee for the Improvement of Industrial Conditions Among Negroes in New York 287
Committee on Civil Rights 289
Committee on Urban Conditions Among Negroes 287
Commodores 501, 502
Comoros 52
Cone, James 376
Conference of Prince Hall Grand Masters 282
Congo 36-39
Congressional Black Caucus 242, 277, 279, 282
Congress of National Black Churches 376
Congress of Racial Equality (CORE) 232, 288-290
The Conjure Woman 417
Connell, Pat 482
Connelly, Marc 435
Connor, Aaron J. R. 512
Constitution House 152
Constitution of the United States 4, 257
Contemporary Craft Center 528
Conwill, Houston 527

INDEX

Cooke, Sam 495-496
Cookman Institute 354
Cook, Will Marion 149, 433
Cooper, Anna 372
Cooper, Chuck 546
Cooper, Jack L. 478
Cooper v. *Aaron* 266
Coppin, Frances Jackson 372
Cordero, Roque 515
Cornish, Samuel 223, 473, 476
Coronado, Francisco 178
Cortes, Hernán 2
Cortor, Eldzier 528
Cosby, Bill 305, 327, 444, 460, 464-465, 470
The Cosby Show 327, 463-464, 470
Costa Rica 70
Côte d'Ivoire (see Ivory Coast)
Cotton Club 450, 507
Cotton Comes to Harlem 456, 466
Counter, S. Allen 138
Cowper, William 368
Cozy Cove 435
Craig, Walter F. 512
Crawford, George Williamson 488
Credo 515
The Creole Show 432
Crichlow, Ernest 528
Crisis 286, 356, 423-424, 476
Crispus Attucks Monument 140
Crockett, Phyllis 485
Crooklyn 461
Crosby, Mattie 170
Crosswhite, Adam 132
Crosswhite Boulder 132
Crowdy, William 380
Crummell, Alexander 170, 223, 249-250, 270, 356, 488
Cry 442
"Crying in the Chapel" 495
Cry the Beloved Country 453

Cuba 60
Cuffe, Paul 10, 141-142, 246, 249, 284
Cullen, Countee 424
Culp, Robert 465
Cunningham, Randall 549
Curaçao 57, 64

D

da Gama, Vasco 45
"Daddy Rice" 432
Dahomey 24
The Daily Challenge 476
The Daily Drum 481
Daily World 476
Daley, Richard 127
Dance Theater of Harlem 442, 443
Dandridge, Dorothy 453-454
Daniel "Chappie" James Aerospace Center 154
Daniel Hale Williams House 125
Daniel, Payne 354
Daniels, Billy 441
Darnell, D. S. B. 354
Dash, Julie 446, 448, 463
Daughters of the American Revolution 169
Daughters of the Dust 448, 463
David Harum 451
Davis, Alonzo 528
Davis, Benjamin O., Sr. 9, 557, 567
Davis, Dale 528
Davis, Gary 492
Davis, Jefferson 225
Davis, Miles 490, 509
Davis, Ossie 436, 440, 441, 456, 466, 481
Davis, Rodney M. 578
Davis, Sammy, Jr. 440-441
Davis v. *Prince Edward County School Board* 359

Day, Tom 163
Daytona Normal and Industrial Institute for Girls 169, 354
"Deadwood Dick" 179
DeBarge 501
Declaration of Independence 4, 76, 86
Dede, Edmond 512
Deep River 150
Dee, Ruby 436, 437
The Defiant Ones 453
DeFrantz, Anita 552
DeKlerk, F. W. 52
de la Beckwith, Byron 266
Delaney, Benford 523
Delany, Martin R. 10, 249, 270
Delany, Samuel 428
de Lavallade, Carmen 444
DeLoatch, Gary 442
Democratic National Convention (1988) 18
Denmark, James 527
Denmark Vesey Conspiracy 219
Denmark Vesey House 164
de Paur, Leonard 517
DePriest, James 516
DePriest, Oscar 127
Derricks, Cleavant 441
de Saint Georges, Chevalier 515
DeShazor, Jacqueline 322
DeShields, Andre 441
Dessalines, Jean Jacques 62
Detroit News 482
Detroit riots 14
Deuce Coupe 524
Devine, Loretta 441
Dexter Avenue Baptist Church 152
Diary of an African Nun 463
A Different World 463, 472
Diff'rent Strokes 469
Dillard, James 155
Dinkins, David 17, 276
Dixon, Alan 280

395

INDEX

Dixon, Ivan 437
Dixon, Lucille 516
Dixon, Thomas 448
Djibouti 40
Do the Right Thing 459, 503
Dominica 60
Dominican Republic 61, 62
Domino, Antoine "Fats" 497
Dominoes 495
Donaldson, Ray 548
Don't Bother Me, I Can't Cope 441
Doo-wop 495
Dorsey, Thomas A. 490-492
Douglas, Aaron 521-523
Douglas, Buster 550
Douglas, John Thomas 512
Douglass, Frederick 1, 4, 8, 85, 137-138, 149, 168, 216, 223, 250, 268, 270-271, 284, 371, 422, 473
Douglass, Sarah Mapp 223
Douglas, Stephen A. 128
Dove, Ulysses 442
Downbeat 509
Downing, Big Al 498
Dozier, Lamont 501
The Drama of King Shotaway 429, 431
Dream Girls 441
Dred Scott v. *Sandford* 249, 257-258, 271
Drew, Richard Drew 165, 541
Drexler, Clyde 546
Drifters 491
Driskell, David C. 532
Drug use 344, 346
Du Bois, W. E. B. 8, 75, 101, 141, 229-230, 250, 262, 272-273, 284, 331, 356, 358, 424, 476, 487, 522
Dubose Hayward House 164
Dudley, S. H. 433
Dukakis, Michael 17, 117

Duke, Bill 448, 462
Dunbar, Paul Laurence 356, 417, 422, 433
Duncan, Todd 434, 435
Duncanson, Robert 520
Dunham, Katherine 435-437, 442
Durham Business and Professional Chain 323
Durham, North Carolina 321
Durham Realty and Insurance Company 322
Durham Textile Mill 322
Du Sable, Jean Baptiste Pointe 4, 125, 126, 316
Du Sable Museum of African-American History and Art 125, 528
The Dutchman 439
Dutton, Charles 472
Duvall, Cheryl 485
Dvorak, Antonin 149
Dwinddie Colored Quartet 493
Dykes, Eva B. 533

E

Earth, Wind, and Fire 501
East Side, West Side 464
Eatonville, Florida 160
Ebenezer Baptist Church 161, 289
Ebony 327, 476-479
Ebony and Topaz 488
Economic Opportunity Act 277
Economics 305-314, 315-328
The Economic Status of the Negro 487
Ecuador 72
Ecumenism 376
Eddie Murphy Productions 445
Edelman, Marian Wright 343
Edge of the City 453
Edison, Thomas 538

Edmonson, William 524, 531
Education 349-364
Edward Kennedy "Duke" Ellington Birthplace 168
Edward Kennedy "Duke" Ellington Residence 147
Edwards, Stoney 498
Eisenhower, Dwight D. 108, 154
El Morro castle 65
El Pueblo Museum 174
Elaw, Zilpha 371
Elder, Lonnie, III 437
Elders, Joycelyn 17, 281
Eldridge, Roy 506-507
Elijah McCoy Home Site 129
Elise, Sister 516, 517
Eller, Carl 548
Ellington, Edward Kennedy "Duke" 147, 149, 168, 442, 507-508, 510-511
Ellison, Ralph 425-426
Ellis, William 250
Elmer Brown 521
Elmwood Cemetery 166
Emancipation Act 257
Emancipation Proclamation 5, 8, 90-91, 143, 216, 225
Emancipation Statue 168
Embry, Wayne 555
Emerson, John 132, 157, 257
Emlen Tunnel 548
Emmett, Dan 432
The Emperor Jones 136, 435, 437, 451
The Empire Strikes Back 446
Employment 305-314
Encyclopedia Africana 356
Endeavor 540
English, Charlotte Moore 483
Ennis, William P., Jr. 569
Entrepreneurship 315-328
Equatorial Guinea 37
Eritrea 40

396

Eritrean People's Liberation Front 40
Erving, Julius "Dr. J" 546
Espy, Mike 280
Essence 473, 478
Estevanico 1, 2, 74, 178
Ethiopia 22, 40, 41
Ethiopian Minstrels 432
Evans, Estelle 436
"An Evening Thought: Salvation by Christ with Penitential Cries" 417
Evers, Medgar 266
Ewe 34
Ewing, Patrick 546
Ex parte Virginia 165
Executive Order No. 8802 (1941) 106
Executive Order No. 9981 (1948) 106
Executive Order No. 10730 (1957) 108
The Exile 446, 449
Exodus of 1879 228
Exodusters 176, 297
Experience; or How to Give a Northern Man a Backbone 417
Extended families 334
Eyes on the Prize 484

F

Face the Nation 481
Fagan, Garth 444
Fair Housing Act (1968) 289
Faison, George 442
Falana, Lola 441
Famous Flames 499
Fanti 29
Fard, W. D. 7, 252
Farmer, Jackie 484
Farmer, James 288, 290
Farrakhan, Louis 253-254, 378, 384

Faso, Burkina 25
Father Augustine Tolton Grave Site 128
Father Divine 375
Faubus, Orval 108
Faubus, Orville 154
Fauset, Jessie 424
Fear of a Black Planet 503
Federal Theater Project 436
Feldman, Nita 444
Fences 440
Ferris, William 250, 532
Fetchit, Stepin 438, 450-451
Fête Noire 443
Fields, Kim 472
Fields, Mary 177
Fifteenth Amendment 94, 225, 227, 257-258, 318
Fifth Amendment 359
54th Massachusetts Infantry Regiment 140, 150, 161, 559
"Fight the Power" 503
Film 446-463
Fine Art 518-532
Fire Baptized Holiness Church 383
Firebird 443
First African Baptist Church 368, 369
First Baptist Church 374
First Black School 180
First Church of Christ 136
First Colored Methodist Protestant Church 380
First Parish Church 137
Fishburne, Laurence 440
Fisher, John 172
Fisk Jubilee Singers 491
Fisk University 159, 354
Fisk University Press 487
Fiske, Pomp 140
The Fist 130
Fitzgerald, Ella 506
Five Blind Boys from Mississippi 493

Five Guys Named Moe 441
The Five Heartbeats 462
Five Royales 495
Fletcher, Dusty 438
The Flip Wilson Show 467
Flipper, Henry Ossian 561
Floyed, Alpha 517
Food Stamp Program 312
Football 547
Foote, Julia A. J. 372
For Colored Girls Who Have Considered Suicide/When the Rainbow Is Enuf 440
Ford, Barney 173
Ford, Carl 440
Forrest, Edwin 432
Forster, James 318
Fort Buford State Historic Site 178
Fort Clatsop National Memorial 179
Fort Des Moines Provisional Army Officer Training School 128
Fort Douglas Military Museum 180
Forten, Charlotte 223
Forten, James 151, 246
Fort Gadsen 160
Fort Manuel Marker 177
Fort Snelling 157
Fort Snelling State Historical Park 132
Fortune, Amos 142
Fortune, T. Thomas 143, 474
Fort Union National Historic Site 178
Fort Washakie Blockhouse 181
48 Hours 445, 457
Foster, Gloria 439
Foster, William 446
Fourteenth Amendment 93, 97, 225, 227-229, 257-259, 266, 318, 357, 359

INDEX

Four Tops 130, 501
Foxx, Redd 438, 444, 466
Frances Ellen Watkins Harper House 150
Franklin and Armfield Office 164
Franklin, Aretha 498-499
Franks, Gary 279
Franzel, Carlotta 435
Fraunces, Samuel 147
Fraunces Tavern 147
Frazier, E. Franklin 331, 355, 487
Frazier, Joe 549
Frederick Douglass House 168
Frederick Douglass Institute 529
Frederick Douglass Monument 138, 149
Free African Societies 248
Free African Society 150, 222, 227, 268, 282-283, 366
Free Haven 143
The Free Negro Family 487
Freedmen's Bureau 350, 352
Freedom National Bank 145, 324
Freedom's Journal 223, 249, 270, 473, 476
Freeman 479
Freeman, Al, Jr. 439
Freeman, Morgan 458
Freeman, Paul 515
Freire, Helena 515
Frémont, John C. 558
French Guiana 72
The Fresh Prince of Bel-Air 472
Friendly Society 246
Friends of Johnny Mathis 282
Front for Liberation of Mozambique (FRELIMO) 47
Frost, Robert 121
Fugitive Slave Act (1850) 249
Fuller, Charles 439
Fuller, Meta Warrick 520, 521
Fuller Products Company 327-328

Fuller, S. B. 327
Funkadelic 501
Furious Five 503
Futch, Eddie 551
Fye, Samba 158

G

Gable, Clark 452
Gabon 36-38
Gaines, Lloyd 263-264, 357
Gaither, Barry 532
Gaither, Edmond Barry 528
Gambia 28
Gandhi, Mohandas K. 7, 289
Gangs 337
Gantt-Blackwell Fort 174
Garnet, Henry Highland 10, 223, 249, 270, 371
Garrison Marker and Bennington Museum 152
Garrison, William Lloyd 151, 152, 223, 352
Garrison, Zina 552
Garvey, Amy Jacques 489
Garvey, Marcus 8, 10, 102, 245, 250-251, 253, 287-288, 375, 380, 385
Gates, Henry Louis, Jr. 305, 313, 418-419, 532
Gaye, Marvin 130, 501
Gebhart v. Belton 359
General Hag's Skeezag 439
Genet, Jean 439
George, David 368
George, R. S. 322
George, U. M. 322
George Washington Carver Birthplace and National Monument 156
George Washington Carver Foundation 154
George Washington Carver Homestead 175

George Washington Carver Museum 154
George Washington Park 180
Gershwin, George 164, 434
Ghana 21, 22, 28, 32, 35, 213
Ghent, Henri 530
Ghost 458
Gibbs, Marla 468, 470
Gibson, Althea 542, 551, 552
Gibson, Truman K., Jr. 570
Gillespie, Dizzy 508
Gilpin, Charles 435
Giovanni, Nikki 417, 427
"The Girl Can't Help It" 497
Giselle 443
Giuliani, Rudolph 276
Glanville, Maxwell 436
Glory 161, 559
Glover, Danny 458
"Go Down Moses" 491
Go Tell It on the Mountain 425
"God's Gonna Cut You Down" 491
God's Step Children 449
Goines, Donald 428
Goldberg, Whoopi 305, 458
Gold Coast 29, 35
Golden Boy 441
Gold Mining Camp 172
Gone with the Wind 11, 446, 452
"Good Golly Miss Molly" 497
"Good Rocking Tonight" 494
Good Times 467-468
Goode, Mal 481-483
Goode, Sarah E. 533
Gooding, Henry 161
Goodin, Prince 135
Goodman, Benny 507, 508
Goodwyn, Morgan 350
Gordone, Charles 439
Gordy, Berry, Jr. 130, 328, 499, 501
Gore, Al 281
Gorleigh, Rex 528

Gospel 490
Gospel Starlighters 495
Gossett, Louis, Jr. 436, 437, 439, 441, 458, 470
Graham, Gordon 485
Graham, Larry 501
Graham, Robert 130
Granary Burying Ground 141
Grand Cayman 60
Grand Comore 53
Grand Ole Opry 498
Grandmaster Flash and The Three MCs 503
Granger, Lester B. 287
Granny Maumee 433
Grant, Cecil 494
Grant, Jacquellyn 375
Grant, Micki 441
Grant, Ulysses S. 4
Gravely, Samuel R. 573
Graves, Earl G. 328, 478
Gray, Samuel 140
Great Plains Black Museum 177
Great Society 312, 338
The Great White Hope 439
Greenburgh, Jack 290
Green, Chuck 444
Green, Dennis 549, 555
Greene, "Mean" Joe 548
Greene, Nathanael 151
Greenfield, Elizabeth Taylor 512
Green Pastures 436
Green, Paul 435
Greenwood, L. C. 548
Gregory, Dick 444
Gregory, Frederick 538
Grenada 62
Grenadines 66
Grier, Rosey 548
Griffith, D. W. 448
Griggs v. *Duke Power Company* 266
Grosvenor, Vertamae 485
Guadeloupe 62

The Guardian 142
Guatemala 70
Guess Who's Coming to Dinner? 454
Guillaume, Robert 441
Guinea 22, 29
Guinea-Bissau 29
Gumbel, Bryant 484
Gunn, Moses 439, 440
Guy, Edna 437
Guy, Jasmine 472
Guyana 72
Guzman, Jessie Parkhurst 487

H

Hagar in the Wilderness 520
Hagler, Marvin 550
Haile Selassie I 40-41, 385
Haines Normal and Industrial Institute 353
Haiti 61, 62
Hale, Edward Everett 352
Haley, Alex 16, 158, 428, 469
Hallam, Lewis 431
Hall, Arsenio 445, 464
Hall, Charles B. 567
Hallelujah 450
Hallelujah Baby 441
Hall, Juanita 435
Hall, Prince 10, 140, 282, 283
Hall v. *DeCuir* 318
Hamblin, Ken 480
Hamilton, Ed 130
Hamlet 431
Hammon, Jupiter 417, 421
Hammons, David 527, 530
Hampton, Eleanor 444
Hampton, Fred 236, 292
Hampton, Henry 485
Hampton Institute Press 487
Hampton, Lionel 507
Hampton University 165
Hancock, John 141

Handy, Dorothy Antoinette 513
Handy, W. C. 152, 159, 432, 490, 493
Hansberry, Lorraine 436, 441
Hardney, Florence 530
Hare, Maude Cuney 488
Haring, Keith 524
Harlan, John Marshall 97, 260
Harlem Art Center 522
"The Harlem Dancer" 423
Harlem, New York 145
Harlem Renaissance 145, 146, 423-424
Harlem Riot (1964) 14, 237
Harlequin 431
Harmon Foundation 526
Harmon, Leonard 573
Harmon, William E. 521
Harper, Frances Ellen Watkins 150, 421
Harpers Ferry, Virginia 133
Harpers Ferry National Historic Park 170-171
Harriet Beecher Stowe House 133
Harriet Tubman House 143
Harris, Barbara 366, 378
Harris, James 548
Harris, Joel Chandler 419
Harris, Leon 485
Harris, Margaret 517
Harris, Neil 439
Harrison, Donald 510
Harrison, Richard B. 436
Harris, Wynonie 494
Harry, Jackee 472
Harry T. Burleigh Birthplace 149
Hartford Inquirer 476
Hartford 156
Hartigan, Linda Roscoe 532
Hastie, William 9, 68, 274
Hatch-Billops Studio 528
Hatch, Jim 528
Hatcher, Richard 15, 242, 277

INDEX

Hausa 33
Hawkins, Coleman 506
Hawkins, June 435
Hayden, Palmer 521, 527
Hayden, Robert 425
Hayes, Elvin 546
Hayes, Rutherford 227
Haynes, Daniel 450
Haynes, George Edmond 287
Haynes, Lemuel 149, 152
Hayward, Dubose 164
Hayward, William 564
Hazel 488
H-D-H 501
Health 344-348
Hearns, Thomas 550
Hearts in Dixie 450, 451
Height, Bob 432
Heights, Dorothy 120
Hemsley, Sherman 468-470
Henderson, Cassandra 485
Henderson, Fletcher 506, 507
Henderson, Gordon 526
Henderson, Julia L. 488
Henderson, Ricky 544
Hendrix, Jimi 497, 501-502
Henry, Andrew 177
Henry, Herbert 436
Henry O. Tanner House 150
Henson, Josiah 139, 224
Henson, Matthew 137-138, 148
Hepburn, Katharine 454
Herc, Cool 503
Here's Lucy 466
Hermenway, James 512
Herrings, James V. 518
Hewlet, James 431
Hickman, Fred 485
Highway No. 1 USA 516
Hill, Abram 436
Hill, Anita 261-262
Hill, Robert 288
Hill, Robert B. 336
Hill, T. Arnold 287, 488

Hinds, Ester 517
Hines, Gregory 441, 444
Hines, Maurice 444
Hinkson, Mary 444
Hinton, William A. 541
His Honor the Barber 433
Hispaniola 61, 62
The History of the Negro 481
Hogan, Ernest 432, 433
Holder, Geoffrey 438, 444
Holiday, Billie 496
Holiday, Jennifer 441
Holland, Brian 501
Holland, Eddie 501
Holley Knoll (Robert R. Moton) House 165
Holly, James T. 370
Hollywood Shuffle 447
Holman, Kwame 484
Holmes, Larry 550
Holmes, Oliver Wendell 263
Holsey, Lucius 374
Holyfield, Evander 550
Home Modernization and Supply Company 322
The Homesteader 449
Hood Theological Seminary 380
Hooks, Benjamin 120, 242, 287, 484
Hooks, Matthew Bones 180
Hooks, Robert 439, 441
Hoover, Herbert 274
Hoover, J. Edgar 14
Horne, Lena 450, 452-453
Horny Horns 502
Horton, Austin Asadata Dafore 437
Horton, George Moses 421
Hoskins, Allen Clayton (Farina) 449
Hot Chocolates 434
Hotel Theresa 146
Hot Fives 507
Hot Sevens 507

Houghton, Katherine 454
House, Colonel Charles Young 134
House Committee on Education and Labor 277
House of Flowers 438
House Party 2 462-463
Houston Hall, Lincoln University 157
Houston Opera Company 517
Howard, Oliver Otis 168, 350, 352
Howard University 169, 354
Howard University Press 488
Howe, Cato 140
Howells, William Dean 133
Hudlin, Warrington 463
Hudson, Cheryl Willis 489
Hudson, Wade 489
Hughes, Langston 145, 423-424, 429, 436, 440
Hughes, Sarah Ann 372
Hulsinger, George 521
Hunter, Clementine 524
Hunter-Gault, Charlayne 476, 484
Hurston, Zora Neale 104, 160, 419, 424, 427
Hustler's Convention 502
Hutu 45
Hyers, Emma Louise 512
Hyman, Earl 436

I

"I Can't Stop Loving You" 498
Ida B. Wells-Barnett House 126
"If We Must Die" 423
"If You See My Savior Tell Him You Saw Me" 492
"I Got a Woman" 496
"I Have a Dream" Speech 11, 13, 109, 162, 169, 228, 232
I Know Why the Caged Bird Sings 121
"I'll Be There." 501

"I'll Overcome Someday" 491
Imam of Oman 44
Imani Temple African-American Catholic Congregation 383
"I'm Black and I'm Proud" 499
Imbokodvo National Movement 52
"I'm Moving On" 497
"I'm Walkin" 497
In Abraham's Bosom 435
Income 305-314, 315-328, 334
Indianapolis World 474
Indian Campaigns 560
In Dohomey 433
Industrial Work of Tuskegee Graduates and Former Students D 487
Infant mortality 344
Ingram, Rex 435, 436
Ingrams, Zell 521
Inkspots 495
In Living Color 471-472
Innis, Roy 289
Interdenominational Theological Center 380-381, 383
Inter-Ocean Hotel 173
Interracial Marriage 342, 343
In the Heat of the Night 454
Invisible Man 425
In White America 439
Ishaw, John W. 432
Isiah Thornton Montgomery House 156
Islam 377, 384
Island in the Sun 453
Isley Brothers 501
I Spy 464-465
It Takes A Nation of Millions to Hold Us Back 503
Ivax Corporation 328
"I've Been Loving You Too Long" 499
Ivory Coast 27
"I Wonder" 494

J

Jackman, Oliver 488
Jack, Sam 432
Jackson, Andrew 172, 246
Jackson, Augustus 533, 535
The Jackson Five 130, 501
Jackson, Janet 460, 462
Jackson, Jesse 1, 17-19, 117, 159, 242-243, 254, 267-268, 278-279, 290, 292-293, 545, 552
Jackson, Joseph H. 375
Jackson, Mahalia 493
Jackson, Michael 490, 501
Jackson, Nigel 526
Jackson, Rebecca Cox 372
Jackson Ward Historic District 166
Jacob, John E. 287
Jaffrey Public Library 143
Jamaica 55, 60, 63, 68
James A. Bland Grave Site 150
James, Daniel "Chappie" 154, 575
James H. Dillard House 155
James, Kay 279
James, King 385
Jamestown, North Carolina 166, 214, 295
James Weldon Johnson House 159
James Weldon Johnson Residence 147
Jamieson, Samuel 512
Jamison, Judith 442
Jan Ernst Matzeliger Statue 142
Jasper, John 166
Jawara, Dauda 27
Jay, Bill 439
Jazz 490
The Jazz Singer 450
Jean Baptiste Pointe Du Sable Homesite 126
Jeff Liberty Grave Site 136

The Jeffersons 464, 467, 470
Jefferson, Thomas 2, 76, 81
Jelly's Last Jam 441
Jemison, Mae C. 540-541
Jet 327, 477, 478
Jewell, K. Sue 338
Jewison, Norman 460
Jim Crow segregation 9, 10, 228, 372, 432
Joel, Lawrence 578
Joe Louis Memorials 130
John Brown House and Grave Site 144
John Brown Memorial State Park 176
John Brown Monument 132
John Brown's Caves 177
John Chavis Memorial Park 163
John Lawson 156
John Mercer Langston House 133
"Johnny B. Goode" 497
John Rankin House and Museum 133
John Roosevelt "Jackie" Robinson House 148
Johnson, Andrew 8, 174
Johnson, Anna 489
Johnson, Anthony 316
Johnson, Benjamin G. 562
Johnson C. Smith University 354
Johnson, Charles Spurgeon 279, 287, 331, 424, 487, 489
Johnson, Dwight H. 578
Johnson, Earvin "Magic" 546-547, 555
Johnson, Francis 512
Johnson, George 327, 328
Johnson, Hazel 557, 575
Johnson, Henry 564
Johnson, James Weldon 21, 101, 147, 159, 287, 433
Johnson, J. Rosamond 101, 159, 433, 435

INDEX

Johnson, Joan B. 328
Johnson, John H. 315, 326-327, 330, 335, 476
Johnson, Larry 526
Johnson, Louis 442, 444
Johnson, Lyndon B. 11, 111, 112, 235, 239, 256, 274, 277
Johnson, Malvin Gray 521, 522
Johnson Products Company 315, 328
Johnson Publishing Company 327-328
Johnson, Richard 216
Johnson, Robert L. 485
Johnson, Virginia 443
Johnston, Joshua 518, 520
John Swain Grave Site 170
Jones, Absalom 150, 222, 268, 282-283, 366
Jones, Alpheus 560
Jones, Casey 158
Jones, Charles Price 381
Jones, Clarence B. 476
Jones, C. P. 382
Jones, David "Deacon" 548
Jones, Elayne 513, 516
Jones, Eugene Kinckle 287
Jones, Gayl 427, 428
Jones, James Earl 439, 440, 446, 458, 470
Jones, LeRoi (see Imamu Amiri Baraka)
Jones, Lois Mailou 527
Jones, Matilda Sisieretta 512
Jones, Quincy 305, 501, 504
Jones, Robert 512
Joplin, Scott 157, 504, 513, 517
Jordan, Louis 441, 493-494
Jordan, Michael 305, 460, 546, 547
Jordan, Vernon E., Jr. 287, 470
Joseph H. Rainey House 164
Journal of Negro History 167, 356

Joyner, Florence Griffith 551-552, 555
Joyner-Kersee, Jackie 305, 551-552, 554, 555
Jubilee 517
Judaism 380
Judith Rutherford Marechal 439
The Juggler of Our Lady 517
Julia 464, 466
Julian, Percy Lavon 541
Jungle Fever 462
Just Above Midtown/Downtown Alternative Art Center 527
Just Us Books, Inc. 489

K

Kansas Exodus 249
Kay, Ulysses 515, 517
Keep Shuffling 434
Kennedy, John F. 11, 111, 121, 277
Kenny, John 487
Kenya 22, 44-45
Kenya African National Union 45
Kenyatta, Jomo 45
Kenyatta, Kwame 362
Kerner Commission 239, 483
Kerner Commission Report 239
Kersands, Billy 432
Kersee, Bob 555
Keyes, Alan 480
Kid Creole 503
Kincaid, Jamaica 427
King, Ben E. 491
King, Coretta Scott 290
King, Don 551, 553
King, Emeline 526
King, Mabel 441
King, Martin Luther, Jr. 1, 8, 11-12, 17, 19, 75, 109, 115, 118, 137, 152, 153, 159, 161-162, 169, 228, 232, 240-241, 243, 245, 267, 277, 279, 289-290, 293, 366, 375, 384, 426, 455, 470, 481, 578
King-Reeves, Hattie 436
King, Rodney 17, 20, 237, 243, 376
Kingsley Plantation 160
Kingsley, Zephaniah 160
Kinshasha Holman Conwill 527
Kongo 37
Kool and the Gang 502
Korean War 573-574
Kountz, Samuel L. 541
Krone, Gerald 439
Ku Klux Klan 5
Ku Klux Klan Act (1871) 94
Kykunkor 437

L

L'Enfant, Pierre-Charles 138
La Guiablesse 437
Lady Sings the Blues 444
Lane, William Henry 432
Laney, Lucy 353
Langston, John Mercer 133
Lanier, Willie 548
Lankfor, John Anderson 164
Lankford, John A. 525
Larsen, Nella 424
The Late Show 445
Lawnside, New Jersey 143
Lawrence, Jacob 523, 532
Lawrence, Robert H. 538
Lawson, James 376
Lawson, Jennifer 464, 484
Laying Down the Law: Joe Clark's Strategy for Saving Our Schools 363
The Lazarus Syndrome 470
Leadership Conference on Civil Rights 289
Lead Story 485
Lean on Me 363
The Learning Tree 456

INDEX

Lear, Norman 466
LeBeauf, Sabrina 472
Ledger 479
Lee, Bertram 547, 555
Lee, Canada 436
Lee, Don L. 426
Lee, Everett 517
Lee, Jarena 371
Lee, Robert E. 4, 558
Lee-Smith, Hughie 521, 523
Lee, Spike 305, 447, 448, 459-460, 503
Lee, Tom 159
Leeward Islands 64
Leidesdorff Street 173
Leidesdorff, William Alexander 173, 315
Leigh, Vivien 452
Leland, John 367
Lemuel Haynes House 149
Leonard, Matthew 578
Leonard, Sugar Ray 550
Leone, Sierra 34
Leopold, King 39
Lesotho 50
Lester Bowie's Brass Fantasy 511
Lethal Weapon 458
Levi Coffin House 128
Lewaro, Villa 144
Lewis and Clark Expedition 179
Lewis, Delano Eugene 476
Lewis, Edmonia 518, 520
Lewis, James 139
Lewis, John 232, 290-291
Lewis, Meriwether 175
Lewis, Norman 523, 528
Lewis, Reggie 555
Lewis, Reginald F. 324-325, 327
Lewis, Samella 523, 528
The Liberator 151, 152, 223
Liberia 21, 22, 30, 222
Liberty, Jeff 136
Liele, George 368
Life 476

Life expectancy 346
"Lift Every Voice and Sing" 100, 148, 159
Like It Is 483
Lilies of the Field 453
Lincoln, Abraham 8, 90, 135, 143, 150, 168, 216, 224
Lincoln Center Jazz Orchestra 510
Lincoln Hall (Berea College) 154
Lincoln Institute 354
Lincoln Memorial 169, 228
Lincoln Picture Co. 449
Lincoln University 156, 354
Lisa, Manuel 177
Liscome Bay 175
Lisle, George 163
Listen Chicago 479
Literature 417-428
Little Cayman 60
Little Ham 436
Little Richard (see Little Richard Penniman)
The Little Colonel 450
The Littlest Rebel 450
Live at the Apollo 499
Livin' Large 462
Living Single 472
Livingston, David 47
Livingstone College 380
Locke, Alain 355, 424, 488, 518, 522
Long, Donald R. 578
Long, Herman 487
"Long Tall Sally" 497
Lorraine Hotel 159
Los Angeles riots 14, 17, 20, 376
Lothery, Eugene 483
Louis Armstrong House 148
Louis, Joe 11, 130, 479, 549
Louis Jordan and the Tympany Five 494
Loury, Glen 279
Love, Nat 179-180

Love Thy Neighbor 451
Lowery, Joseph E. 289
Lucas, Sam 446
The Lucy Show 466
Lunceford, Jimmie 507
Lundy, Lamar 548
Lyles, Aubrey 434
Lynching 100, 228, 487
Lynching by States, 1882-1958 487

M

Mabley, Jackie "Moms" 438, 443-444
Madagascar 53, 54
Madah Hyers, Anna 512
Madhubuti, Haki R. 426, 489
The Mad Miss Manton 452
Mae C. Jemison Academy 540
Magazines (see Media)
Maggie Lena Walker House 166, 167
Majors and Minors 133
Makeba, Miriam 291
Malagasy Republic 53
Malawi 46, 48
Malcolm X 7, 10, 11, 13, 145, 148, 235, 245, 252, 288, 375, 426, 455, 460, 503, 578
Malcolm X 459, 461
Malcolm X Academy 362
Malcolm X Residence 148
Mali 21, 28, 30, 34, 213
Malinke 29, 30
Malone, Moses 546
Man about Town 451
Mandela, Nelson 52, 293
Manelik II 40
Manumission Society 350
"Maple Leaf Rag" 157
Marbury, Donald L. 484
March on Washington 12-13, 169, 232, 243, 290

INDEX

Maria Baldwin House 141
Mariam, Mengistu Haile 41
Mariel boatlift 55, 300
Markham, Pigmeat 502
Markings 515
Marley, Bob 385
Maroons 3, 34
Marsalis, Branford 510
Marsalis, Wynton 510
Marshal, Jim 548
Marshall, George C. 567
Marshall, Thurgood 11, 107, 112, 255-256, 261, 263, 359
Martel, Linda 498
Martha and the Vandellas 130, 501
Martin 472
Martin Beck Theater 441
Martin, Dewey "Pigmeat" 432
Martin, Helen 436, 439, 441
Martinique 64, 66
Martin Luther King Day 17, 243
Martin Luther King, Jr. Center for Nonviolent Social Change 162, 290
Martin Luther King, Jr. National Historic Site 162
Martin, Nan 439
Martin, Sallie 493
Marvellettes 500
Mary Ann Shadd Cary House 169
Mary Church Terrell House 169
Mary McLeod Bethune Memorial 169
Mary Tyler Moore Show 467
Mason, Charles H. 382
"Master Juba" 432
Matney, William C., Jr. 481-482
Matthew Henson Memorial 137
Matthew Henson Residence 148
Matthews, Benjamin 517
Matzeliger, Jan 142, 533, 535
Maude 467

Mau Mau rebellion 45
Maurice, Prince 54
Mauritania 32
Mauritius 54
Maverick, Samuel 140
"Maybelline" 497
Mayfield, Curtis 498, 501
Mayflower 2, 216
Mayhew, Allen B. 177
Maynard, Robert 473
Mayotte 53
Mays, Willie 544
Mbuti 39
McAdoo, Bob 546
McAlpin, Harry 476
McBride, William, Jr. 528
McCall's Pattern Company 325
McCannon, Dinga 527
McClendon, Rose 435, 436
McClenny, Cheryl 530
McClinton, O. B. 498
McCormick, Cyrus 534
McCoy, Elijah 327, 533, 535
McCullers, Carson 436
McDaniel, Hattie 11, 446, 452
McDuffie, Arthur 16, 20, 242
McElroy, Guy C. 531
McGovern, George 293
McGuire, George Alexander 380
McKay, Claude 147, 423-424
McKayle, Donald 442, 444
McKee, Clarence 483
Mckenna, Maureen A. 532
McKenney, Morris 436
McKenzie, Vashti 378
McKenzie, Vinson 525
McKinney, Nina Mae 450
McKissick, Floyd 289
McLaurin, G. W. 264
McLaurin v. *Oklahoma State Regents for Higher Education* 264
McMillan, Terry 427
McNair, Lesley James 571
McNair, Ronald 538

McNamara, Robert 577
McNeil, Claudia 437
McPhatter, Clyde 495
McQueen, Armelia 441
McQueen, Butterfly 436, 452
McShine, Kynastan 529
McTell, Blind Willie 492
The Meanest Man in the World 452
Media 473-489
Medicaid 312, 348
Medicare 312
Meharry Medical College 539
Meharry Medical School 159
Mel, Melle 503
Meltzer, Milton 429
Member of the Wedding 436
Memoria 442
Memphis Blues 490
Memphis Free Speech 476
Menellik, King 41
Merina 53
Metronome 509
Mexican-American War 221
Mexico 55, 74
Mfume, Kweisi 281
Miami riots (1980) 16, 242
Micheaux, Oscar 446, 448-449
Michigan Chronicle 482
Midnighters 496
"Midnight Hour" 499
Mighty Clouds of Joy 493
Miles, George L., Jr. 484
Military 556-579
Miles, William H. 381
Miller, Dorie 174, 570, 572
Miller, Flournoy 434
Mills, Florence 434, 437
Mills, Stephanie 441
Milton House and Museum 135
Milton, John 141
Milton L. Olive Park 127
Mingus, Charles 510
Minton's Playhouse 508

INDEX

Missouri Compromise 221, 271
Missouri ex rel. Lloyd Gaines v. *Canada* 263, 357
Mitchell, Abbie 435
Mitchell, Arthur 438, 443
Mitchell, Nellie Brown 512
Modeliste, Ziggy 501
Modern Sounds in Country Music 497
Modern Sounds in Country Music Volume 2 498
Moheli 53
Momeyer, William M. 567
Moms Mabley at the Geneva Conference 444
Moms Mabley at the UN 444
Monagas, Lionel 481
Mondale, Walter 112, 279-280
Monk, Thelonius 490, 508
Monroe, James 30, 222
Monroe, Marilyn 453
Monrovia 30, 222
Montgomery, Barbara 440
Montgomery Bus Boycott 11
Montgomery Improvement Association 11, 289
Montgomery, Isiah Thornton 156
Montserrat 64
Moon, Warren 549
Moore, Charles 444
Moore, Gatemouth 492
Moore, Kermit 516
Moore, Melba 441
Moore, Tim 438
Moorish Science Temple 251
Moorland-Spingarn Collection 169
Morehead, Scipio 519
Morehouse College 161, 354
Moreland, Mantan 450
Morgan, Garrett 533
Morris Brown College 161
Morrison, Toni 305, 417-421, 427, 463
Morton, Joe 441

Mosell, Sadie T. 533
Mosely, Robert 517
Moshoeshoe I 50
Moskowitz, Henry 284, 285
Mossi 25
Mother Bethel African Methodist Episcopal Church 150
Motley, Archibald 521, 522
Moton, Robert R. 165
Motown Museum 130
Motown Record Corporation 130, 328, 499, 501
Mott, Lucretia Coffin 223
Mount Pisgah African Methodist Episcopal Church 143
Movement for the Liberation of São Tomé and Príncipe 38
Mowry, Tamera 472
Mowry, Tia 472
Moynihan, Daniel Patrick 338
Mozambique 47
Mr. Ed 466
Mr. Lord of Koal 433
Mswati 52
Muhammad, Clara 360
Muhammad, Elijah 7, 11, 13, 251-252, 254, 360, 375, 378, 384, 566
Muhammad, Sister Clara 360
Muhammad, Wallace Fard 252
Muhammad, Warith D. 384
Muhammad's Temple No. 2 Publications Department 486
Mulatto 429, 436
Mules and Men 419
Multicultural teaching 364
Murphy, Eddie 444, 445, 457-458
Murphy, John Henry 475
Murray, Ellen 164
Murray, Joan 476
Murray, Oliver E. 573
Muscle Shoals Sounds 500
Museum of African Art 528

Museveni, Yoweri 46
Music 490-517
Muslim Mosque, Inc. 13
Mutual Black Network 479
Mutual Building and Loan Association 322
Muzorewa, Bishop 49
Myers, Milton 442
Myers, Pauline 436
"My Jesus Is All the World to Me" 496

N

NAACP Legal Defense and Educational Fund, Inc. 288, 359
NAACP v. *Alabama* 286
Nairobi Day School 360
Namibia 24, 50
Narrative of the Life of Frederick Douglass 422
Natchez National Cemetery 156
National Aeronautics and Space Administration (NASA) 540
National Afro-American Museum 134
National Association for the Advancement of Colored People (NAACP) 8, 101, 228, 231-232, 242-243, 255, 273, 283, 284, 288, 290, 314, 356, 476, 488
National Association of Colored Women 169, 284
National Association of Colored Women's Clubs 168
National Baptist Convention 366
National Baptist Convention of America, Unincorporated 383
National Baptist Convention of the U.S.A., Inc. 375, 383-384
National Baptist Educational Convention of the U.S.A. 384
National Baptist Publishing Board 486

405

INDEX

National Black Caucus of State Legislators 277
National Black Network 479
National Black Political Convention 15
National Center of Afro-American Artists 528
National Conference of Black Mayors 277
National Conference on a Black Agenda for the Eighties 277
National Council of Churches 376
National Council of Negro Women 277
National Endowment for the Arts 518
National Freedmen's Relief Association 352
National Institute Against Prejudice and Violence 243
National League for the Protection of Colored Women 287
National League on Urban Conditions Among Negroes 287
National Medical Association 284
National Museum of African Art 169
National Museum of the Tuskegee Airmen 131
National Negro Business League 273, 284, 305, 318
National Negro Committee 284
National Negro Finance Corporation 322
National Negro Newspaper Publishers Association 474
National Primitive Baptist Convention of America 384
National Rainbow Coalition 293
National Training School for Women and Girls 353

National Union for the Total Independence of Angola (UNITA) 35
National Urban League 231, 232, 243, 283, 287, 290, 314, 488
Nation of Islam 7, 13, 148, 251, 254, 279, 360, 378, 384, 486, 503
Native Son 418, 425
Naylor, Gloria 427
Negritude 521
Negro American Labor Council 232
The Negro and Economic Reconstruction 488
The Negro and His Song 487
Negro Digest 327, 476, 477
Negro Ensemble Company 439, 440
The Negroes in Medicine 487
Negro Membership in Labor Unions 489
Negro Poetry and Drama 488
Negro Society for Historical Research 355
Negro Soldiers Monument 151
"The Negro Speaks of Rivers" 423
The Negro World 250, 489
The Negro Yearbook 487
Negro Yearbook Publishing Company 487
Nell, William C. 141
Netherlands Antilles 57, 64
Nevis 56, 64, 66
New Bedford Whaling Museum 142
New Concept Development Center 360
New England Anti-Slavery Society 284
New England Freedmen's Aid Society 352
New Jack City 448, 462

New Jersey-based Education, Training and Enterprise Center 323
New York Manumission Society 222
New York African Free School 350, 351
New York Age 143, 474
National Foundation for Teaching Entrepreneurship 323
Newman, Rock 551
The New Negro, 424
Newspaper Boy 520
Newspapers (see Media)
Newton, Huey P. 14, 15, 113, 236, 291
Newton, John 368
Nez Percé National Historical Park 175
Nguema, Francisco Macias 38
Niagara Movement 230, 284
Nicaragua 70
Nicephore Soglo 25
Nichols, Denise 439
Nicodemus Colony 176
Nicodemus, Kansas 297
Niger 32
Nigeria 32
Nilotic 44
Niño, Pedro Alonzo 1, 2, 216
9th Cavalry Regiment 180-181, 560
Nixon, L. A. 262
Nixon v. Condon 263
Nixon v. Herndon 262
Nkrumah, Kwame 28
Nobel Peace Prize 51
Noble, Gil 473, 482, 483
Nonviolent philosophy 235
Norris Wright Cuney 488
North Carolina Mutual Life Insurance Company 163, 322
Northern Star 223
North Star 149, 270, 473

INDEX

Northrup, Solomon 88
Northwest Ordinance 221
Norton, Eleanor Holmes 267
No Way Out 453
Ntozake Shange 440
Nyasaland 47

O

Oak and Ivy 133
Oak Hill Cemetery 172
Oakland Memorial Chapel and Alcorn State University 156
Oberlin College 133
Obote, Milton 46
The Octoroon 432
Odets, Clifford 441
An Officer and a Gentleman 458
Officer Training School 557, 564
Of Mice and Men 452
"Oh Freedom" 491
Ohio Players 502
Oklahoma movement 249
Old Courthouse 157, 178
Oldsmobile Achieva SC 526
O'Leary, Hazel R. 281
Olive, Milton 578
Oliver, Joe "King" 485, 506
Oliver Otis Howard House 168
O'Neal, Frederick 436
O'Neal, Shaquille 305, 546
O'Neill, Eugene 435
One More Spring 451
On the Pulse of Morning 121
101 Ranch 179
Onesimus 539
Open Hand Publishing Inc. 489
Opera Ebony 517
Opera/South 516
Operation Breadbasket 293
Operation PUSH (People United to Save Humanity) 242, 292-293
Opportunity 423, 424

O'Ree, Willie 542
Organization of African Unity (OAU) 24
Organization of Afro-American Unity 13
Oriental America 432
The Original Colored American Opera Troupe 512
Original Dixieland Jazz Band 506
Orioles 495
Orozco, Jose Clemente 523
Oscar Micheaux Corp. 449
Oscar Staton DePriest House 127
Othello 431
Ottolenghi, Joseph 350
Our Gang 449
"Out of Sight" 499
Ovington, Mary White 284, 285, 488
Owens, Jesse 542-543
Oyo 33
Oyster Man 433

P

The Padlock 431
Page, Allan 548
Page, Clarence 476
Page, Ken 441
Page, Ruth 437
Paige, Satchel 470
Palmer, Henry 125
Palmer Memorial Institute 353
Panama 70, 72
Panama Hattie 453
"Papa's Got a Brand New Bag" 499
Paradise Lost 141
Paris 470
Parker, Charlie "Bird" 508-511
Park, Robert E. 487
Parks, Gordon, Sr. 476, 478, 456, 528

Parks, Rosa 1, 11, 118, 228, 231-232, 289
Parliment 501
Parliment-Funkadelic 502
Partners in Ecumenism 376
Party of the Hutu Emancipation Movement (PARMEHUTU) 45
Paul Cuffe Farm and Memorial 142
Paul Cuffe Memorial 141
Paul Laurence Dunbar House 133
Paul Robeson Residence 135, 148
Paul, Willard S. 571
Payne, Daniel A. 354, 366, 371
Payne, Les 473
Payne Theological Seminary 379
Payton, Walter 548
Peace Corps 540
Pearl Harbor, Hawaii 174
Pearl Primus Dance Language Institute 438
Peary-McMillan Arctic Museum 137
Peary, Robert E. 137, 148
Pecanha, Nilo 72
Peebles, Melvin Van 456
Pendleton, Clarence M., Jr. 16
Penniman, Little Richard 497
Penn School Historic District 164
Pennsylvania Society for Promoting the Abolition of Slavery 222
Pentecostalism 366, 374
"People Get Ready" 498
People's Building and Loan Association 322
People versus Property 487
Pepper Jelly Lady 523
Pepsi Bethel 444
Performing Arts 429-445
Perry, Julia 515
Perry, Regina 530, 532

INDEX

Pershing, John J. 564
Persian Gulf War 577-579
Person to Person 481
Peters, Clark 452
Peterson, Louis 436
Peterson, Oscar 506
Philadelphia Female Anti-Slavery Society 223
Philadelphia Tribune 474
Philander-Smith College 154
Philip, Randolph, A. 10, 290
Phillips, Channing E. 268
Phillips School of Theology 381
Phillis Wheatley Folio 141
The Philosophy and Opinions of Marcus Garvey 489
Pickett, Bill 179
Pickett, Wilson 499
Pierce, Delilah 523
Pilgrim Baptist Church 492
Pinchback, P. B. S. 268
Pindell, Howardena 527, 529
Pinklon, Thomas 553
Pinkney, Jerry 526
Pinkney, William 574
Pinto da Costa, Manuel 39
Pioneers' Home 170
Pippin, Horace 524
Pittsburgh Courier 479, 481, 566
Pitts, Riley L. 578
Pittsylvania County Courthouse 165
The Plantation Revue 434
Planter 558
"Please Mister Postman" 500
Plessy, Homer Adolph 228, 260
Plessy v. Ferguson 96, *107*, 228, 229, 232, 257, 260, 318, 356
A Poetic Equation: Conversations between Nikki Giovanni and Margaret Walker 488
Poetic Justice 462
Poitier, Sidney 436-437, 446, 453-455, 457

The Policy Players 433
Pollock, Jackson 523
Ponce de León, Juan 2, 65
Poole, Elijah 252
"Poor People's Campaign" 290
Poor People's March on Washington 481
Poor, Salem 140, 557
The Poor Soldier, Obi 431
Pope, Alexander 419
Pop music 501
Popular Movement for the Liberation of Angola (MPLA) 35
Population 295-304
Porgy and Bess 164, 434, 453
Positively Black 473
Poverty 309, 341
Powell, Adam Clayton, Jr. 145, 268, 275-276, 577
Powell, Adam Clayton, Sr. 145
Powell, Adam Clayton, III 485
Powell, Clilan B. 476
Powell, Colin L. 17, 556, 557, 576-577, 579
Power of the Ballot: A Handbook for Black Political Participation 489
Precipice 442
Presbyterian Church, U.S.A. 366
Price, Florence 514, 515
Price, Leontyne 514
"Pride and Joy" 501
Pride, Charley 498
Primus-Borde School of Primal Dance 438
Primus, Pearl 437, 442
Prince 305, 460
Prince Goodin Homestead 135
Prince Hall and His Followers 488
Príncipe 38
Progressive National Baptist Convention, Inc. 366, 375, 384
Project Headstart 312

Prosser, Gabriel 247
Provident Hospital 125, 533
Provident Hospital and Training School 127
Provincetown Theatre 435
Pryor, Richard 444, 457
Public Enemy 503
Publishing (see Media)
Pueblo, Hawikuh 178
Puerto Rico 64
Pulliam, Keshia Knight 472
Purlie Victorious 441
Purviance, Florence 522
Purvis, William 535
PUSH-EXCEL 293
Pygmies 26

Q

Quarles, Norma 482, 485
Queen Latifah 305, 472, 503
Quintet 442
Quitman, Cleo 440

R

Rabah 37
"Rabbi Matthew" 380
Race, Fear and Housing in a Typical American Community 489
Racism 242
Radio (see Media)
A Rage in Harlem 448, 462
Ragtime 504
The Railroad Porter 446
Rainbow Coalition 19
Rainey, Gertrude "Ma" 432
Rainey, Joseph Hayne 164
Raisin 441
Raisin in the Sun 437, 441
Ralph Bunche House 149
Ranch, E. J. "Lucky" Baldwin 172
Randolph, A. Philip 10, 262, 267, 275, 289-290, 566

INDEX

Rangel, Charles 288, 579
Rang Tang 434
Rankin, John 133
Ransom, Reverdy 295, 304, 375
"Rapper's Delight" 503
Rashad, Phylicia 472
Raspberry, William 473
Rastafarians 385
Ray, Marcus H. 570
"Reach Out I'll Be There" 501
Reagan, Ronald 16-17, 243, 280
Reconstruction 8, 9, 227, 249
Recorder 479
The Redd Foxx Comedy Hour 467
The Redd Foxx Show 467
Redding, Otis 499
Redd, Veronica 439
Redman, Don 506, 507
Red Sea Press 489
Reed, Ishmael 426
Reed, Napoleon 435
Reed, Willis 546, 555
Reflections in D 442
Regal Theater 438
Reid, Tim 472
Religion 365-385
Réunion 54
Revelations 442
Revels, Hiram R. 6, 8, 164, 268, 271-272, 372
Reverend George Lisle Memorial 163
Revolutionary War 556
Reynolds, Joshua 519
Rhode Island Black Heritage Society 151
Rhodesia 47, 49
Rhythmetron 443
Rice, Jerry 548
Rice, Thomas Dartmouth 432
Richard Pryor—Live in Concert 457
Richard III 431

Richie, Lionel 501
Rich, Matty 448
The Rider of Dreams 433
Riggs, Marlon 485
Riley, Clayton 480
Ringgold, Faith 527
Riots 14, 237
"Rip It Up" 497
Rivera, Diego 523
The River Niger 439
Rivers, Ruben 571
Roach, Hal 449
Roach, Max 506
Robert S. Abbott House 128
Robert Smalls House 163
Robertson, Don 527
Robeson, Paul 129, 135, 148, 435, 449, 451
Robinson, Bill "Bojangles" 166, 434, 437, 450
Robinson Crusoe 431
Robinson, Frank 16, 544, 545
Robinson, Jackie 146, 148, 481, 542-544
Robinson, Lavaughn 444
Robinson, Max 482
Robinson, Randall 293-294
Robinson, Smokey 130
Robinson, Sugar Ray 549
Roc 472
Rodgers, Jonathan 483
Rodgers, Moses 172
Rogers, Joel Augustus 250
Rogers, Rod 444
Rogers, Timmie 464
Rohan, Shelia 443
Roker, Roxie 439
Rolle, Esther 439, 467-468
Rollins, Sonny 510
Roman Catholic Church 376, 383
Romare, Eleo 442-443
Romney, George 519
Roosevelt, Franklin D. 8, 106, 160, 274, 518, 566, 572

Roosevelt, Theodore 149
Roots 16, 121, 158, 428, 464, 467, 469, 470
Roots: The Next Generation 470
Rose, Edward 177
Rosenwald Fund 518
Ross, Diana 501
Ross, Ted 441
Rotardier, Kelvin 442
Roundtree, Richard 456, 470
Rowan, Carl T. 473, 573
Rowland and Mitchell 322
The Royal Family 467
Royal Knights Savings and Loan Association 322
Royal Sons 495
Roy Wilkins House 149
Rozelle, Robert V. 532
Rudolph, Wilma 470, 542, 551
Rufus Rastus 433
Runnin' Wild 434
Rush, Christopher 371
Russell, Bill 546, 547
Russell, Jane 453
Russwurm, John B. 223, 249, 270, 473, 476
Rustin, Bayard 289, 290
Rwanda 44, 45

S

Sackler, William 439
Saddler, Joseph 503
Saint Christopher 56, 66
Saint Croix 68
Saint-Gaudens, Augustus 140
Saint John 68
Saint Kitts 64, 66
Saint Lucia 66
Saint Thomas 68
Saint Vincent 66
Sakalava 53
Salem, Peter 140, 557
Sallee, Charles 521

INDEX

Salt-N-Pepa 503
Sam, Alfred C. 250
Sanchez, Sonia 427
Sanders, Wayne 517
Sands, Diana 437, 439
Sanford and Son 444, 466
Sanford, Isabel 468-469
San Salvador Island 58
Santa Anita Race Track 172
Santería 366
Santo Domingo 62
Santomee, Lucas 533, 539
Sao Tomé 38
Saratoga 452
Sargent, Ruppert L. 578
Sasser, Clarence E. 578
Saturday Night Live 445, 457
Saunders, Wallace 158
Savage, Augusta 521
Savory, P. M. H. 476
Savoy Ballroom 507
Saw the House in Half, a Novel 488
Saxon, Luther 435
Sayers, Gayle 548
Scarborough, William Sanders 356
Scheherazade 443
Schindler's List 458
Schmeling, Max 130, 549
Schmoke, Kurt 276
Schomburg, Arthur A. 146, 355, 528
Schomburg Center for Research in Black Culture 146, 527
School Daze 459
Schuller, Gunther 511
Science 533-541
Scotia Seminary 354
Scott, Charlotte 168
Scott, Dred 132, 157, 257-258
Scott, Emmett J. 487
Scott, Hazel Dorothy 464
Scott Joplin House 157

Scottsboro Boys 11, 104, 105
Scott, Tasha 472
Scott, William Edouard 521
Seale, Bobby 14, 113, 236, 291-292
Search for Missing Persons 479
Segregation 228
Selida, Marie 512
Selway, Robert R. 567
Selznick, David O. 452
Senegal 32, 34
Senga Nengudi 527
Senghor, Leopold Sedar 34
Sensational Nightingales 493
Separate but equal doctrine 229
704 Hauser 467
"Seven Rooms of Gloom" 501
Seychelles 54
Shaft 456
Shaka 51
Shakesnider, Wilma 517
Shakespeare, William 431
Shaw, Bernard 485
Shaw, Robert Gould 140, 161
Shaw University 354
Sheba, Queen of 41, 385
Shell, Art 549, 555
Sheridan Broadcasting Corporation 479
She's Gotta Have It 447, 459
The Shoo-Fly Regiment 433
Shook, Karel 443
Show Boat 136, 451, 452
Shrine of the Black Madonna 375
Shuffle Along 434
Sickle Cell Anemia 345
Silver Bluff Baptist Church 366, 367
Silver Streak 457
Simms, Hilda 436
Simon the Cyrenian 433
Simpson, Carole 484
Simpson, Georgiana Rose 533

Sims, Lowery 530, 531
Singleton, John 446, 448, 462
Sipuel, Ada Lois 263
Sipuel v. *Board of Regents of the University of Oklahoma* 263
Siqueiros, David Alfero 523
Sissle, Noble 434
Sister, Sister 472
Sitting Bull 178
Six Degrees of Separation 472
The Six Million Dollar Man 467
60 Minutes 482
Skies of America 515
Sklarek, Norma Merrick 525
Slave trade 22, 368
Slavery 213-226
Sloane, Paul 449
Sly and the Family Stone 501
Small Business Administration 324
Small, Mary J. 372
Smalls, Robert 163, 558
Smith, Abiel 139
Smith, Bessie 432, 495
Smith, Bragg 162
Smith, Freeman M. 322
Smith, Gerrit 143, 144
Smith, Ian 49
Smith, James McCune 539
Smith, Lowell 443
Smithsonian Institution 169
Smithsonian Jazz Masterpiece Ensemble 510
Smith v. *Allwright*.) 256
Smith, Will 472
Smith, Willi 525-526
Smith, William E. 521
"Snakes Crawl at Night" 498
Snelling, Josiah 132
Snow, Hank 497
Sobhuza II 52
Social Gospel Movement 375
Society for the Propagation of the Gospel in Foreign Parts 350

Society of California Pioneers 172
Sojourner Truth Grave Site 129
The Soldier's Play 439
Solomon, King 385
Somalia 23, 41
Sonata for Piano and String Quartet 515
Song of Solomon 420
Songhai 21, 28, 213
So Nice, They Named It Twice 439
Sons of Ham 433
Soul Train 328, 464
Sounder 456
South Africa 22, 51-52, 294
South Central 472
Southern Christian Leadership Conference (SCLC) 13, 232, 283, 289-290, 292
The Southerners 433
The Southern Workman 487
South View Cemetery 162
South West Africa People's Organization (SWAPO) 50
Southwest Atlanta Youth Business Organization (SWAYBO) 323
Sowell, Thomas 16, 279, 312, 314
Soyinka, Wole 418
Spanish-American War 180, 561
Spelman College 161
Spencer, Peter 369, 380
Spielberg, Steven 458
Spingarn, Joel E. 287
Spingarn Medal 287
Spinks, Leon 550
Sports 542-554
Spriggs, Edward 527
Spruill, James 439
S.S. *Liberia* 250
Stabat Mater 515
Stallings, George A., Jr. 377, 383

"Stand by Me" 491
St. Andrew's African Methodist Episcopal Church 172
Stand Up and Cheer 451
Stanley, W. Jerome 555
Stans, Jacob 512
Stanton, Elizabeth Cady 223
Star Trek: The Next Generation 470
Star Wars 446
Stars of Faith 440
The State of Black America 489
Stax Records 500
Steele, Shelby 16, 279
Steinberg, Benjamin 516
Stephenson, Dwight 548
Stevenson, Mickey 500
Stevens, Thaddeus 150, 271
Steward, Susan McKinney 533
Stewart, Maria 247, 371
St. George's Church 366
St. George's Episcopal Church 149
Still, William Grant 143, 513, 515, 517
Stimpson, Henry L. 570
Stir Crazy 444, 457
St. Jacques, Raymond 439
"St. Louis Blues" 152
St. Louis Woman 435
St. Luke Penny Savings Bank 167
St. Luke's Episcopal Church 170
St. Mark's Theater 439
Stokes, Carl 277
Stono River Slave Rebellion Historic Site 164
Stormy Weather 453
Stowe, Calvin 137
Stowe, Harriet Beecher 4, 133, 134, 137, 139, 446
Stowe House 137
Stowers, Freddie 565
Straight out of Brooklyn 448, 462

Strait, George 484
Strange Incident 452
Strictly Business 462
Strode, Woodrow 548
St. Thomas's Protestant Episcopal Church 366
Student National Coordinating Committee (SNCC) 290
Student Non-Violent Coordinating Committee (SNCC) 13, 290-291, 232
Studio Museum in Harlem 527
Suber, Jay 485
Sudan 43
Sugar Hill 146
Sugar Hill Gang 503
Sugar Hill Times 464
Suicide 347
Sula 420
Sumner, Charles 174, 271
Sumner Elementary School 177
Sunday School Publishing Board 486
Super Fly 456
The Supremes 130, 500, 501
Suriname 73
Survival of the Black Family: The Institutional Impact of U.S. Social Policy 338
Sutton, Percy 293, 476, 480
Swain, John 171
Swan Lake 443
Swazi 52
Swaziland 52
Sweatt, Herman Marion 264, 358
Sweatt v. *Painter* 256, 264
Sweet Auburn Historic District 162
Sweet Charity 441
Sweet Daddy Grace 375
Sweet Sweetback's Baadasssss Song 456
Swing High 451
Symphonic Concertante 515

INDEX

Symphony in E Minor 514, 515
Symphony of the New World 516

T

Take a Giant Step 436
"Take the A Train" 147
"Take These Chains from My Heart" 498
Talladega College 354
Talladega College and Swayne Hall 153
Tallman Restorations 134
Tallman, William M. 134
Tan 477
Tandy, Vertner Woodson 144
Taney, Roger Brook 157, 258
Tanganyika 46
Tanksley, Ann 527
Tanner, Henry Ossawa 150, 153, 518, 520, 531-532
Tanzania 45
Tar Baby 419, 420
Tate, Larenz 472
Tatum, Art 507
Taureg 32
Taylor, Cecil 510
Taylor, Robert 525
Taylor, Susan 478
Teenage pregnancy 310, 343
Television 446, 464-472
Tell My Horse 419
Temple, Lewis 142
Temple, Shirley 450
The Temptations 130
10th Cavalry 181, 560
Terrell, Mary Church 169, 284
Terry, Lucy 417
Tex, Joe 499
Thaddeus Stevens Grave Site 150
Tharp, Twyla 524
That's My Mama 468
Thea 472

Theater Four 439
Theodore Drury Colored Opera Company 512
Third World Press 489
Thirteenth Amendment 92, 225, 227, 257-259
Thirty Years of Lynching in the United States, 1889-1918 488
Thomas Baily & Sons 322
Thomas, C. Edward 515
Thomas, Clarence 17, 257, 261-262
Thomas, Debi 552
Thomas, Edna 436
Thomas, William Henry (Buckwheat) 449
Thompson, Bob 527
Thompson, Clive 440, 442
Thompson, Robert Ferris 532
Thompson, William 575
Thrash, Dox 522
Threadgill, Robert 527
Three Black Kings 442
Three Years in Europe 417
Thriller 490
Tidal Basin Bridge 170
"Tight Like That" 492
Tilden, Samuel 227
Timbuktu 213
Tindley, Charles Albert 491
TLC Beatrice International Holdings Inc. 315, 325, 327
Tobago 67
Togo 33, 34
The Toilet/The Slave 439
Tolson, Melvin B. 425
Tolton, Augustine 128
Tom and Jerry 431
Tombalbaye, François 37
Tom Lee Memorial 159
Tones 443
Tongues Untied 485
Tony Brown's Journal 473, 484
Toomer, Jean 424

Toomes, Lloyd 527
Torrence, Ridgely 433
To Sir with Love 454
Tougaloo College 354
Toure, Kwame (see Stokely Carmichael)
Toure, Samory 29, 32
Toussaint L'Ouverture 62, 247
Towne, Laura 164
Townsend, Robert 447-448
Townsend, Ronald 484
T. P. Parham and Associates 322
Tracy, Spencer 454
Trading Places 457
Trail, William 128
TransAfrica 294
Travis, Dempsey 489
Travis, Jack 525
Treemonisha 513, 517
Trinidad 67
Trip to Coontown 429, 432
The Triumph of Love 431
Trotter, William Monroe 142, 284
Troubled Island 436
Troy Game 443
Truman, Harry S 10, 106, 160, 228, 289, 574
Truth, Sojourner 129, 223, 271, 371
T. Thomas Fortune House 143
Tubman, Harriet 4, 143, 224, 270-271, 284, 470
Tucker, Lem 482
Tucker, William 1, 2, 216
Turks and Caicos Islands 68
Turnbull, Walter 517
Turner, Big Joe 494
Turner, Henry McNeal 250, 372
Turner, Nat 82, 163, 248, 371
Turner, Ted 485
Turner Theological Seminary 379
Tuskegee Airmen 154, 568

Tuskegee Institute Press 487
Tuskegee Normal and Industrial Institute 8, 153, 156, 165, 229, 273, 353, 487, 525, 539
Tutsi 45
"Tutti Frutti" 497
Twelve Years a Slave 88
24th Infantry Regiment 172, 180, 560
25th Infantry Regiment 560
Twilight, Alexander Lucius 268
Two Trains Running 440
227 470
Tyson, Cicely 439, 456, 458, 464, 469-470
Tyson, Mike 550, 553

U

Uganda 46
Uggams, Leslie 441, 470
"Uncle Jack" 371
Uncle Remus: His Songs and His Sayings 419
Uncle Tom's Cabin 4, 133, 134, 137, 139, 446
Underground Railroad 4, 7, 15, 74, 135, 143, 177, 224
Underground Railroad Marker 132
Unemployment 306
Union Church of Africans 380
Union Insurance and Realty Company 322
United Negro Improvement Association 380
United States Colored Troops 559
United States Commission for the Relief of the National Freedm 352
United States Constitution 218
Universal Negro Improvement Association (UNIA) 102, 245, 250, 287, 489

University of Islam 360
Unseld, Wes 546
Up against the Wall 462
Upper Volta 25
Up Tight 455
Uptown Saturday Night 457
Urban Research Press 489
Uridin, Jalal 502
U.S. Episcopal Church 366
U.S.S. *Arizona* 573
U.S.S. *Arizona* Memorial 174
U.S.S. *Enterprise* 574
U.S.S. *George Washington Carver* 574
U.S.S. *Intrepid* 573
U.S.S. *Iowa* 563
U.S.S. *Jesse L. Brown* 574
U.S.S. *Liscome Bay* 573
U.S.S. *Maine* 561
U.S.S. *Miller* 574
U.S.S. *San Francisco* 574

V

Van Buren, Martin 136
Vanderhorst, Richard 381
Van Der Zee, James 527
Vann, Robert 566
Van Peebles, Mario 448
Varick, James 369, 380
Vaughn, Lyn 485
Venezuela 72, 73
Vereen, Ben 444, 470
Vesey, Denmark 164, 247, 370
Victoria, Queen 50
Victory Monument 128
Vidale, Thea 472
Vidor, King 450
Vietnam War 574-575
Vincent, Eddie "Cleanhead" 494
Violence 336, 337
Virginia Union University 354
Virgin Islands 68
Voodoo 366

Voter Education Project 277
Voting Rights Act (1965) 235, 241, 257, 277, 289

W

Walcott, Derek 418
Walk Hard 436
Walker, Alice 160, 427, 428, 458, 463
Walker, David 223, 247
Walker, George 433, 437, 438, 515
Walker, Jimmie 467-468
Walker, Madame C. J. 144, 315, 319-320
Walker, Maggie Lena 166, 167
Walker, Rachel 512
Walker, T-Bone 494, 497
Wallace, George 153
Waller, Thomas "Fats" 441
Walling, William English 284, 285
Walters, Alexander 285
Warbourg, Eugene 519
Ward, Billy 495
Ward, Douglas Turner 437, 439
Ward, Francis 242
Ward, Theodore 430
Wardlaw, Alia J. 532
Waring, Laura Wheeler 521
Warmoth, H. C. 268
Warner, Malcolm-Jamal 472
War on Poverty 235, 277
Warren, Earl 107
Washington Bee 474
Washington, Booker T. 6, 8, 95, 153, 156, 165, 167, 229, 262, 273, 284, 305, 318-319, 353, 474, 487, 539
Washington, Denzel 440, 461
Washington, George 79, 147, 557
Washington 136

INDEX

The Washington Post 481
Water Boy 521
Waters, Ethel 435, 436
Waters, Maxine 237
Waters, Muddy 497
Watson, Clifford 362
Watson, Johnny "Guitar" 501
Watts Riot (1965) 14, 238-239
Wayans, Damon 472
Wayans, Keenan Ivory 472
Wayans, Kim 472
Wayans, Shawn 472
"We Are the World" 501
W. E. B. Du Bois Homesite 141
Weaver, Faith 530
Weaver, Robert 9
Weaver, Robert C. 268
The Weekly Anglo-African 249
Welburn, Edward T. 526
Wells-Barnett, Ida B. 100, 126, 228-229, 476
Wells, Mary 130, 501
"We're a Winner" 498
"We Shall Overcome" 491
Wesley, John 367
Western World Reporter 479
West Indies 62
Westside Preparatory School 361
Wharton, Clifton R., Jr. 281
"What I'd Say" 496
What's Happening 468-469
Wheatley, Phillis 133, 141, 417, 419, 422, 519
Whitaker, Hudson "Tampa Red" 492
White, Bill 545, 554-555
White, Charles 521, 523, 528
White, Dwight 548
White, Effie Melody 441
Whitefield, George 367
White, Maurice 501
White, Michael 276
White, Slappy 438, 444
White, Walter 287

Whitman, Walt 150
Whitney, Eli 8, 216, 218
Whitney Foundation 518
"Whole Lotta Loving" 497
Wilberforce University 354, 379
Wilberforce, William 354
Wilder, Gene 457
Wilder, L. Douglas 17, 268
Wilkins, Roy 149, 287, 289, 290
Wilks, Gertrude 360
William C. Nell House 141
William Christopher Handy Birthplace 152
William Christopher Handy Park 159
William Monroe Trotter House 142
Williams, Armstrong 480
Williams, Bert 432, 433, 437-438
Williams, Billy Dee 458
Williams, Daniel Hale 125, 127, 533, 539
Williams, Delores 375
Williams, Doug 548
Williams, George Washington 355
Williams, Hank 498
Williams, Marion 440
Williams, Marshall 439
Williamson, Richard 280
Williams, Paul R. 525
Williams, Peter 249
Williams, Randy 527, 530
Williams, Vanessa 17
Williams, Walter 16, 314
Williams, Walter E. 279
Willis, Ben 548
Will Marion Cook Residence 149
Wilson, Arthur Dooley 436
Wilson, August 440
Wilson, Billy 442
Wilson, Brenda 485

Wilson, Dooley 435
Wilson, Dudley 442
Wilson, Flip 444
Wilson, Margaret Bush 286-287
Wilson, Teddy 507
Wimberly, Frank 527
Winchester, Jesse 498
Winfield, Hemsley 437
Winfield, Paul 456
Winfrey, Oprah 17, 305, 458, 460, 473, 476, 484
Winslow, Vernon 495
Winter, Marian Hannah 432
Wisconsin Historical Society 135
Within Our Gates 448
The Wiz 429, 441
The Wizard of Oz 441
Woman Resting 529
Women in Sports 551
The Women of Brewster Place 458
Wonder, Stevie 130
Woodard, Charlene 441
Wood, Donna 442
Woodruff, Hale 153, 521, 522, 527
Woods, Granville T. 535
Woods, Love B. 146
Woodson, Carter G. 167, 356, 488
Woodson, Robert L. 279, 305
Woodson, Robert, Sr. 16
Woodward, Sidney 512
Wordlaw, Gary 484
Work, John W. 487
Work, Monroe N. 487
Works Project Administration 518
"Work with Me Annie" 496
World Community of Al-Islam in the West 384
World Saxophone Quartet 511
A World View of Race 488
World War I 562-564

INDEX

World War II 565
Wright, Dolores 530
Wright, Elizabeth 279
Wright, Richard 418, 425
Wright, Will 484

Y

Yaraborough, Sara 442
The Yellow Tavern 163
Yordan, Philip 436
York 175, 179
Yorkin, Bud 466
"You Beat Me to the Punch" 501
"You Don't Know Me" 498
Young, Charles 134
Young, Charles A. 561
Young, Graylian 485
Young, Lester 507
Young, Whitney M., Jr. 287, 290
"Your Cheating Heart" 498
"You're on My Mind" 498
"You Send Me" 496
Youth Unemployment 310
Yucca Plantation 155

Z

Zaire 39, 45
Zambia 47, 48
Zanzibar 46
Zenobia 451
Ziegfield Follies 433
Zimbabwe 48, 49
Zora Neale Hurston Grave Site 160
Zora Neale Hurston Memorial 160
Zulu 51, 52

SEP - 9 1994
21.00

474132

JR Estell, Kenneth
973 The African-American
     Almanac (Volume 2)

Reference
Children
Dept.

South Huntington Public Library
Huntington Station, New York
11746

005

DISCARDED

For Reference

Not to be taken from this room